The Performance of Nationalism

Imagine the patriotic camaraderie of national day parades. How crucial is performance for the sustenance of the nation? *The Performance of Nationalism* considers the formation of the Indian and Pakistani nation, in the wake of the most violent chapter of its history: the partition of the subcontinent. In the process, Jisha Menon offers a fresh analysis of nationalism from the perspective of performance. Menon recovers the manifold valences of "mimesis": as aesthetic representation, as the constitution of a community of witnesses, and as the mimetic relationality that underlies the encounter between India and Pakistan. The particular performances considered here range from Wagah border ceremonies, to the partition theatre of Asghar Wajahat, Kirti Jain, M.K. Raina, and the cinema of Ritwik Ghatak and M.S. Sathyu. By pointing to the tropes of twins, doubles, and doppelgängers that suffuse these performances, this study troubles the idea of two insular nation-states of India and Pakistan. In the process, Menon recovers mimetic modes of thinking that unsettle the reified categories of identity politics.

JISHA MENON is Assistant Professor of Theatre and Performance Studies at Stanford University.

CAMBRIDGE STUDIES IN MODERN THEATRE

Series editor
David Bradby, *Royal Holloway, University of London*

Advisory board
Martin Banham, *University of Leeds*
Jacky Bratton, *Royal Holloway, University of London*
Tracy Davis, *Northwestern University*
Sir Richard Eyre
Michael Robinson, *University of East Anglia*
Sheila Stowell, *University of Birmingham*

Volumes for Cambridge Studies in Modern Theatre explore the political, social, and cultural functions of theatre while also paying careful attention to detailed performance analysis. The focus of the series is on political approaches to the modern theatre with attention also being paid to theatres of earlier periods and their influence on contemporary drama. Topics in the series are chosen to investigate this relationship and include both playwrights (their aims and intentions set against the effects of their work) and process (with emphasis on rehearsal and production methods, the political structure within theatre companies, and their choice of audiences or performance venues). Further topics will include devised theatre, agitprop, community theatre, para-theatre and performance art. In all cases the series will be alive to the special cultural and political factors operating in the theatres examined.

Books published

The Performance of Nationalism

India, Pakistan, and the Memory of Partition

Jisha Menon

CAMBRIDGE
UNIVERSITY PRESS

CAMBRIDGE
UNIVERSITY PRESS

University Printing House, Cambridge CB2 8BS, United Kingdom

One Liberty Plaza, 20th Floor, New York, NY 10006, USA

477 Williamstown Road, Port Melbourne, VIC 3207, Australia

314-321, 3rd Floor, Plot 3, Splendor Forum, Jasola District Centre, New Delhi - 110025, India

79 Anson Road, #06-04/06, Singapore 079906

Cambridge University Press is part of the University of Cambridge.

It furthers the University's mission by disseminating knowledge in the pursuit of
education, learning and research at the highest international levels of excellence.

www.cambridge.org
Information on this title: www.cambridge.org/9781108468565

© Jisha Menon 2013

First published 2013
First paperback edition 2018

A catalogue record for this publication is available from the British Library

Library of Congress Cataloging in Publication data
Menon, Jisha, 1972–
    The performance of nationalism : India, Pakistan, and the memory of
    Partition / Jisha Menon.
        pages   cm. – (Cambridge studies in modern theatre)
    Includes bibliographical references and index.
    ISBN 978-1-107-00010-0
    1. Indic drama–20th century–History and criticism.   2. Nationalism
in literature.   3. Partition, Territorial, in literature.   4. Motion
pictures, Indic.   5. Nationalism in motion pictures.   6. India–History–
Partition, 1947–Influence.   7. India–In literature.   8. Pakistan–In
literature.   9. India–In motion pictures.   10. Pakistan–In motion
pictures.   I. Title.
    PK5421.M46 2012
    891´.1–dc23
    2012033994

ISBN 978-1-107-00010-0 Hardback
ISBN 978-1-108-46856-5 Paperback

Contents

Illustrations

viii

Acknowledgments

The journey of writing this book has revealed to me the numerous ways in which I am sustained by the support of friends and strangers. This book bears the traces of mentors, friends, family, colleagues, and students over the past several years. I am blessed not only to have been the student of extraordinary scholars but also the beneficiary of their kindness. The critical generosity of Harry Elam continues to nurture and inspire me. Purnima Mankekar and Akhil Gupta opened the doors of postcolonial anthropology to me and demonstrated the rewards of pursuing interdisciplinary scholarship. To Peggy Phelan I owe a greater debt than I can convey for her brilliance and mentorship. For their intellectual nurture, I thank Jean-Marie Apostolides, David Palumbo-Liu, Patricia Parker, Michael Ramsaur, Alice Rayner, Rush Rehm, and Carl Weber. Ania Loomba and Lata Mani inspire me to live a life of the mind with courage, vitality, and a sense of harmony.

The Fab Four were my first home away from home: Thanks to the cheer and camaraderie of Brandi Catanese, Faedra Carpenter, Shawn Kairschner, and Zack. Lalaei Ameeriar, Patrick Anderson, Susan Bennett, Nandi Bhatia, Renu Capelli, Manishita Das, Chandan Gowda, Edith Gimm, Aleta Hayes, Michael Hunter, Bakirathi Mani, Janelle Reinelt, Freddie Rokem, Natalia Roudavskova, Rebecca Schneider, Steve Wilmer, Bill Worthen, Haiping Yan, and Patricia Ybarra offered a vibrant intellectual community at Stanford and beyond. Maya Dodd and Gauri Gill have been the source of solidarity, wisdom, and joy across the globe from the dazzling beaches of Carmel to the rough waters of monsoon Goa.

This is also the place to register some older debts: Suryakumari Dennison, Ranita Hirji, Srikrishna Ayyangar, Sandeep Bakshi,

x

Priyo Bannerjee, Saugata Bhaduri, Damayanti Bhattacharya, Piyas
Chakrabarti, Reena Chakrabarty, Nitoo Das, Paromita Das, Prachi
Deshpande, Sharmistha Ghosh, Alexis Halkovic, Shruti Kapila, Laura
Luktisch, Franson Manjali, Nayanika Mookherjee, Misa Oishi, Shruti
Pant, G.J.V. Prasad, and the late Professor Meenakshi Mukherjee at
Jawaharlal Nehru University offered a formidable intellectual com-
munity and laid the groundwork for me to pursue a career in aca-
demia. Deepa Chikermane, Pushpa Menon, Anita Raj, Priya Raman,
and Sonali Sattar ensure that I never feel like a stranger at home: Their
homes and hearts have always remained open to me.

I cherish my former colleagues in the Department of English
at UBC for their collegiality, humor, and compassion; I am especially
grateful to Patsy Badir, Sarika Bose, Richard Cavell, Mary Chapman,
Sian Echard, Sneja Gunew, Stephen Guy-Bray, Tina Lupton, and Laura
Moss. My colleagues at Stanford push me to do the best work that I possibly can: Conversations with Jennifer Brody, Michele Elam, Thomas
Blom Hansen, Leslie Hill, Allyson Hobbes, Branislav Jakovjevic,
Aishwary Kumar, Sangeeta Mediratta, Cherrie Moraga, Paula Moya,
Helen Paris, Janice Ross, Parna Sengupta and Anna Schulz have cru-
cially informed my thinking. My thanks to the administrative staff
in the Drama Department at Stanford, especially Patrice O'Dwyer,
Stephany Baker, and Christina Hartung for their patience and inspir-
ing proficiency.

I thank my interlocutors at the various venues where I have
presented parts of this research, including American Society for
Theatre Research; the Modern Language Association; Women and
Theatre Program; Duke University; Yale University; University of
California, Davis; Tufts University; Brown University; University
of British Columbia; Swarthmore College; International Centre
for Advanced Theatre Studies (Helsinki); Alternative Law Forum,
Bangalore; Azim Premji University, and Clayman Institute, Stanford.
My thanks to Shahzad Bashir, Suvir Kaul, and Miyako Inoue for reading drafts of chapters and offering valuable advice. I have thought
through most of the ideas in this book with my brilliant students who
will find a trace of their voice in the text that follows. In particular, I thank Jessica Nakamura and Lindsey Mantoan for their superb

research assistantship. Generous support from the Social Science and Humanities Research Council of Canada, the Annenberg Faculty Fellowship, and the Clayman Institute for Gender Research at Stanford University facilitated my research and offered opportunities for excellent critical feedback on my project.

I have been very fortunate to have the firm support of Cambridge University Press. I am especially grateful to the late David Bradby for his enthusiasm for this manuscript. Vicki Cooper and the anonymous readers offered excellent advice and detailed reports, which pushed me to sharpen my arguments. I am indebted to Rebecca Taylor and Fleur Jones for their unflagging attentiveness to this manuscript.

My thanks to the artists who assisted me with this project: Rukhsana Ahmad, B. Gauri, Kirti Jain, Basir Kazmi, Sheema Kermani, Shahid Nadeem, and Asghar Wajahat have offered important insights into the many questions I explore in the pages that follow. M.K. Raina went beyond the call of duty to help me with my project for which I remain very grateful.

Sections of individual chapters have appeared in different versions. I thank the publishers for their permission to reprint and the editors for their feedback and advice. Different versions of Chapter 3 and Chapter 4 appeared in *Modern Drama* (Volume 46, Number 2, Summer 2003) and *Feminist Review* (Volume 84, Sept. 2006), respectively.

Finally, thanks to my family: This project would not have been possible without the support and everyday acts of generosity of Sanjay Rajagopalan. My sisters, Roji Menon and Jyothi Menon; my brother, Manoj Menon; and their families have been a source of great strength to me. The rapturous delight of my son, Rahil Menon, makes me believe in and grateful for the power of miracles. Finally, I thank my parents: My father's robust sense of humor and my mother's faith and serenity carried me through my darkest moments. I dedicate this book to my parents as thanks for giving me my life a second time.

1 Introduction

My whole soul rebels against the idea that Hinduism and
Islam represent two antagonistic cultures and doctrines.

M.K. Gandhi

In July 1993, just seven months after the demolition of the Babri
mosque in Ayodhya and the subsequent riots in Bombay, Sahitya
Akademi–winning playwright Mahesh Dattani directed the premiere
production of *Final Solutions* in Bangalore.[1] The plot unfolds in the
midst of Bombay riots as two Muslim boys, Bobby and Javed, seek refuge in the house of the Gandhis, a Hindu family. Exasperated by their
sense of the everyday humiliations of untouchability perpetrated on
Muslims, Bobby and Javed expose the insidious exclusions on which
the safety of the Hindu home is predicated.

The arrival of these two Muslim boys rekindles the memory
of an old family secret. The secret returns us to the scene of the 1947
Partition of India and Pakistan when, in the rising tide of religious violence, the Gandhis set fire to their Muslim neighbors' shop. Torching
the shop was not an expression of religious intolerance but rather a
devious attempt to quash the business of their Muslim rivals. As a
result, the burgeoning friendship between Zarine, the shopowner's
daughter, and Daksha, the young Gandhi bride, comes to an abrupt
end. Daksha's father gets brutally murdered in the violence that occurs
in the wake of the Partition.

The Partition resurfaces as a repressed historical memory that
continues to mold both secular and religious identities. The narrative

Gandhi, in Tendulkar, *Mahatma*, 333–334.

I

action moves back and forth between 1947 and 1992, thus illuminating two historical moments that capture the crisis of secularism in India. Unfinished negotiations with the past fuel both Ramnik's generosity and his mother's hostility toward Muslims: Whereas Daksha harbors a festering resentment toward Muslims, her son Ramnik is guiltily aware of the family's complicity in demolishing the shop and repeatedly placates his guilt by overzealous acts of generosity toward Muslims.

Final Solutions dramatizes the self-interest that drives the violence in this case. Rather than explain violence as a "natural" explosion of primordial religious difference, Dattani considers the unstable historical conditions in 1947 and in 1992 as catalysts that generate essentialist religious identities. Set in this context, religious violence is a response to anxieties over material resources, insecurities generated by the implosion of former certitudes, and panic over the sudden collapse of long-standing social and political orders. Dattani deliberately invokes the specter of Hitler's "final solution" to the "problem" of exterminating Jews in Europe. By drawing analogies to Hitler's fascist politics, Dattani mounts his critique against violent and exclusivist Hindu nationalism in India.

The character of Daksha – as the grandmother and the young bride – is shared between two actors: The younger one is set in 1947 and removed from the action and other characters of the play, whereas the older one is set in 1993, appearing with all the other actors onstage. The narrative action is punctuated by flashback scenes in which the younger Daksha records in her diary her experience of being a young bride, her anguish when her father gets murdered during the Partition riots, her sorrow over Zarine's betrayal of their friendship, and her love of the legendary singer Noor Jehan's haunting melodies. Daksha's diary bears witness to the intrusion of the nation's public and political life into her private chambers.

In the 1993 Bangalore production, I played the role of the younger Daksha. Inhabiting Daksha's character required taking a leap back into a dark moment in the nation's history. Through her diary, I glimpsed a moment in Indian history, often overlooked in celebratory textbook accounts of India's nonviolent path to independence.

The character of Daksha offered me a lens with which to traverse the transformation of what Dipesh Chakrabarty has termed "practices of proximity" into the "politics of identity." Chakrabarty offers proximity and identity as alternative ways of dealing with difference, where identity refers to a congealed fixity and proximity refers to negotiation of difference.[2] When, for example, does Daksha withdraw from the practice of negotiating difference with her neighbor and petrify Zarine as her absolute other? How does this fixity of identity structure the Gandhi home as Hindu and foreclose the possibility of hospitality to the Muslim boys? By tracing the contingent and particular ways in which negotiated practices of proximity transform into strident and implacable politics of identity, Dattani exposes how Hindu liberals, such as Ramnik Gandhi, are unable to attend to the critique of unthinking Hindu privilege launched by Javed and Bobby.

The character of Daksha reveals the encrusted prejudices of people who grapple with the tenacious hold of the Partition on their everyday life. Embodying the character of a seventeen-year-old bride who experienced the vicissitudes of a violent political history required me to imagine and inhabit the extreme ruptures that the Partition produced in the everyday lives of its survivors. Indeed, it made me ponder how entire worldviews crumble under the weight of tumultuous events. It was during the production of *Final Solutions* that I first considered the enduring ways in which discourses of the Partition interpellated religious and secular as well as regional and national identities.

I vividly recall the sense of political urgency that drove the cast and crew of this production. Our first attempt to stage the play was thwarted when the sponsor – one of the city's premier newspapers – pulled us out of a regional theatre festival, fearing further clashes between religious communities. When we finally mounted the production in July 1993 – with the support of Maadhyam, a local nonprofit organization – the political situation had stabilized and offered the audience the opportunity to speculate on the growing crisis of secularism within the nation. The Hindu right's disturbing ascendancy to power in the intervening years gradually strengthened the emergent project of the Sangh Parivar to redefine India, both culturally and politically.[3] Indeed, the comparatively insipid public response to the violent pogroms against the Muslims in Gujarat that broke out in 2002 suggests the insidious ways in which the Hindu right normalizes spectacular forms of violence against minorities. It is within such a political and social context that this present project acquired its critical urgency.

The specter of the Partition returns to mold contemporary subjects of religious conflicts: Survivors and witnesses of post-1947 conflicts evoke the Partition as a recurrent point of reference. For example, in the wake of the assassination of Prime Minister Indira Gandhi in 1984 by her two Sikh bodyguards, the widespread pogroms against the Sikh community constituted a pivotal moment that evoked the Partition in public memory. One survivor eloquently describes the betrayal and bewilderment: "The memory of '47 came flooding back, except that I feared this might be much worse.... When the Hindu mobs shouted 'Traitors, get out!' I asked myself, 'Traitors? Is this what I sang songs of Independence for? Was handcuffed at the age of six for?' Which is our home now? ... 1947 was no shock, the shock is now."[4] Pioneering oral historians Ritu Menon and Kamla Bhasin reiterate the significance of the 1984 pogroms in reviving anxieties about national and ethnic belonging. In their words, "1984 changed the way 'history' concealed our past from us. Here was Partition once more in our midst, terrifying for those who had passed through it in 1947.... Yet this was our own country, our own people, our own home-grown violence."[5] In her groundbreaking work, Urvashi Butalia also acknowledges that the 1984 pogroms played a pivotal role in her undertaking the project of collecting oral histories of the Partition: "It took the events of 1984 to make me understand how ever-present Partition was in our lives, too, to recognize that it could not so easily be put away inside the covers of history books."[6] Another survivor reiterates the sense of panic, apprehension, and deep disillusionment the 1984 pogroms evoked: "We didn't think it could happen to us in our own country," she recalls, "this is like the Partition again."[7] The aforementioned remarks rehearse the eruption of an older memory during a moment of historical crisis; the 1984 pogroms evoked the specter of the Partition.

The diachronic doubleness of these memories that shuttle between 1947 and 1984 reveal that the Partition as "event" had not

4

ended – that the religious tensions that sparked in post-Independence India were haunted by the traumatic memory of the Partition.[8] The Partition resurfaced at other volatile moments in the history of the subcontinent. Preceding and during the demolition of the Babri Masjid in 1992, the Partition reemerged in the hate speech of the Hindu right. Likewise, Muslims displaced from their homes during the ensuing Bombay riots allude to the Partition in an effort to make sense of the violent ruptures the ethnic conflict produced. Indian novelist Shama Futehally remarks that the Babri Masjid demolition has "made it impossible, so to speak, to keep the lid on Partition any more."[9] Victims and witnesses of these riots frequently reference Partition as a touchstone of their experience of violence. The 1998 nuclear tests conducted by India and Pakistan conjured yet again the Partition. Suvir Kaul writes eloquently about the "extraordinary irony" that undid the Partition when the highly policed border between India and Pakistan was threatened into obliteration by "the power of mutually assured nuclear destruction."[10] Ashis Nandy argues that the Gujarat pogroms in 2002 confirmed that the Partition continues to resurrect "fantasies of orgiastic violence" that taunt us to both exterminate the enemy as well as compel him/her to live in abject humiliation and disgrace.[11]

The uncanny doubleness of memory that mimetically evokes the Partition discloses, rather than closes, the specters of the past. These recurrent associations reveal that it is not only a former time that binds one to the memory of the Partition but also a former self. The Partition simultaneously possesses and dispossesses its survivors: Its spectral memory holds subjects in thrall to the dispossessed dimensions of their self, precluding any possibility of self-possession. Despite the institutional strategies of redress and reparation and the redemptive accounts of the nation's nonviolent path to freedom, the unruly memories of the Partition resist efforts toward a harmonizing closure. The memory of the Partition continues to shape social relations between Hindus, Muslims, and Sikhs in the subcontinent; conversely, contemporary religious conflicts shape and revise past narrations of the Partition.

The Performance of Nationalism: India, Pakistan, and the Memory of Partition explores the affective and performative constitution of the Indian and Pakistani nation in the wake of the most violent chapter of its history: the Partition of the subcontinent. I recuperate the idea of mimesis to think about the mimetic relationship between political history and the crisis of its aesthetic representation. I also consider the relationship between India and Pakistan as constituted through a mimetic relationality, which evokes the fraternal metaphor of twins separated at birth. The particular performances I examine trouble the idea of two coherent, autonomous nation-states of India and Pakistan by pointing to the trope of mimetic doubles that suffuse the dramas of Partition. These performances reveal that the shadowy underbelly of antagonistic politics is constituted by the promise and betrayal of mimetic kinship. This study attempts to recover mimetic modes of thinking to unsettle the reified categories of identitarian politics. First, however, let us turn to a brief history of the Partition of the subcontinent.

Ruptures of Partition

In August 1947, when the British finally ceded political interest in India after colonial rule for nearly two centuries, they transferred their power to two separate nation-states: India and Pakistan. Not only did the mounting anticolonial nationalist movement put pressure on the British empire to evacuate India; the economic exigencies that a greatly impoverished Britain faced in the aftermath of World War II also reinforced the British decision to "quit" India. The return of the Labour Party to power in Britain further expedited the decolonization process. The ideological commitment of the Labour Party to postwar reparation and decolonization rapidly changed the Indian political scene. Britain's desire to relinquish its interests in India to a centralized national government, one capable of defending British economic and political interests in the regions of the Indian Ocean, appeared unfeasible. Lord Mountbatten, the last British viceroy, was sent to India to transfer power and consider alternatives to Partition. Instead of deliberating over these complex issues in the allotted ten-month period, Mountbatten took a mere two months to announce the date for the transfer of power and for Partition.

6

The division of the subcontinent into India and Pakistan was triggered by a combination of factors in the metropole and the colony: In addition to the shifting colonial position on retaining India as a colony, the demand for Partition was articulated within the context of a colonial state's framing of provincial politics and intra-elite factional conflicts within India that had already prepared the ground for irreconcilable differences. The two-nation theory, driven more by politics than religion, grew in momentum from the fears stoked by democratization in the 1930s, the Indian National Congress's anti-war stance, the growing empowerment of the Muslim League, and the British announcement to quit India. Add to this the more immediate factors expediting the process: Mountbatten's hasty and ill-conceived exit strategies and the rising tide of religious violence.[12]

Between June 3, 1947, when the decision to divide India was announced, and August 15, 1947, the day of formal Indian independence from British rule, roughly 15 million people were displaced. What the government euphemistically called "the exchange of populations" of Muslims into Pakistan and Hindus and Sikhs into India resulted in the largest human exodus ever recorded. According to *Millions on the Move*, a report published by the government of India, between August and November 1947, as many as 673 refugee trains moved approximately 2,300,000 refugees within India and across the border.[13] From mid-September to late October, 24-foot convoys, each consisting of 30,000 to 40,000 people, marched 150 miles to cross the border into India. Roughly 32,000 refugees had been flown in either direction; nearly 133,000 people had been moved to India by steamer and country craft boats. The disputed death toll ranges from 200,000 to 2 million: People died as a result of communal clashes, floods, starvation, exhaustion, and the proliferating cases of famine and cholera caused by unhygienic conditions. Approximately 83,000 women were abducted, raped, and killed.[14] Innumerable children disappeared. Many who were unable to travel with speed got left behind: the elderly, the infirm, the disabled, children, and women. Thousands of people were forcibly converted; many others voluntarily opted to convert in order to stay in their homeland. At least 500,000 people were massacred on the trains referred to as "gifts" that people were sending across to the new nation.

The official territorial award was announced on August 16, one day after the independence of India and two days after the formation of Pakistan. The massive dislocation, however, had been set in motion by the cycle of violence that began with the Great Calcutta Killings of August 16–19, 1946, which left nearly 6000 dead and displaced 100,000 people. In addition, the Noakhali riots drove out the Hindus from a region where they constituted about a fifth of the population, and the Rawalpindi massacres in Punjab in March 1947 left 40,000 Sikhs homeless. The killings in Bengal in the 1950s prompted a further flood of refugees.[15] People were on the move, uncertain of where they would settle down and whether they would eventually belong to India or to Pakistan.

The Partition was unlike any other religious conflict in the region. Talbot and Singh identify crucial features that distinguish the violence of the Partition from more traditional communal riots: ethnic cleansing of minority populations, political desire for power and territory, sadistic violence, intrusion into the domestic sphere, and organized violence through the use of paramilitary groups, which included the complicity of state agents.[16] Talbot and Singh further point out that the organized violence of the Partition must be located within the framework of the Second World War and the widespread presence of weapons and demobilized soldiers in north India who trained volunteer groups through spectacular parades and drills. Seen in this light, the violence was far more organized than "spontaneous"; not an atavistic feature of fanatically religious groups, the violence was produced in a mimetic encounter with a European fascistic culture of hostility that was refracted ideologically and materially within the subcontinent.[17]

Colonialism, religion, enumeration

Edward Said reminds us that "rhetorically speaking Orientalism is absolutely anatomical and enumerative, to use its vocabulary is to engage in the particularizing and dividing of things Oriental into manageable parts."[18] British administrative policies consolidated Hindus

8

and Muslims as separate "enumerative communities" through the introduction of a range of bureaucratic measures, which mimetically reproduced western analytical categories of classification. For example, the introduction of the colonial census throughout India in 1881 had far-reaching effects in the ossification of religious identities. By imposing orientalist grids, such as the census, the British calcified fluid, flexible, and heterogeneous cultural practices into the antinomies of religious majority and minority.

Several South Asian scholars have developed Said's insights about the relationship between enumeration and the ossification of identities. David Ludden establishes the dialectical production of communalism from its interaction with orientalism when the latter institutionalized oppositions between Hindus and Muslims in colonial administrative, bureaucratic, and legal practices.[19] Gyanendra Pandey argues that British officers treated Hindu-Muslim antagonism as a given "fact" that then became a touchstone in colonial bureaucratic practices.[20] When quantitative technologies of colonial state governance turned their lens to religious identities, it had the result of gradually turning what political theorist Sudipta Kaviraj has termed "fuzzy communities" – "a relative lack of clarity of where one's community, or even region, ended and another began" – into enumerative communities.[21] Dipesh Chakrabarty also accentuates the "pervasive marriage between government and measurement" that he suggests is constitutive of the "deep structure of the imagination that is invested in modern political order."[22] Arjun Appadurai further develops the relationship between the logic of arithmetic and the production of religious violence: The categories of majority/minority are haunted by an "anxiety of incompleteness," which diminishes the project of national purity and consequently triggers ethnocidal mobilization.[23]

The interdependence of governance and enumerative strategies was central to the production of religious differences between Hindus and Muslims of British India.[24] By the early twentieth century, religious differences had been institutionalized on the principle of communal representation. In 1861, the Indian Councils Act introduced separate electorates to increase Muslim representation through the system of elective local government. Constitutional reforms in 1919 and 1937 further democratized and consolidated Muslim political constituency. These changes increased opportunities for the Muslim political majorities in Punjab and Bengal to correct the educational and economic imbalance in favor of Hindu and Sikh populations. The Muslim backlash against the Congress administration in Uttar Pradesh (1937–1939) was to provide the critical catalyst in the demand for a separate homeland. Following the Government of India Act of 1935 – which introduced a substantial measure of representative government through provincial autonomy and represented one of the important efforts at transferring limited power to Indians – provincial elections were held in 1937 based on the notion of a communal representation.

The creation of separate electorates according to religious identity consolidated the idea that people sharing a particular faith constituted an identifiable group with common interests, which marked them off from another group, which practiced a different faith. This particular way of imagining community affirmed certain commonalities through the category of religious identity while underestimating other axes of similitude and association. This idea was embedded in everyday life, "the idea that (Indian) society consisted of groups set apart from each other.... The result was the flowering of a new communal rhetoric, and ultimately, of the Pakistan movement."[25]

Performance and the nation

What can a performative approach to the study of the nation make visible?[26] *The Performance of Nationalism: India, Pakistan, and the Memory of Partition* considers the ways in which logocentric, cognitivist ideas of "the imagined community" acquire their affective and material force through embodied performances. Moving beyond dominant considerations of politics underpinned by institutional policies, theories of rational choice, and Habermasian critical-rational public spheres, this study considers the centrality of performance as a tactic of political power. The relationship between power and performance has been theorized as far back as Machiavelli's *The Prince* and continues to reverberate today from the quotidian secular Wagah ceremonies to the disruptive *rathyatras* (chariot processions) coordinated by the Hindu right.[27] This book makes visible the double-edged power

of performative politics – the aesthetic and spectacular representations of the state are not simply absorbed by its citizen-subjects but
contested, contradicted, and negotiated through other enduring imaginaries of kinship and belonging.[28]

Dominant accounts of nationalism foreground how capitalist
production, print technology, and monoglot reading publics combined
to create the conditions for imagining the nation.[29] The consumers
of the novel and the newspaper accessed the same information, and
this served to link the mass-reading publics within the same imagined boundaries. Media such as newspapers contribute to the formation of public opinion, enabling civil society to exercise surveillance
over the state. A good deal has been written about the centrality of
print journalism, of literature – especially novels – in the creation of
national identity. For example, Benedict Anderson examines "print-
capitalism" as the institutional form through which the "imagined
community" of nation is forged; Timothy Brennan argues that nations
depend for their existence on a system of cultural fictions in which
"imaginative literature" plays a decisive role; Homi Bhabha encounters the nation "as it is written" and examines its narrative address to
draw attention to its language and rhetoric and thereby reexamine the
conceptual object of nation itself.[30]

The analysis of embodied performance in public spaces brings
new questions to studies of nationalism. It places centerstage the role
of performance in understanding the complex processes of nation
formation. The internalization of an ideational construct of nation
depends for its success on its affective translation into material symbols such as the flag, the military uniforms, and the national anthem.
Sandria Freitag has argued that central to the act of imagining a community is the pictorial image where "spectatorship meets creation
in a complex interplay between visuality, apparatus, institutions,
discourse, bodies and figurality."[31] Although performance certainly
engages a visual vocabulary, it resists ocularcentric notions of the general dominance of the visual in late modernity and does not reinforce
an artificial dichotomy between the visual and the linguistic.[32]

I also draw on deconstructive notions of the performative
to think about the iterative constitution of refugees into national

subjects. How are people persuaded to attach their loyalties to abstractions rather than to the embedded, concrete relationships in their everyday life? The process by which colonial subjects are produced as national citizens through complex iterative practices is exemplified at the moment of Partition when national identities were still gestational. Those displaced were enjoined to resignify themselves as Indian/Pakistani, an identification with which some may have had little prior affiliation. The assumption of this new macro-identity also served to make official and permanent the displacement from their prior homes. The performative insists on the processual, unfinished, and constantly renewed function of national belonging – what Renan calls "the daily plebiscite"– rather than assume the unchanging, static, a priori ontology of national identity. It is within the context of a compulsory citationality that the reconstitution of refugees as national subjects needs to be thought.

The performative speech act fundamentally revises our understanding of the stability and given-ness of national and religious identities. By paying attention not only to the descriptive features of language, meaning, and intentionality of speech acts, but also to their ability to effect through their very utterance, performative speech acts demonstrate the world-making and world-shattering power of discourse. Conferring national and religious identities through the power of performative speech acts radically refigures the citizen-subjects of the Partition. The illocutionary force of performative speech acts, in the context of the Partition, makes visible that the very terms of recognition of one's existence had to be articulated through the address of the state. The act of state recognition differentially interpellates the citizen: It is through the address of the state that the citizen acquires an ontological status.

Although the analytical categories of performance theory offer ways to think about the spectacular and iterative practices through which citizen-subjects were constituted in the wake of the Partition, I turn to the trope of mimesis through which to consider the undoing of the national and religious ontology. The conceptual richness of mimesis enables me to ask a range of questions with regard to the Partition, and it is to mimesis as a fertile conceptual lens that we will now turn.

Introduction

Mimesis as aesthetic representation

A protean and capacious concept, mimesis has been used over millennia to convey a range of meanings from falsehood, fiction, *imitatio* (tradition, convention, emulation), *mimesthai* (representation), and nonsensuous correspondence, among others. The concept traverses a spectrum of semantic and performative possibilities that range from aesthetic theories to accounts of self- and world-making. Rather than serving a strictly referential function, mimesis evokes a world of similitude; semblance rather than sign connotes mimetic modes of thinking. A brief consideration of some of the leading theorists and critics of mimesis gives a sense of the heterogeneity of associations generated by the concept.

Traced back to at least the fifth century BC, mimesis derives from *mimos*, designating both a person who imitates and a genre of performance based on imitation of stereotypical character traits. The first probing analysis of mimesis in ancient Greek thought emerges in Plato's *The Republic* (c. 375 BC), which advances a rich, complex, and multivalent conception of mimesis. Here Plato uses the figure of his mentor, Socrates, to mimetically address questions regarding the constitution of an ideal republic, where psychic and civic integrity are key to the governance of the city.[33] Mimetic arts could provoke the destabilization and disintegration of self-possessed, composed citizen-subjects, which could then precipitate the disintegration of the civic constitution.

The Socratic resistance in Plato's *Republic* to mimetic arts emerges not from a dismissal but rather from an acknowledgment of the transformative power of art to influence audiences. Plato cautions against irresponsible appeals to emotions that paralyze the critical-rational faculty. Losing self-possession through a mimetic identification with the charismatic actor/character/orator can disable critical distance and sway audiences to act in ways that are ethically dubious and politically treacherous.[34] Mimesis, in the Platonic conception, threatens the integrity of the autonomous subject, and therefore must be proscribed from the ideal republic.

Aristotle resuscitates mimesis from the Platonic conception of it as threat to civic and psychic integrity by suggesting that mimesis

13

offers us a means to understand past events and to make sense of the world we inhabit. Aristotle distinguishes the Platonic conception of mimesis as *pseudos*, or falsehood, from mimesis as fiction. The aware-ness of the fictional status of an artistic work enables the viewer to derive pleasure from otherwise painful memories.[35] The ontological otherness of a parallel, imaginary world enables a safe distance from which to reflect on our own world.[36] By highlighting the capacity of art to enable a deeper awareness of our world and our lives, Aristotle rejects Platonic moralism that proscribes mimesis. The transforma-tion of painful past into aesthetic pleasure through mimetic practice depends on the capacity of the mimetic art to offer a renewed under-standing of the event. Whereas philosophy is concerned with abstract universal, and history with contingent particular, poetry offers a sen-suous understanding – at once concrete and contemplative – of the world we inhabit.[37]

During the thousand years that constitute the Middle Ages and up until the end of the eighteenth century, mimesis was frequently reimagined as *imitatio*, which consisted predominantly in the con-ventional emulation of authoritative literary texts.[38] Emulating exem-plary texts not only offered artists the opportunity to aspire to the highest role models beyond their time; the intertextual tissue of meanings and resonances also established a sense of traditional con-tinuity between classical authors and their mimetic counterparts.[39] Although second, the imitated work was not secondary; reconfiguring and retelling offered the possibilities for structured play while still drawing on classical models. Renaissance writers in turn drew on the artistic resources of the Roman tradition. Imitation was central to education by supplying both the method of repetition and the model of exemplary figures to inculcate and inspire virtue in readers.

The decline of imitation's significance at the end of the eighteenth century owed something to the emergence of detached, instrumental rationality, which privileged reason and disinterested-ness. Whereas thinkers such as René Descartes and Immanuel Kant championed science, progress, innovation, and genius, others such as Alexander Pope continued to emphasize the importance of learning from past masters.[40] For Descartes the subject is the creator of the world, a world idealized and formulated in mathematical language – abstract and universal; the language of abstract universality departed from that of mimetic similitude. Setting aside the incommensurable particularity of embodied experience, Descartes pursued science, which consisted of universal rules supplied in nature.

The quarrel between the ancients and the moderns polarized venerable tradition and innovative modernity, and definitively privileged originality over *imitatio*. Unsurprisingly, the Romantic period, which stressed uniqueness, also saw the emergence of copyright laws that legally bound creativity to individual private property. *Imitatio* now raised specters of plagiarism or intellectual piracy. The romantic genius struggled to break free from the shackles of tradition, to rebel against authority. The resultant devaluation of mimetic modes of thinking continues to circulate in the modern world.[41]

Mimesis as world-making

The Performance of Nationalism: India, Pakistan, and the Memory of Partition argues that recovering mimetic modes of thinking about the relationship between India and Pakistan stresses similitude over semiotics, kinship over referentiality, and troubles the reified categories of identity politics. How do mimetic practices discohere the sovereign subject, enabling her to enter into a radically rearranged relationship with the other? Complicating theories of autonomous subject formation, I argue that mimesis re-enchants a Cartesian split between subject and object, self and other by reintroducing the specter of enigmatic semblance.

To make this argument I draw on mimesis as both aesthetic practice and social relation. As we have seen, the discussions of mimesis co-implicate aesthetics with ideas of subject formation. Even as early as Plato's *Republic* we find the dual connotations of mimesis as both dramatic representation and mimetic identification. Linking action to virtue, mimesis oscillates between aesthetic practice and subject formation.[42] More recently, critical theory has resuscitated the fertile concept of mimesis. For Walter Benjamin, the translator of Charles Baudelaire, Marcel Proust, and Theodor Lessing, language constitutes an archive of nonsensuous similarity in a predominantly disenchanted world. Unlike a disinterested, neutral, instrumental approach that consolidates the subject-object split, sensuous knowledge attends to the proliferation of mimetic similitude. Likewise, Horkheimer and Adorno argue that the reified subject-object relationship supplants the manifold affinities that exist between things. Human beings are turned into mere examples of species, identical to one another through isolation within the compulsively controlled collectivity. Ruled by the principle of equivalence, dissimilar things are made identical by reducing them to abstract qualities, subsuming diffe-rence under sameness.

The rich contributions of Rene Girard, Michael Taussig, and Elin Diamond have augmented our understanding of mimetic practice and its relation to questions of desire, colonialism, and sexual differ-ence. Girard complicates the dyadic structure between subject and object by exposing the triangulation within which mimetic desires are enmeshed; the desire to emulate the model draws the subject toward the object. He plumbs the varying implications of mimetic desire, depending on whether the subject is drawn to an idealized model or a rival. Far from autonomous or original, desires are mimetically gener-ated, ignited by a mimetic rivalry with someone else. Girard's concep-tion of mimetic desire cautions us against uncritical celebrations of mimesis by exposing its potential for insidious violence.

Taussig develops Benjamin's conception of the "mimetic faculty" to consider its ramifications within colonial encounters.[43] Defined as "the nature that culture uses to create second nature," the mimetic impulse carries a vestige of a compulsive need for people to become/behave like something else. The wonder of mimesis lies in the copy drawing on the character and power of the original to the point where the representation may even assume that character and that power. Taussig combines Benjaminian insights with Marxist ideas of alienated labor: The spectral commodity denies its historicity and multiple sensuous interactions and emerges as pristine fetish object, its particularity grindered into an abstract identity.

Elin Diamond's astute analysis of feminist performance insists on mimesis as a creative interpretive process. Counterposing iden-tity with identification, she argues that identifications produce and

16

destabilize identity; in assimilating the other the subject doubles herself. If identity works to sustain a believable and mobilizing fiction that binds each individual into an imagined unity, identification is a "passionate mimesis," drawing another into oneself, projecting oneself onto another. Whereas identity operates through a logic of exclusion – my being or consciousness affirms its self-sameness by not being you – identification is trespass, to be the other is a loss of self. "Identification," according to Diamond, "violates identity."[44]

The Performance of Nationalism: India, Pakistan, and the Memory of Partition develops the idea of mimesis in three crucial directions: as aesthetic practice, as social relation, and as worldmaking. Considering the Partition of the subcontinent through its aesthetic representations offers a *sensuous understanding* of the events of political history. Charting a space between the contingent particular of history and the abstract universal of philosophy, aesthetic mimesis enables a sensuous knowledge that attends to the particular lives of protagonists while simultaneously enabling a bigger-picture understanding of events through *theoria* or contemplation.[45]

As social relation, mimesis takes seriously the promise and peril of similitude that does not dissolve into sameness. Mimetic relationality offers productive political possibilities for imagining cross-border affiliations. Recognizing the mimetic doubleness of political subjects moves us away from the shrill polarities of identity politics. The agon of the Partition illuminates the irresolvable doubleness at the heart of the fraternal encounter between India and Pakistan. Building on Elin Diamond's perceptive remark, "Mimesis is impossibly double," I argue that mimetic thinking moves from identity and the principle of equivalence endemic to abstract rationality to an insistence on incommensurable difference. This "impossibly double" attribute of mimesis, however, also cautions us to its contradictoriness. Although mimesis offers a powerful challenge to dominant ideologies of ethnic and national identity, it is not necessarily a benevolent or "progressive" force. For example, Chapters 5 and 6 consider mimetic desire as triangulated among masculinist institutions of community and state, where the possession of women and territory (Kashmir, in this case) becomes the means to stage rivalry between implacably hostile groups.[46]

Finally, *The Performance of Nationalism: India, Pakistan, and the Memory of Partition* considers the ways in which publics are constituted through mimetic practices.[47] Can mimesis initiate a process of renewed world-making? Theatre, the most social of all arts, moves us beyond the merely private or domestic sphere toward a larger, common civic philia – an emotionally charged public sphere of kinship and community. Aesthetic pleasure derives not only from dramatic action, but also from a sense of shared witnessing. The public recognition of the sufferings one has endured reconnects the grieving individual to a wider community of witnesses. Plato's warning that mimesis disintegrates the unity of the subject could point the way to a radical rearrangement of the discoherent subject, dispersed in the wake of grief. Could mimesis then offer the opportunity to rearrange the self and fashion a new ethical relation to the other? *The Performance of Nationalism* argues that grief can offer the occasion for reimagining community. Rather than privatizing grief, such acts of collective witnessing offer the ground to generate a powerful sense of solidarity.[48]

In addition, all the productions I consider in this book bear conscious semblance to earlier works. The mimetic practice of adaptation allows the artist to embed creative difference by retelling a story that is similar but not identical to the original. In the words of Edward Said, "The writer thinks less of writing originally, and more of rewriting. The image for writing changes from original inscription to parallel script, from tumbled-out confidence to deliberate fathering-forth, ... from melody to fugue."[49] Each of the works considered here is shaped through mimetic engagements with other texts: M.S. Sathyu draws on Ismat Chugtai; Kirti Jain draws on Saadat Hasan Manto; Ritwik Ghatak draws on Shaktipada Rajguru; Asghar Wajahat draws on Nasir Kazmi; and M.K. Raina draws on Shakespeare. Mimetic semblance points not only to the doubleness of characters within these stories but also to the palimpsestic doubleness of the narratives themselves.

This book examines dramatic and filmic representations of the Partition from the 1960s to 2010. What can varying narrations of the Partition tell us about the particular historical moment of its creative articulation? Contemporary retellings of the Partition do not simply reflect the past but inscribe within their very narration the stories one wants to tell of the present. The following chapters hold the mimetic discourses of performance and history in contrapuntal tension without dissolving their discursive differences into a unifying closure.[50] The discrepant discursive fields of performance and history have discrete agendas and internal formations, and critically interanimate each other. Weaving together in contrapuntal tension aesthetic, political, and historical discourses without harmonizing closures allows us to pay attention to individual, sometimes dissonant, narratives and attend to their incommensurable heterogeneity.

Focusing on the symbolic, affective, and embodied dimensions of state-making, Chapter 2 considers the role of political performance as a key technique in the constitution of publics. It lays the groundwork for the book by considering the performative dimensions of political power through a consideration of high political debates and spectacular displays of state power. From a brief account of the high politics of the Partition played out by the colonial and nationalist elite, I turn to the Retreat ceremony at Wagah, at the border of India and Pakistan. The border ceremonies at Wagah exemplify the spectacular strategies that not only reify and make visible the power of the state but also insidiously inscribe social power onto the bodies of its spectators. The spectacular representation of the nation at Wagah attempts to secure the mimetic political relationship between the representative and the represented through the sensuous evocation of patriotic philia. The mimetic rituals across the border performed by Indian and Pakistani border guards, however, ironically destabilize both accounts of identity within and difference without the nation. This chapter argues that mimetic semblance across the border unsettles the spectacular production of political power.

Chapter 3 turns to the cinema of avant-garde Bengali filmmaker Ritwik Ghatak, which explores the mimetic relationship between person and place in partitioned Bengal. For Ghatak, love of country cannot be subsumed within accounts of nationalism and political contestations over territoriality. Ghatak systematically rejects the logic and lure of the nation by invoking the nonsensuous similitude between person and place in the riverine Bengal. Ghatak demonstrates the affinity between place and person through the trope of nonidentical twins; the relationship between the twins is analogous to the bond between the twin Bengals. By insistently depicting two orphaned siblings as analogous to the partitioned East and West Bengal, Ghatak forwards kinship as the terrain on which the Partition played out its antagonistic politics.

In Chapter 4 I continue to explore the ramifications of the Partition's displacement by turning from the eastern to the western border between India and Pakistan. This chapter specifically addresses the ways in which Hindu and Muslim minority communities configured questions of displacement, national belonging, and gender. Does the concept of accommodation offer a spectral mode of cohabitation between the self and the other? By looking at two performance texts, M.S. Sathyu's film *Garm Hawa* (1973) and Asghar Wajahat's play *Jis Lahore Ne Dekhiya* (1988), I argue that home, property, and the idea of accommodation provide an urgent lens through which to consider the anxieties regarding national belonging in the partitioned subcontinent. I explore how the dialectical production of Hindus and Muslims, India and Pakistan pivots around the question of semblance. The mimetic doubleness disturbs the symmetries of insider/outsider, and destabilizes the sovereign subjects of the Partition.

Chapter 5 turns to the gendered dimensions of the violence that occurred in the wake of Partition. The constitutive role played by gendered violence during the Partition took on an uncanny mimetic dimension. As bearers of the nation, women ensured the perpetuity of both the religious community and the nation. By desecrating the possession of the rival, mimetic violence reveals that women themselves were evacuated of subjectivity. Not only were members of one community responding to violence done across the border but the nation-states, too, participated in this scenario of mimetic violence. Kirti Jain's 2001 production, *Aur KitneTukde*, depicts the circulation of female bodies between men from opposing communities and nations. This chapter takes up the relationship between embodiment and discourse in a context where bodies themselves circulated as "somatic texts." I argue that marking female bodies through specific acts of gendered violence constitutes a mode of transcription for men to communicate with their mimetic counterparts.

If "woman" was the token of exchange in a conflict between warring men, Chapter 6 considers the ways in which the valley of Kashmir becomes the object of desire in the mimetic fraternal encounter between India and Pakistan. This chapter considers the ways in which the Bhand Pather, a satiric form of Kashmiri folk theatre, negotiates the hostility of antagonistic politics in the region. Through an analysis of M.K. Raina's folk adaptation of *King Lear, Badshah Pather*, I consider the ways in which mimesis offers the occasion for the constitution of a witnessing public. *Badshah Pather* oscillates between the satiric critique of Bhand Pather and the tragic awareness of human vulnerability. In the process, the performance moves the audience toward an affective public sphere of kinship and solidarity. The public witnessing of grief, particularly of parents mourning the untimely deaths of their children, generates a powerful sensuous solidarity among the audience.

In the final analysis, *The Performance of Nationalism: India, Pakistan, and the Memory of Partition* argues that recovering mimetic modes of thinking potentially unsettles the reified certitudes of community and nation. Mimetic semblance does not dissolve difference into sameness but rather exposes the doubleness of the self, the nonidentity of the self with the self, thus fracturing the unity and uniformity on which civic and religious nationalisms depend.

2 Bordering on drama: the performance of politics and the politics of performance

Borders are scratched across the hearts of men
By strangers with a calm, judicial pen
And when the borders bleed we watch with dread
       The lines of ink across the map turn red.

This chapter considers the role of political performance as a key technique in the constitution of publics. I argue that spectacular and quotidian political performance affectively binds its audience – a word derived from *audentia*, an assembly of listeners, into publics. The focus on performance allows us to consider the symbolic, affective, embodied dimensions of state-making, which redresses the social-scientific focus on Weberian and rational choice accounts that concentrate on institutions and interests respectively.[1] I begin with an account of the routine performances of the "high politics" of the Partition that deployed rhetoric as a strategy to advance political goals.[2] From the performance of high politics, I turn to the Retreat ceremony at Wagah, at the India–Pakistan border, to examine the politics of performance. The sensuousness of political life as experienced through spectatorial and auditory practices does not interpellate pre-given subjects; rather, the persuasiveness of rhetoric and ceremony hegemonically produces the desired forms of political subjecthood, the basis for social cohesion and political unity.

The border ceremonies at Wagah exemplify the spectacular strategies that not only reify and make visible the power of the state, but also insidiously inscribe social power onto the bodies of its spectators.

Mannes, *Subverse*, 12.

22

Reading the Retreat ceremony as a spectacular theatre of nationalism allows us to consider the relationship between aesthetic and political representation. The aesthetic representation of the nation attempts to secure the political relationship between the representative and the represented; however, the identical rituals across the border performed by Indian and Pakistani border guards ironically destabilize both accounts of identity within and difference without the nation. This chapter argues that mimetic similitude across the border unsettles the aesthetic representation of the nation.

Rather than binarize history and fiction, statist and humanist accounts, I suggest that a performative reading of the political troubles the dichotomies through which we narrate the Partition and generates a more labile understanding of our histories and our politics. Moving beyond questions regarding the causes and effects of the Partition, this study considers the ways in which bodies carry stories. Archives and repertoires are co-constituted, drawing from elite policies and mass mobilizations through a dialectical inter-animation of performance and history.[3] Let us turn first to explore the performative practices of the high politics of the Partition.

The drama of high politics

Anticolonial nationalist politics was an exemplary instance of political performance. The strategic deployment of language, theatrics, and the interplay of speech and silence in the political debates between the Muslims League and the Congress constituted the grounds on which the questions surrounding the Partition were articulated. South Asian political theorist Sudipta Kaviraj may well have been referring to Pakistani Governor-General Jinnah's masterful manipulation of language when he observed that "politics often becomes a contest over the use of language, a matter of defiance of linguistic and symbolic norms. Indeed the whole world of colonialism seemed perfectly suited to a theater of a typically Austinian defiance....Politics in colonial society is a world of performatives."[4] Their educational background in law gave leaders such as Nehru, Jinnah, and Gandhi an acute awareness of the performative power of rhetoric. The formation of publics through the cultivation of audiences, an assembly of listeners, suggests the central role played by rhetoric and persuasion in the formation of imagined communities. Further, the growing momentum of the anti-colonial movement provided the perfect opportunity to illustrate, in J.L. Austin's words, "how to do things with words." Jinnah's performative manipulation of language clearly illustrates this point.

The dominant account of Partition in India has been rooted in two central assumptions:

1. The Muslim League, headed by Jinnah (who later became the first governor-general of Pakistan) stood for Partition. The Muslim League vigorously disseminated the two-nation theory, which held that Muslims and Hindus had incommensurable differences and thus constituted two different nations.
2. The Congress rejected the Partition proposal and stood for unity. They were, however, forced to concede to the demand for Partition because of the mounting religious violence.

The histories of the Partition's high politics recall a Habermasian model of a critical-rational public sphere. Such a model of the public sphere foregrounds its dispassion, neutrality, and transparency, obscuring the drama, ambition, and manipulation that surrounded these discussions. The passionate speech acts of the high politics of the Partition illustrate the ways in which words perform actions; moving beyond a consideration of language as a neutral, inert channel of communication, an analysis of the performative dimensions of speech foregrounds the world-making and world-shattering power of speech acts.[5]

The revisionist critique, pioneered by Ayesha Jalal, locates the ambiguity in Jinnah's demand for Pakistan in the supplementary space of the unspoken. Jalal attends to the crucially significant aspect of the performative – the shared language of expressive behavior – and restores the significance of the performative to historical debates. She argues that the Muslim League used the bogey of Pakistan as a bargaining counter with the Congress. The Muslim League demanded representative parity with the Congress, independent of numerical proportions on the basis of the inherent dichotomy between Hindus and Muslims.[6] The effort was to coerce the concerned parties into conceding substantial representation of Muslims at the center, with the threat of Partition. Thus, Ayesha Jalal makes an intervention into the assumption that the League stood for Partition by revealing the slippage between the rhetoric and practice of Jinnah.

The famous speech by Jinnah in 1940, known as the Lahore Resolution, has often been cited as the first clear articulation of Pakistan. The Resolution, however, made no mention of the Partition but spoke eloquently of "two nations" and of Muslims having "their homelands, their territory and their state." Refuting notions of composite nationhood, Jinnah passionately argued that "it is a dream that the Hindus and the Muslims can ever evolve a common nationality, and this misconception of one Indian nation has gone far beyond the limits, and is the cause of most of our troubles, and will lead India to destruction, if we fail to revise our notions in time."[7]

By declaring the Muslims a nation, Jinnah's speech clearly rejected his former position that the Muslims constituted a minority. When Jinnah's secularist idea of resolving the problem of Muslim minoritization through substantial representation at the center and provisional autonomy was thwarted, he shifted his rhetorical strategy. He realized the only way to be taken seriously was to shift from empiricist, enumerative, and bureaucratic accounts of "Muslims" as minority to an aspirational account of Muslims as a "nation." Subsequently, he realized that "an honorable settlement can only be achieved between equals and politics means power and not relying only on cries of justice or fair play or goodwill."[8] Thus evolved his claim for parity at the center based on the claim of being a separate religious nation, and this in turn provided the foundation for the two-nation theory. Dominant explanations suggest a radical change in Jinnah's personality from a secular politician to a communalist one.[9] Jalal, among other revisionist historians, has shifted our attention from preoccupations with Jinnah's political beliefs, his "interior" personhood, to his political persona, his public performance. Jinnah's shift in rhetorical position serves as a tactical maneuver and signals no serious change in his political goals.

Despite the fact that the Lahore Resolution does not explicitly mention Pakistan, it soon acquired the status of the first cogent articulation for the creation of Pakistan and was, in fact, referred to as the Pakistan Resolution. As Jinnah himself lashes out, "When we passed the Lahore Resolution, we had not used the word 'Pakistan.' Who gave us this word? ...You know that Pakistan is a word which is really foisted upon us and fathered on us by some section of the Hindu press and also by the British press."[10] Jinnah rejects the conflation of the Lahore Resolution with the demand for Pakistan.

Jinnah's momentous address at Lahore is ambiguous, as he refused to define his "nation," leaving it open to diverse interpretations. Its very vagueness, however, played an important role in securing Jinnah some strategic leverage with the Congress. The elusiveness of the Resolution, Jalal suggests, confirms that Jinnah was always less interested in the creation of a real Pakistan than he was in using the notional Pakistan to secure the needs of Indian Muslims. Seen this way, the two-nation theory was a means to advocate parity, while Congress stood for majority rule.

According to Ayesha Jalal, the Lahore Resolution was a rhetorical performance advanced to secure an equal say for Muslims in India's political future. Although Jinnah framed his demand using the rhetoric of Muslim "nationhood," his oratory was incommensurate with his political objectives. The key to unpacking this conundrum lies in asking not only what Jinnah's words *mean* but also what they *do*. The shift from hermeneutic to performative modes of analysis bears rich insights: The affective force of the Lahore Resolution constituted a powerful audience through its address that claimed Muslims not as a minority but as a nation. In addition to the discursive constitution of a public, it served to shift from an enumerative economy of political representation to an aspirational one. The Lahore Resolution aimed to generate an unequivocal recognition of Muslim nationhood that could then redress the political disadvantage of a minority status in a federal constitution. South Asian historian Asim Roy explains it thus:

> The thrust of Jinnah's political strategy underpinning the
> resolution was initially to secure the recognition of the
> Indian Muslim nationhood on the basis of the acceptance of

the "Pakistan" demand by the British and the Congress, and thereby gain an equal say for Muslims in any arrangement about India's political future at the centre. Once the principle of the Muslim right to self-determination as embodied in the Lahore Resolution was conceded, the resultant Muslims state or states could either "enter into a confederation with non-Muslim provinces on the basis of parity at the center" or make as a sovereign state, "treaty arrangement with the rest of India about matters of common concern."[11]

By shoring up evidence of the complicity of the Congress in the Partition of the subcontinent, Ayesha Jalal also makes an intervention into the widespread assumption that the Congress stood for unity.[12] For example, Jalal persuasively argues that faced with the choice between a strong center and territorial unity, the Congress chose the former. The League sought to create a negotiated pattern of sharing power at the center with the Congress on the basis of a substantial League representation at the centre. A solid center was integral to Nehru's socialist vision of a united and modernized India, capable of economic reconstruction, based on centralized planning and a strong army. Further, the increasing ethnic tensions of the provincial Congress ministries after 1937 reinforced Congress's reluctance to seek political accommodation with the League. Having a strong center would enable the Congress to stem the centrifugal tendencies and frame a constitution unhampered by communal considerations. Ultimately, the Congress did not want to forfeit control by sharing power with the Muslim League and thus preferred Partition to giving up control in a unified India.

Jalal's path-breaking scholarship has been criticized for being too exclusively focused on high politics and diplomacy.[13] For example, Mushirul Hasan points out that Jalal's analysis does not account for the growing movement for Partition drawn from different regions as well as classes. It does not deconstruct the notion of a monolithic Islam by foregrounding dissenting Muslim voices against the creation of Pakistan. There is little analysis of the ideological content of the movement, the social base of the Muslim League, its mobilization techniques after the Lahore Resolution, or its ability to use Islam as a rallying symbol.[14] Further, certain questions remain unanswered in Jalal's theory. Why, for instance, does Jinnah not dispel the conflation of the Lahore Resolution with the demand for Pakistan? Why not opt to be more straightforward and mature and put forward the demands of the Muslims in minority areas along with those in majority? Why does Jinnah play into the hands of the Congress by persisting on "Pakistan?"[15] By forwarding sincerity in politics, these criticisms obscure the central role played by performance in the field of politics. Jalal's scholarship radically intervened into orthodox histories surrounding the Partition and circumvented textual fetishization by examining the performative dimensions of political rhetoric.

The debates between the Muslim League and the Congress over the Partition issue exemplify the performative deployment of language by both political parties; the performance of political positions plays on the subterfuge of language. In playing with the idea of Pakistan as a bargaining counter, both parties "said what they did not mean, stood for what they did not want and what they truly wanted was not stated publicly but only betrayed in their vital and purposive political decisions and actions."[16] Words take on a life of their own, however, and Jinnah's rhetorical ingenuity exceeded his intentions and generated unpredictable effects.

Attending to the performative dimension in the political debates decenters a linguistically overdetermined scrutiny of pedagogical history and allows us to consider rhetoric not only for its meaning but also for its generative effects and affective force. Dwight Conquergood reminds us, "A whole realm of complex, finely nuanced meaning that is embodied, tacit, intoned, gestured, improvised, co-experienced, covert – and all the more deeply meaningful because of its refusal to be spelled out" gets left out by textually overdetermined analyses.[17] The world-making perlocutionary force of the rhetorical address of powerful, charismatic leaders played no small role in the generation of counterpublics that gained momentum and culminated in the division of the subcontinent. It is to the moment of Partition that we will now turn.

The Radcliffe boundary

The Radcliffe Boundary, which separates India from Pakistan, materially instantiates the two-nation theory, which held that Muslims and Hindus were essentially incompatible and could not coexist within the same nation-state. By exploring some of the genealogies of that idea, as well as its contemporary reverberations in South Asian politics, I now examine the discursive, material, and ideological production of the India–Pakistan border at Wagah.

To begin with, let us turn to "Partition", a poem written by British poet W.H. Auden.[18] In 1966, nearly two decades after the Partition of British India into two separate nation-states, Auden's "Partition" ironizes the high drama just prior to British India's independence after a century of colonial rule. Auden's unnamed protagonist is Cyril Radcliffe, a British lawyer, called in from England to delineate the precise territorial boundary between the two independent nation-states of India and Pakistan.

W.H. Auden (1907–1973), radical-leftist British poet, pithily captures the sweat and nerves of Radcliffe, the trusty barrister, assigned with the momentous task of allocating the precise boundary between the two nation-states. Following on the heels of Leonard Mosley's influential account, *The Last Days of the British Raj*, published in 1962, Auden's poem appeared at a political moment when the question of international partitions resurfaced in the public sphere (for example, the partition of North and South Vietnam in 1954, and the erection of the Berlin Wall in 1961). By highlighting the restiveness of the final days, "Partition" punctures the facade of order that the departing British empire struggled to present to the world. The poem also interrupts the dominant account of a peaceful decolonization on the subcontinent.[19]

Cyril Radcliffe, the beleaguered protagonist of "Partition," is significantly unnamed, referred to only as "he." In devaluing Radcliffe's authorial agency, Auden affirms his role as merely another institutional player in the political theatre of colonialism and violently emerging nationalisms. Through the brisk anapestic meter of the poem, Auden conveys not only the urgency of the times but also ironizes the serious business of partitioning nations. The poem dramatizes the manner in which Radcliffe was sucked into the political vortex: The paucity of time in which he was to delineate the territorial boundaries made his task all the more daunting. Radcliffe had the onerous responsibility of reconciling the demands of the key political players: Jinnah of the Muslim League, Nehru of the Indian National Congress, and Lord Mountbatten, the governor-general of British India.

Auden's poem captures the frantic urgency under which Radcliffe had to produce his Boundary Award. Mountbatten, the governor-general of India, understood that appearance was a key technique of power and maintained a Machiavellian facade of order, rational deliberation, and due process.[20] In reality, disorder, haste, and poorly conceived and executed exit strategies marked Britain's departure from India. Mounting evidence suggests that the violence in the wake of Partition had less to do with "religious fanaticism" than with the panic generated in the aftermath of the collapse of political negotiations, which were widely anticipated by British officials at the highest levels.[21] Radcliffe then offered a convenient scapegoat not only for colonial officers but also for Indian politicians who were fully aware that the new border would provoke further unrest.

Radcliffe was only one node in the colonial discursive machine but as the final authority of a Boundary Award that eventually frustrated all concerned parties, he provided an expedient shield. Auden's poem punctures the notion of a monolithic omnipotent colonizer. He reminds us colonial power was disseminated through multiple and shifting channels: Radcliffe was at once both architect and scapegoat.

Auden's poem also offers an interesting point of entry into the Radcliffe Boundary Award because it rehearses many of the widespread assumptions about the final days of the British empire in India. Radcliffe, a wealthy and successful barrister, well known for his loyalty to the British government and his perspicacious intelligence, was selected for the momentous task of delineating the boundary between the two nation-states. A surprising choice, Radcliffe had little expertise in matters of boundary allocation; he had no experience of India, never having visited the region. Radcliffe himself expected to have two years to complete his task, which was subsequently curtailed to six months. On his arrival in India, however, he was informed that he must produce the Boundary Award within seven weeks.[22] And so, "in seven weeks it was done, the frontiers decided, A continent for better or worse divided."[23]

Auden's poem captures the careful arithmetic of the British empire: "We can give you four judges, two Moslem and two Hindu, To consult with, but the final decision must rest with you."[24] The Boundary Award Commission consisted of two committees: one for Punjab and another for Bengal, both headed by Radcliffe. The Muslim League and the Congress nominated two judges each to the committees. This political arithmetic ultimately culminated in a deadlock, thus making Radcliffe the final arbiter on contentious issues. The appointment of four political nominees casts a judicial veneer of balance and orderliness to the boundary allocation process, which obscured the increasingly unstable situation on the ground. The representatives from both parties conceded little, creating a political impasse in the discussions around the Punjab Partition.[25] In addition, the members of the Boundary Commission were all judges with a background in criminal law and with little experience in matters of boundary allocation.

In Bengal, the Bengal Legislative Assembly arrived at the decision to partition by dividing the assembly into two units, one part representing Muslim majority districts and the other part Hindu majority districts. On June 20, 1947, these two units voted on the question of Partition, with the Hindu majority unit in favor and the Muslim majority unit opposed.[26] Foregrounding the territorial considerations that drove the decision to partition, Joya Chatterji reminds us that the Bengal Assembly consisted of representatives of territorial rather than communal units, thus reinforcing that communal autonomy had to take the shape of territorial sovereignty.

Auden evokes the image of a sickly Radcliffe: "Shut up in a lonely mansion, with police night and day, Patrolling the gardens to keep the assassins away, He got down to work, to the task of settling the fate, Of millions. . . . The weather was frightfully hot, And a bout of dysentery kept him constantly on the trot."[27] Perspiring and petrified, poring over inaccurate maps and census data as fanatical and murderous, unruly masses lurked in the shadows, threatening to infringe into a precariously ordered world. The image at once recalls the enumerative practices of colonial administration: census reports, maps, land surveys, and other modes of governance that insistently relied on techniques of measurement.

Radcliffe's knowledge of the territory to be partitioned was predominantly textual – the urgency with which he was required to work meant that he did not have the time for field surveys – or even any visits to the regions in question.[28] The confidence in empiricist methods of boundary allocation – a variety of discursive texts ranging from maps, surveys, and censuses, reinforces a particularly orientalist mode of apprehending place, one that simplifies and sanitizes the complex embeddedness and intermingling among communities of Hindus, Sikhs, and Muslims into orientalist maxims about bounded and polarized religious communities.[29] Auden's poem reinforces the colonial taxonomies of Hindus and Muslims as "two peoples fanatically at odds, with their different diets and their incompatible gods."[30]

I take up questions of the sedimentation of religious identities in the public sphere again in the chapters that follow. For now it is sufficient to note that it is within the colonial enumerative categories such as the census that religious identities such as Muslim and Hindu began to calcify as political groups. Thus, "communalism" or what Auden calls "two peoples fanatically at odds" was insidiously consolidated by enumerative practices of the colonial state that finally also provided the flawed tools for partitioning British India.

In fewer than six weeks, the Radcliffe Boundary drew 2,500 miles of boundary in Punjab, allocating 64 percent of the area of undivided Punjab to Pakistan, with slightly less than 60 percent of the populace. To Pakistan, the award gave 63,800 square miles of Punjabi territory, whereas India received 35,300 square miles.[31] In Bengal, the award gave India an area of 28,000 square miles, with a population of 21.19 million people, of which nearly 5.3 million (29 percent) were Muslim. East Pakistan was awarded 49,000 square miles for a population of 39.11 million, of which 29.1 (11.4 million) were Hindu. West Bengal got 36.36 percent of the land to accommodate 35.14 percent of the population, whereas East Bengal got 63.6 percent of the land to accommodate 64.85 percent of the population.[32]

The commission's terms of reference emphasized the importance of contiguous religious majorities, making religion – rather than infrastructure, kinship relations, or topography – the governing rationale behind the boundary allocation. The commission was advised to "demarcate the boundaries of the two parts of the Punjab on the basis of ascertaining the contiguous majority areas of Muslims and non-Muslims. In doing so, it will also take into account other factors."[33] The new boundary traced the major administrative divisions, but cut across well-developed infrastructural systems disrupting road, telephone, and telegraph communications and most importantly, interfering with the region's vital irrigation system, the repercussions of which extend to the contentious question of Kashmir.[34]

The Radcliffe Award was announced on August 17, two days after the Independence of India and three days after the formation of Pakistan. Lord Mountbatten, who replaced Lord Wavell in February 1947, advanced the date of this award by almost a year. Despite his deadline of June 1948 for Britain to withdraw from India, Mountbatten rushed to decolonize India within six months of his arrival. Chester warns that perhaps even alternative borders may not have helped to divide the Hindus, Sikhs, and Muslims amicably into two separate nations.[35] It did, however, placate the primary political players: The British, hastily leaving the scene of religious violence, exonerated themselves from their responsibilities of a peaceful transfer of power; the Indian National Congress saw the culmination of decades of anti-colonial nationalism as it held the political reins of an independent India; the Muslim League carved out of India a separate sovereign Islamic state, Pakistan.

The uncertainty about the boundary allocation exacerbated the mayhem and communal violence that was rapidly spiraling out of control. The massive dislocation was set into motion as soon as rumors about the partition of India along religious lines began to circulate. People were on the move, uncertain if where they would settle down would eventually belong to India or Pakistan. In this context, the dominant rhetoric of India's "nonviolent" path to independence obscures the magnitude of the violence of the Partition. Britain no doubt strove to appear efficient while handling the transfer of power to the two nations; the newly independent nation-states marked their independence with celebrations. For the victims and survivors of the Partition, however, the violently attained "freedom" was a shattering experience.

In what follows I consider the ways in which the official narratives of the Partition are dramatized at Wagah, the border in Punjab that cuts Amritsar in India from Lahore in Pakistan. Moving away from the role of print culture as the modality through which the nation is imagined, here I consider performance as crucial in affectively sustaining the imagined community. The Retreat ceremony dramatizes the power of the state through performative practices that subtly insert hegemonic power into the bodies of its onlookers. Through a consideration of the mimetic practices of the border ceremonies, I interrogate the production of the border as the marker of national differences and argue that the drama at Wagah inadvertently highlights the nonidentity within the national political subject.

Bordering on drama

The Radcliffe Line cuts Amritsar in India from Lahore in Pakistan at the Wagah border. Amritsar and Lahore, "twin cities" prior to British colonization of Punjab, 36 miles apart, were now strategic border towns of the two new rival nations.[36] The Punjab region witnessed the mass migration of approximately 5.5 million Hindus and Sikhs from its western (Pakistani) area, and 6 million Muslims from its eastern (Indian) area.[37] Ian Talbot reminds us that

> almost 40% of Amritsar's houses were destroyed or damaged and its Muslim population fell from 49% on the eve of the Partition to just 00.52% in 1951. 6000 houses were damaged in Lahore and its Hindu and Sikh population who formed over a third of the population departed for India ... the cities' proximity to the border meant that they received large numbers of refugees. There were a million in Lahore alone in April 1948, two-fifths of whom were housed in camps.... Refugees formed two-fifths of Lahore's population, while Amritsar suffered the greatest physical destruction of any Punjabi city.[38]

34

The 1,500-mile border, which runs through the provinces of Sindh (Pakistan) and Rajasthan (India) and touches on Gujarat (India), can be crossed at two points: the pedestrian crossing at Wagah, typically inaccessible to Indian and Pakistani citizens, and the train track a few miles south at Attari. The red line inscribed by Radcliffe's "calm, judicial pen" is rendered visible at Wagah through elaborate theatrical, architectural, and bureaucratic practices of state.[39] The checkpoint at Wagah is 15.5 miles east of Lahore and 17.5 miles west of Amritsar. The elaborate scaffolding, barbed wire, steel gates, and uniformed border guards contribute to the highly structured production of national difference.

The 10-mile drive from Amritsar in India to the Wagah border appeared uneventful at first.[40] As my taxi speedily rattled along, I gazed at the congested roads teeming with signs marking the end of a long day. In the cold December afternoon, cycle-rickshaws carrying schoolchildren competed with angry busdrivers and irate motorcyclists. Along the way were signs of an earlier time: The striking 300-acre Khalsa College building, founded in 1892, lay adjacent to the newer sprawling campus of Guru Nanak Dev University established in 1969. As we approached the border, the many faces of a bustling city gave way to the solitariness of the Grand Trunk Road, which grew quieter and more forlorn. Occasionally, a large, gaudy film billboard would suddenly interrupt the seamless gray road that wound its way ahead of me.

The languorous streets were flanked on either side by mustard and maize fields, resplendent in the sun. On closer scrutiny, I discerned military tanks lurking behind the tall fields. My taxi driver, Chetan Singh, informed me that the gently sloping hillocks in the distance were in fact camouflaged barracks.[41] Intermittently, all the bright greens and gold of the countryside gave way to fields with rotted corn. The recently planted underlying landmines made harvest impossible; consequently, crops turned rancid on the stalks. Red signs of warning were posted along the way. We were approaching the border.

Chetan Singh suggested that I visit the Attari Railway Station in the town of Attari, named after Sardar Sham Singh Attariwala, Maharaja Ranjit Singh's governor of Kashmir who died in 1846 at the

battle of Sabraon during the First Anglo-Sikh War.[42] Formerly a driver
for the Immigrations Office, Singh spoke fondly of his interaction with
Pakistani officials. When we arrived, I was struck by the ghostly and
deserted look at the station. The Attari Railway Station consisted of a
massive shed with a corrugated tin roof that covered a wide platform.
A steel mesh fence separated the central platform into two sections, in
order to divide the passengers traveling in opposite directions. "India:
The World's Largest Democracy" exclaimed a large, tattered poster,
pasted on a wall. The Samjhauta Express, a cheerless, bleak Northern
Railways biweekly train, has the distinction of being the only train
in the world that covers the shortest rail route of just under 2 miles,
between Attari in India and the Wagah Railway Station across the border; the train returns to Attari the same evening. The train was oper-
ated by the Pakistan Railways for six months of the year and by the
Indian Railways for the other six months, demonstrating the careful
arithmetic and mimetic relationality at play in the relations between
the two nations.[43] Following the Shimla Agreement, the train was
started on July 22, 1976, and ran between Amritsar and Lahore, covering a distance of about 26 miles. Due to security reasons, Indian
Railways decided to terminate the service at Attari, where bureaucratic surveillance practices, customs, and immigrations take place.[44]

If Wagah spectacularizes the power of state through highly
theatrical border rituals, then the railway station at Attari allows
us to consider the technologies of border surveillance. Spectacle and
surveillance offer competing techniques of national governmental-
ity to insert the hegemonic power of the state into the bodies of its
citizens.[45] The government functionaries are important players in the
bureaucratic machine; the delays, harassments, intrusive interroga-
tions, and suspicious attitudes of the customs officials attest to the
material production of the border through fastidious and intimidating
processes.[46] Further, the minutiae of immigration measures, forms to
be filled out in triplicate, customs restrictions, and security checks all
contribute to the aura of the gravity of borders. In the words of travel-
writer and novelist Stephen Alter, "Their illegible signatures and the
smeared patterns of rubber stamps, bearing national insignia, are all
part of an effort to give the border some kind of shape, to make it real

and understood."[47] The iterative bureaucratic and ceremonial procedures at the railway station inscribe the hegemonic power of the state on the bodies of its citizens.

In his travelogue, *Amritsar to Lahore: A Journey across the India-Pakistan Border*, Alter captures the palpable tensions and power dynamics within the railway station at Attari. After the complicated immigration procedures, he passes through the metal detectors to reach the other side of the platform. The railway journey was unnecessarily protracted with short spurts of activity followed by long periods of delay. Prolonging the time taken to traverse such a short distance deliberately stretched out the conceptual space between the two nations. The ensuing sense of physical and mental strain attempted to make the passengers believe that the two countries were much farther apart than they really were.[48] Several travelers complained that the visceral power of the state manifests itself in the harassment and intimidation, the deliberate fastidiousness and unpleasantness that makes travel between the two nations an arduous and complex affair.[49]

After our brief stop at the railway station, we got back into the taxi and drove to the Wagah border. The Grand Trunk Road runs from Amritsar in India to Lahore in Pakistan and cuts the border post at Wagah. Previously known as Sher Shah Suri Marg after the Moghul ruler (1540–1545) who originally constructed the route, it established a sophisticated administrative and communications system. The road was subsequently renamed Grand Trunk Road after British colonization of the Punjab. Sher Shah Suri Marg was the main artery that connected the breadth of the territory and ran from Sonargaon in Bengal to Peshawar in the northwest of Pakistan.[50]

The taxi pulled over at a somewhat deserted parking space. Walking toward the closed gate that admitted visitors, I observed the vendors – sedentary as well as itinerant – for whom the border was serious business.[51] Several stalls served refreshments, including tea, tobacco, popcorn, and groundnuts. Others sold souvenirs of India, trinkets, and gift items. Some young boys besieged me with postcards of the ceremony and miniature Indian flags. Several of these trinkets and postcards reiterated that India was the world's largest democracy. Even a year after the attacks on the Indian Parliament House in

December 2001, business was slow. Trade between the two countries had come to a standstill, and few people crossed the border except diplomats of the two countries and "foreigners," conferring a strange sense of kinship to the citizens of either nation.

The border outpost consists of an elaborate complex of buildings, roads, and barriers with electrified barbed wire on either side. India has fenced hundreds of miles of its border with Pakistan, consisting of two 8-foot-high barbed-wire fences with razor-sharp concertina wire running in between. Facing the Indian border, another signboard relentlessly reiterates, "India: The largest democracy in the world welcomes you." Across the Indian border, I discerned an impressive Pakistani seating arena. The Pakistani Baab-e-Azadi (Gate of Freedom) was built in 2001 as a memorial to the Muslims who were killed during 1947.

Soon after Independence in 1947, the border post consisted of a few whitewashed drums and a rubble of stone. "Ours was a difficult task," writes Brigadier Mohinder Singh Chopra of the Indian Army, "there were no pillars or markers to suggest which was our land and which theirs."[52] At the behest of brigadiers of the Sixth Royal Battalion, Mohinder Chopra of India, and Nazir Ahmed of Pakistan, a few tents were pitched on either side. Further, two sentry boxes painted in the two countries' national colors in addition to a swing gate, to regulate the refugee traffic, were also set in place. Two flag masts were erected on either side of the border, and a brass plaque, commemorating the Partition, was installed. On October 11, 1947, the Wagah border was formally established after the brigadiers and former regimental executives officially signed and endorsed the establishment of the border post. The ceremonies commenced in 1959.

Radcliffe's boundary was materialized by the architectonics of government that separated India from Pakistan. It appeared to stretch out endlessly, but the Zero Point is the only place where one was allowed to cross. A thin white line drawn on a tar road signified the Zero Point. A brick gateway flanked either side of the border. The Indian gate had a large sign that read: *"Mera Bharat Mahan"* (My India Is Great), and the Pakistani side had an Urdu inscription: *"Pakistan Zindabad"* (Long Live Pakistan.) The two gates separating India and Pakistan were painted with the colors of the respective flags. A few

feet ahead of us, in Pakistan, was a Pakistani guard looking noncha-
lantly at the eager and curious faces on the other side.

After a scrupulous body inspection, the guards let in the hundred or so people cheerily assembled at the gates. Two guards escorted
us on a long, meandering route behind the army barracks to the Zero
Point. We were then escorted away from the barbed wire and toward
the military edifice where we were asked to sit down. The theatricality of this event was further affirmed by the newly constructed "viewers' gallery" that allowed the spectators to organize themselves in a
more orderly fashion. The border police then warned us that cheering
slogans should be limited to three: *"Bharat Mata Ki Jai," "Hindustan
Zindabad,"* and *"Vande Mataram."* We were explicitly warned not to
jeer at the Pakistanis.

As we were being seated, the invisible stereos started blaring
out old patriotic songs from popular Hindi movies.[53] The music was
carefully chosen to evoke nostalgic memories and elicit a particular emotional response from the audience. The songs played on the
emotions and attachments of the audience and sonically reinforced
shared cultural memories. Ravi Vasudevan reminds us, "images and
sounds do not only course around us, they also reside, affectively,
in us. They are layered in the space of memory, where public and
personal archives intermesh, where for example, music provides
a soundtrack that traverses public history and personal biography.
Within the immediacy of audio-visual experiences rest other images
and sounds that clamour, contest, and dialogue with their own histories."[54] In this case, the music was carefully selected to suggest a
benevolent Nehruvian patriotism and was drawn primarily from early
socialist-inspired Hindi cinema of the 1950s and 1960s. It steered clear
from more recent jingoistic numbers churned out by the Hindi film
industry. As old Hindi favorites such as *"Meri Desh ki Dharti"* and
"Wo Bharat Desh Hai Mera" blared out of the stereos, there was a
clear attempt to revive an idealized nostalgia that reinforced the harmonious, affective dimensions of patriotic fellow-feeling. This was
the house music as the audience settled down with their teacups and
paper cones of piping hot groundnuts. The Pakistanis chose to play
more religious and devotional music.

The audience consisted primarily of young Sikh men, but there were some Sikh and Hindu families there as well. Many of the young middle-class men, couples, and families were on a religious pilgrimage to the Golden temple at Amritsar, and included Wagah as part of their itinerary.[55] I also noticed quite a few non-Sikh Indian and foreign tourists. The Pakistani audience organized themselves into separate groups of men and women, but I could not discern much more than that.

A group of about fifty uniformed schoolboys between the ages of ten and thirteen arrived with their teachers. What followed made vivid the risks of politically indoctrinating the young into unthinkingly imbibing national ideologies. At first, they belted out a few patriotic songs, adhering to those of Hindi cinema in the 1950s. Their songs reiterated a Nehruvian patriotism, consonant with the recorded music, and affirmed the importance of rising above religious, ethnic, and regional divisions. What followed after the singing was the prologue to the real show. Two adolescent Sikh boys consecutively carried a huge 10-foot flag of India and vigorously ran up to the gates, swirling it in a show of insolence toward Pakistanis. Their flagbrandishing mirrored identical moves by their Pakistani counterparts. The Pakistani contingent, however, consisted of young adults skilled at the art of brandishing their flags. High-spirited audiences cheered the adolescent schoolboys as they sprinted with the flags, which turned out to be rather unwieldy. After about fifteen minutes of pre-Retreat warm-ups of flag brandishing, the guards directed the schoolboys to sit down in the audience.

The categorical production of docile and patriotic citizens through performative practices encourages the citizen-viewers to behold the grandeur of the state while participating through programmed responses of sloganeering and cheering, thus inscribing on the citizen body itself the repressive rhythms of the state.[56] Despite the patriotism that some of the audience displayed, many more chuckled at the hapless antics of the schoolboys getting entangled in their flags. There was a healthy dose of humor, cynicism, and curiosity in the audience that December evening.

If the schoolboys demonstrated the politicization of children through pedagogical and somatic inculcation of a patriotic subjectivity, a small group of about six Shiv Sainiks in the audience disrupted the carefully composed rhythms of civic nationalism. It appeared that these young men, brandishing saffron scarves, were no strangers to the rituals at the Retreat ceremony. They were there with the express intention of provoking the audience. The pre-ceremonial rituals of flag-brandishing were punctuated by their belligerent cheers. They began their sloganeering almost immediately. Although many tried to ignore these rabble-rousers, some in the audience watched their belligerence with a scornful amusement. In the words of Thomas Blom Hansen, there is something "profoundly excessive" in the public style of Shiv Sena, which combines "visual, theatrical, urban, violent, masculine performances" into a new politics of presence.[57] This style of claiming public space through dress, speech, gesture, and comportment ensured the visibility of the Shiv Sainiks. They cultivated and promoted the identity of their group through their iterative somatic and embodied performances; their excessive manner attempted to incite passions, influence opinions, and convert Hindu audiences into their fold.

The hordes of spectators goaded the soldiers on and cheered their own side as they would at a cricket match. The rabble-rousers barely even looked at the performance. They wound their way through the audience shouting patriotic slogans. It was impossible to ignore them as their presence intruded into the aural and visual fields of perception. The Sainiks audaciously inserted themselves into the secular space of the civic ceremony deploying the body as an instrument of defiance against the disciplinary regimes of institutional power.

The agitators drew on and refracted the Retreat ceremony's ideal of masculinist nationalism. They frequently taunted the less vocal male audiences: "*Chup kyon ho? Agar chup hi rehna hai to ghar pe choodi pehen ke baitho!*" (Why are you silent? If you want to stay silent then wear bangles on your hands and sit at home.) Using clichéd insults, these rabble-rousers accused the audience of effeminacy, unwittingly excluding women from the scene of national belonging, while simultaneously engendering the fraternal imagined community.

Throughout the Retreat ceremony, the Shiv Sainiks kept up their sloganeering. As the ceremony progressed, they began to introduce new slogans; two were especially interesting. The first, *"Chatrapati Shivaji ki Jai,"* or "Long Live Shivaji," referenced the historical Maratha leader Shivaji, who fought against the Mughal rulers, and circulates as an icon of Hindu nationalism in contemporary India. Given that the majority of the people in the audience were, in fact, from the Sikh community, this was an especially clear marker of the ways in which the Shiv Sainiks assimilate heterogeneous religious identities into an imagined, uniform community effected through the slippage from Hindu to Indian identity. The fraternity of the "imagined community" invoked here then clearly excludes women and religious minorities but nevertheless claims to represent them.

The second moment was when the agitators began to deride Pakistan and started shouting, *"Pakistan Murdabad"* or "Death to Pakistan." The guards immediately responded to the disobedient act and warned them to be quiet; the raucous youth reverted to the sanctioned slogans for a while to appease the guards. The unruly members of the audience routinely played up as well as against the magnificence of state power. In this way, their belligerent patriotism alternatively reified as well as challenged the state's power. The hooliganism illustrates the ways in which live spaces constitute communities through processes of identification as well as intimidation. Through acts that toy with state power, the rowdy youth perform their allegiance to the nation not in the passive and obedient register of dispassionate spectatorship but through affective performances that flouts institutional authority. By capitalizing on emotion, the Shiv Sainiks tap into the affective vacuum of secular public culture and turn passionate and sensuous fellow-feeling toward their own political ends.

Further, such moments reveal the potentially disruptive power of live performances in public spaces and point to the constitutive unknowability that makes up live performance.[58] By introducing liveness as an analytical category, I am less concerned with its temporal economy and questions about its nonreproducibility.[59] These energetic debates have generated rich insights, but my interest here is to reclaim the spatiality of liveness. Live performance in public space draws us out of our secure, individualistic viewing practices into different – sometimes dangerous –spatial configurations of "contact zones," thereby exposing our vulnerability. The agency of the audience and the performers to interrupt or change the performance is crucial to "liveness," unlike in mediatized live events where the audience is "screened out." Here, liveness works not as an unexamined celebration of community but rather as an exploration of how such contact zones offer opportunities for spontaneous or planned action that interrupts totalizing powers of state representation. The particular contingencies of live action – its unpredictable provocation, response, and reaction – all contribute to its disruptive power. Liveness, then, invokes an electrical metaphor: just like a live wire, the current between performer and spectator goes both ways and can be deadly.

The juxtaposition of the schoolboys and the Hindu agitators offers not only a moment to consider the competing performances of politics at play that evening but also the pedagogical and somatic inculcation of political ideologies. While the boys in their school uniforms performed a civic, Nehruvian nationalism, the unruly Shiv Sainiks seized on a militant, heteronormative Hindu register. While the latter subscribed to a culturally exclusivist and aggressive brand of Hindu nationalism, the former evoked a kind of civic nationalism that produces citizens with strong national sentiment but also with confidence in liberal values of "equality" and "composite" culture.[60] While the Shiv Sainiks' display of Hindu cultural nationalism gained legitimacy through rhetoric and practices of religious intolerance and exclusion within the nation, the civic nationalism of the schoolboys evoked allegiances based on abstract citizenship rights and democratic equality.[61] Although there was a strong, all-encompassing anti-Pakistani sentiment that united both factions, blurring the distinctions between cultural and civic nationalisms, the civic nationalists purportedly locate the "anti-nationals" outside India, and the Hindu cultural nationalists position "the enemy" both within and without the nation.

The performances of the Shiv Sainiks on the one hand, and the students on the other, index mimetic modes of evoking sensuous fellow-feeling in the audience through an aesthetics that subsumes difference into sameness.[62] The powerful performative claims made on empathy by both civic and religious nationalisms is premised on dissolving the affective distance between the actor and the spectator, so they become one with the performance. This empathetic dissolution of difference is in stark contrast to the inadvertent mimetic doubling of the Retreat ceremony, which foregrounds the doubleness and nonidentity of the political subject.

The flag-brandishing prologue set the stage for the mimetic play of the soldiers. The piercing Hindi music stopped abruptly as the bugles picked up the pitch, announcing the beginning of the "invented traditions" at the India–Pakistan border.[63] A dozen of the choicest military men from both India's Border Security Force (BSF) and the Pakistani Rangers (PR) performed a ritual that reiterates the militancy and machismo of nationalism.[64] One Pakistani and one Indian soldier appeared simultaneously from their respective army barracks at the call of the bugles. The BSF soldiers wore khaki uniforms: ornate red, yellow, and black cummerbunds around their waists and vivid, tall, impressive turbans with tassels. The PR soldiers wore long military green *kurtas* over matching pants; they also wore cummerbunds and tasseled headgear.

A militant demonstration of martial prowess followed: The soldiers glowered at each other, stomped their feet, and shook their weapons in a highly stylized fashion. A ceremonial parade marks the beginning of the proceedings. From about thirty yards across the border, the soldiers belligerently goose-stepped toward the other. A few yards short of the white line separating India and Pakistan, the soldiers stopped and performed a one-quarter turn in perfect harmony. Both groups now stood at attention, bodies perpendicular to the border, chests distended as they stared piercingly at one another over their near shoulders. Next, a lone sentry marched out along with his Pakistani counterpart; two more border guards joined him. They approached a higher official and requested permission to open the gates and lower the flag. In a loud, clear, and staccato voice, the officers responded: "*Ijaazat di jati hai*" (Permission granted). Several border guards joined in and the ceremony proceeded with coordinated stamping, wheeling, shouted commands, and saluting. They approached the respective gates, unlocked them, and with great power swung the gates open in one, swift motion. They briefly

Figure 2.1 A Pakistan Ranger and an Indian Border Security Force soldier marching during the Wagah border ceremony. Photo: AP/Aman Sharma.

shook hands and then proceeded to lower their respective flags that were placed high on poles planted at the foot of the gates. Buglers on either side played in perfect unison as both flags are lowered simultaneously and were then folded and carried away to their own stations. The commandants of both sides finally saluted each other, very briefly shook hands, and shut the respective gates with a ferocious crash.

45

The semiotic excess of this performance of nationalism hardly needs to be belabored. The composition of the event with the house music, flag-brandishing prologue, and arena seating, frames it as nationalist theatre. Furthermore, the plethora of signs – for example, the iconic representation of the encoded soldiers' bodies as actors, civilians as audience, the corresponding stage settings on either side, the identical use of stage props (including weapons and flags), and finally the significance of the flag coming down as curtains marking the end of the show – all circulate within a theatrical economy. The hyperbolic performance of consummate nationalism is also unsurprisingly the performance of a robust masculinity. Both nation-states appropriate an ideal of martial masculinity to affirm their potency to protect their motherland; the male body of the performing soldier inscribes militarism with patriotism and patriarchy. The Retreat ceremony derives its performative idiom from imperial systems of displaying power, which themselves were invented traditions carefully crafted to symbolically assert the authority of Britain over India.[65]

In addition to drawing on imperial iconography of power in India, the uniforms, music, and military drill also draw on the symbolic genealogies of Britain's Beating Retreat ceremony, referred to as Watch Setting as early as 1554, which symbolically enacts the culmination of the day's fighting, a return to camp, and the mounting of the guard for the night.[66] The Beating Retreat ceremony continues to be performed in England as a major event in the army's ceremonial calendar, delivering an evening of spirited marches as well as hymns and anthems.

Given that the Retreat ceremony at Wagah derives from the wartime rituals of its British predecessor, it becomes significant to ponder the extent to which the border rituals symbolically enact a state of permanent, quotidian war between India and Pakistan. For the two nations symbolically at war the retreat suggests a temporary cessation of hostilities for the evening to be resumed again the next day. The border rituals aesthetically represent the nation as one at war and performatively inscribe, sustain, and perpetuate a narrative of antagonistic hostility between the two nations. The location of the Retreat ceremony at the Wagah border, which cuts Amritsar from Lahore, is

also significant: The chaos, panic, and bewilderment that characterized the massive forced migrations is reshaped into a crisp, structured
ceremony that keeps alive a particular account of the Partition in
order to legitimize state monopoly of violence.

The Wagah border rituals dramatize the national mimicry
between India and Pakistan. The competitiveness and one-upmanship
that shapes the relations between the two nations converge on ideas of
identity and difference. This national mimicry, however, is amply demonstrated in other arenas as well; for example, in May 1998, Pakistan
carried out six nuclear tests in response to India's five. Thus, the logic
of this national mimicry extends to the more dangerous nuclear race
between the two countries, explicitly dramatizing what is at stake in
the serious play of theatre that at once marks and troubles the notion
of national difference.

Performance offers a crucial political technique in the affective constitution of publics. We considered the rhetorical strategies
of high politics as well as the spectatorial performances that make
visible the authority of the state. These performative practices insidiously inculcate the compulsory narratives of the state within its
audience. The hyperbolic display of nationalism during the border
ceremonies at Wagah oscillates between high realism and parody.
The power of the parodic mode derives from its manipulation of a
recognizable norm, citing it with a twist that resignifies the action.[67]
The inadvertent parodic performance of the border guards denatu-
ralizes the affective realism of patriotism and exposes its construction as artifice and theatre. The gradual accretion of symbolic and
gestural language, done in the competitive spirit of one-upmanship,
steadily turns the seriousness of militaristic might into a parody of
uber-patriotism. The inflated and highly exaggerated performative
idiom dramatizes the absurdity of the extreme antagonism between
the two nations and offers an opportunity to read the border ceremony against the grain and meditate on the histrionics that under-
gird political performances. Haunted by its own inadequacy, the
border rituals require magnified and exaggerated performances to
establish and augment their authority and reveal themselves as anxious performances of nationalism.

Figure 2.2 Soldiers glare at each other at the Wagah border. Photo: AP/Vincent Thian.

The Wagah ceremony displays the magnificent power of the state at the same time that it dramatizes the antagonism between India and Pakistan. According to anthropologist Richard Murphy, the identical gestures of the soldiers across the border acquire a mirror effect through a logic of binary opposition. Drawing on theories of Lacanian psychoanalysis, he observes, "The mirror stage at Wagah is a dramatic illustration that Pakistan is defined as that which India is not.... On close examination this definition collapses into a dance of similitude: while the border ritual enacts difference, it also illustrates the fundamental similarities that Pakistani nationalist discourse seeks to deny."[68] Murphy suggests that the rhetoric of difference melts into a "dance of similitude" and confounds Pakistan's two-nation theory that held Hindus and Muslims as incommensurable ethnic groups.

While the identical mirror play of Lacanian psychoanalysis dissolves the Retreat ceremony's play of national difference into a dance of similitude, I argue that the familial trope of twins can offer important insights into the constitution of political subjectivity. The border ceremonies inadvertently reflect popular Partition discourse that casts the event in the image of twins, violently separated at birth by the nation's founding fathers. This image circulated widely in representational public spheres, including newspapers, political cartoons, and popular Hindi cinema.[69] It holds accountable the founding fathers of both nations (Jinnah and Nehru) and divests the innocent newborn nations – and by extension, "the common people" – of complicity.[70] By casting the people as guiltless victims of the founding fathers' political games, sundered by overwhelming political forces, these popular representations also forestall an examination into the violations perpetrated by "ordinary people."

The Retreat ceremony expressed through identical moves and gestures uncannily evokes the image of twins mimetically reinscribing kinship as the terrain on which the antagonistic politics of state is played out. Furthermore, the trope of twins disallows dissolving difference into identical mirror images and pushes us to consider the nonidentity within dialectical images that contain the incommensurable contradiction of being similar and different simultaneously.

Nationalisms are structured around the dialectic of identity within the nation and difference without. However, the trope of twins makes vivid the doubleness that complicates unifying certitudes of national identity and difference. The border rituals at Wagah unwittingly stage the drama of the twins separated at birth, thus reinforcing the mimetic relationality rather than the oppositionality between the two nations. Doubles disallow the dissolution of self and other by holding multiple selves in nonreducible constellation with each other. Brecht's idea of the doubleness, the nonidentity between actor and character in his epic theatre, is instructive here: "The actor must show his subject, and he must show himself. Of course he shows his subject by showing himself, and he shows himself by showing his subject. Although the two coincide, they must not coincide in such a way that the difference between the two tasks disappears."[71] Paying attention to the mimetic doubleness prevents us from collapsing difference into sameness, and resisting the empathetic aesthetics of civic and religious nationalism.

In addition, the exaggerated theatricality of the antagonisms between both nations opens up the possibility to read the border display itself as a parody of patriotism. The aggressive posturing of the Shiv Sainiks further demonstrates the heterogeneity rather than the uniformity of the nation's imagined community. Finally, diverse audience responses at Wagah introduce a disjunctive temporality that uncannily doubles and disorders the monological state performance of the Partition.[72]

As the resounding bugles marked the end of the ritual performance, the flags were lowered and the two iron gates were shut with a colossal clamor. The bemused spectators slowly began to disperse. The audience was now permitted to go up to the gates and glimpse the other side of the border. About 15 feet separate the two gates. Several of the audience left after the display, excited and invigorated by the spectacle. Many continued to linger at the gates, staring into the other nation. Likewise, many of the Pakistanis on the other side, too, gathered at the gate looking toward us.

In conclusion, I turn to two vignettes that illuminate competing modes of avowing friendship across the border. In his book *The Falcon in My Name: A Soldier's Diary*, Major General K.S. Bajwa recalls meeting his old friend Captain Zulfikar Ali of the Pakistan Army across the border at the Wagah checkpoint. Ali and Bajwa were close friends as army cadets in Dehradun under the British Guards in pre-Independent India. They met by accident after the 1971 India–Pakistan War when Bajwa was coordinating the repatriation of Pakistani prisoners of war through the gates at Wagah. As he recalls, "Both brigadiers now, it took us only a few seconds to rush into a warm embrace, oblivious to the touchy dignities of the victors and the vanquished.... We both laughed and years of the invisible barrier fell away.... Then I became acutely aware of the hostile glares of an adversary posture from his people from across the border and we parted.... We had relived for fleeting moments the bonds of human friendship that knew no geographical barriers."[73]

Consider now an account from Suketu Mehta's essay "Reflections: A Fatal Love." Mehta recounts the story of Harjeet Singh, whom he met in Lahore in 1997. Singh told him about the madness that overcame him for one day in August 1947. "We killed one third of the people in that village. About 50 to 60 men were killed in those few hours." Mehta notes that Harjeet Singh was "weeping profusely by now, his handkerchief going now to one eye, now to the other." Harjeet Singh continues, "I don't get angry on anybody else but myself. I did not sleep all that night, I did not stop thinking about it for a single minute. That's the worst memory for me."[74] At the Wagah border, Harjeet Singh met one of his former Muslim friends. Suketu Mehta describes Singh's frequent visits to Wagah as a compulsive attempt to assuage his guilt:

> Harjeet Singh went forward ... beyond the fence and his friend came forward to meet him. They embraced each other; what could be said? How does one condense the highlights of three decades? ...
>
> Then the soldiers separated the two men and his friend went back into Pakistan and Harjeet Singh started walking slowly back into India. He was stopped by agents from the Intelligence Bureau, and they asked him, "Who were you talking to?" "To my brother," Harjeet Singh answered. How can that be, they demanded, he was Sikh, the man who came to meet him was Muslim. "I said that is exactly what I mean, he is my brother. He has land on that side, I have land on this side, that's why we're separated." The Intelligence men said, "Don't fool us." I said, "I have told you what I told you, I have said what I have said, he is my brother."[75]

These accounts frame cross-border friendship divergently, the first invoking the call of abstract humanism, the second insisting on incommensurable particularities. In the first account the soldiers impulsively embrace each other but withdraw when they become aware of hostile glances that tacitly rebuke them for transgressing the bounds of patriotic duty. Their withdrawal from each other, despite their obvious affection for each other, suggests their commitment to the higher imperatives of patriotic duty. Although cognizant of the political realities that pervade this encounter, Major Bajwa temporarily transcends them and invokes an abstract human friendship that knows no geographical barriers. However, the evasive and neutral vocabulary of universal humanism lacks the power through which to mount a pointed, robust critique of narrow nationalisms because its abstract categories of liberal humanism refuse to take seriously the given-ness of political identities.

Whereas the first account proffers a humanizing imperative to dissolve differences in the service of a higher, abstract ideal of human friendship, the second approaches friendship, acutely aware of the particular contingencies that shape these encounters and position them as distinctive political subjects. In the second instance, Harjeet Singh acknowledges the particularity of given political identities at a given historical moment, and then proceeds to challenge it anyway. For Singh there is no turning away or disavowal of the given-ness of their political identities at this historical moment. Rather it is through acknowledging the "political facts" of their identities, insisting on their kinship, that they powerfully refute the narrative of implacable hostility enacted at the border.[76]

Harjeet Singh's challenge to the given citizen role acquires its particular affective force from his sense of betrayal. The traumatic memory of the Partition emerges from the horror that people were more attached to abstract ideals than to their friends, their kin, their neighbors. Singh's powerful affirmation: "Yes, he is my brother" derives its power from an earlier denial of this friendship, which he sacrificed at the altar of the abstractions of nation and religion. Both accounts expose the limits of hegemonic political ideologies: While the first affirms friendship in the idiom of abstract humanism, the second offers an account that negotiates difference and particularizes friendship.

Political friendship acquires its power to critique antagonistic nationalism not through a disavowal of difference in the name of abstract humanism but through recognition and refutation of the given roles of identity taxonomies. Cognizing the contradictoriness of political subjectivity – "Yes, I am a Sikh; yes, he is my brother" – discloses the *doubleness* at the heart of political subjectivity that is denied by the unifying discourses of civic and religious nationalism, and of abstract humanism. The mimetic relationality, the proliferation of doubles, turns not on the principle of identity but of difference. Mimetic semblance does not dissolve difference into sameness but rather exposes the doubleness of the self, the nonidentity of the self within the self, thus dispersing the deceptive coherence of civic and religious nationalisms. This allows the work of building solidarities across differences, rather than dissolving plurality into a specious unity.

In Chapter 3, we travel from the western border at Wagah across the breadth of the nation to the eastern border in Bengal. Looking at the Partition cinema of Ritwik Ghatak allows us to return again to the trope of twins, which structures the non–sensuous similitude between person and place in riverine Bengal. Not only does the intimate bond between the twins provide an analogue to the kinship between the two Bengals, it also offers the occasion to consider the ways in which mimetic relationality exposes the nonidentity at the heart of the national subject.

3   Ghatak's cinema and the discoherence of the Bengal Partition

I am frightened of an abstraction that is willing to ignore living reality.

Rabindranath Tagore

In his Partition cinema, which comprises *Meghe Dhaka Tara* (1960), *Komal Gandhar* (1961), and *Subarnarekha* (1965), avant-garde Bengali filmmaker Ritwik Ghatak disperses the unifying certitudes of Partition narratives. Introducing interrelated motifs of cross-gender twins, secular and sacred topos, visual and sonic disruptions, and gestus, Ghatak demonstrates the nonidentity of the purported sovereign national subject. Ghatak demonstrates the nonsensuous similitude between place and person through the trope of nonidentical twins; the relationship between the twins is analogous to the bond between the twin Bengals.[1]

Through the trope of twins, Ghatak explores the larger theme of partitions and unions in his cinema. By insistently depicting two orphaned siblings as analogous to the partitioned East and West Bengal, Ghatak forwards kinship as the terrain on which the Partition played out its antagonistic politics. Whereas dominant representations of the Partition cast the event through the fraternal metaphor of twins, Ghatak foregrounds gendered inequities through his depiction of cross-gender twins. No sense of parity structures the relationship between the pairs; indeed, Ghatak reflects on the gendered disparities that the sibling pairs suffer in the wake of Partition.[2] The predominance of orphans, sibling disunions, missing mothers, and incestuous

Rabindranath Tagore, *An Anthology*, 171.

54

unions in his cinema exposes kinship as destructured and fraught with betrayal and desertion. The crisis of kinship constitutes the ground on which larger spatial, social, and psychic displacements are played out in Ghatak's cinema.

Thematically, Ghatak's mode of narration concatenates and brings into relief mythological and modern epistemes. In his films, mythological and modern abstractions converge on "the public woman," whom Ghatak depicts as clerical employee in *Meghe Dhaka Tara*, stage actress in *Komal Gandhar*, and singer-prostitute in *Subarnarekha*, respectively. The significant feminist scholarship on the Bengal Partition has cautioned us against flattening out the gendered dimensions of the Partition by recuperating instances of feminist agency, particularly in Bengal, that enabled women to emerge into the public sphere as breadwinners. Ghatak's depiction of this breadwinner offers a nuanced portrayal of the promise and peril of entering into the public sphere as a gendered laborer.

By braiding competing epistemes – Brechtian-inspired epic narrative with Tagorean romanticism, modernist expressionism with Hindu mythology – Ghatak plays with form to disorient his viewers. Through the interweaving of secular and sacred tropes, Ghatak conjoins Brechtian epic with Bengali mythological epics and offers a narrative that resists the programmed pleasures and reassuring closures of social realist cinema. As a result, Ghatak's trilogy achieves formal and thematic discoherence through the tropic structuring of mimetic siblings, dialectical juxtaposition between mythological and public womanhood, and visual and sonic disjunctures. Together these tropes multiply, disperse, and discohere the unified subjects of social realism. Ghatak follows Brecht's advice to eschew the naturalistic model of an "integrated work of art" and rather pursue a mode of presentation where various elements on stage discohere and mutually alienate each other.[3] This methodology reflects Ghatak's vision of the Partition itself – its repeated and unpredictable incursions into the everyday reveals precisely its incoherence and the inability to bring this event to a comforting closure.

Inspired by Brecht, Ghatak's epic style avoids centralizing the dramatic action.[4] Like Brecht, Ghatak takes a cohesive narrative plot and shreds it into several animated, lively in dividual pieces. Ghatak himself reveals his preference for a centrifugal narrative: "I have joined the different phases of the narrative, one to another, to make a story of fateful coincidences ... the author is not concerned with telling a story but more concerned with attitudes as they evolved with the events. Such coincidences, even if they occasionally appear incredible, would not really jar as long as there is a verisimilitude to it all."[5] The idea of "fateful coincidence," two things occurring simultaneously, recovers the sense of the nonunitary present in a manner that complicates the telos of individual agency within a progressive historicist frame.

Although Ghatak borrows his repertoire of images from Tagore's pastoral romanticism, the sonic register insistently subverts its harmonizing closures.[6] The various sound effects that Ghatak uses, from whiplashes to discordant notes, rupture the sense of utopic nostalgia set up within the diegetic frame. In *Subarnarekha*, Sita counsels her son, "Listen, and you will see," when he inquires about rice fields in rural Bengal, and this advice on nonidentical sensuous registers offered by the eye/ear provides a clue on how to unpack his films. Ghatak exploits the aural soundscape to render discoherent the soothing narrative closures of social realism.

In all three films Ghatak portrays characters who have lost their ground – both literally, as refugees, but also metaphorically. What are the implications of this perpetual disorientation? What larger comment does Ghatak make about the loss of certitudes when people are literally and metaphorically deterritorialized, pulled away from the familiar sustenance of home, family, geography? It is to these questions that this chapter will turn.

Ritwik Ghatak

Ritwik Ghatak was born on November 4, 1925, at Jindabazar, Dhaka, the cultural heart of East Bengal. The Partition of British India suddenly turned Ghatak into a foreigner in his own country, and like many thousands of refugees, his family moved to Calcutta in West Bengal. His films depict the sudden loss of power that middle-class migrant Bengalis experienced in the wake of the Partition. The son of a magistrate in rural East Bengal, Ghatak and his twin sister were the youngest of nine children. Ghatak migrated to Calcutta and joined Calcutta University in 1948 to complete his studies.

As a member of the Communist Party and the left-wing Indian People's Theatre Association, political theatre exerted a significant influence on Ghatak's cinematic imagination. He was drawn to Brecht and translated *Life of Galileo* and *Caucasian Chalk Circle* in addition to acting in and directing numerous plays. In 1955, he joined Filmistan Studios in Bombay as a script writer, but he soon returned to Calcutta. He completed a total of eight feature films, four short films, and four documentaries. In 1965, Ghatak took over the position of vice principal of the Film and Television Institute of India, India's premier film institute. He inspired a whole generation of avant-garde Indian filmmakers, including Mani Kaul, Kumar Shahani, and Ketan Mehta, among others. In 1976, at the age of fifty, Ghatak died prematurely of alcohol-related disease and tuberculosis.

The traumatic events of the 1940s – World War II, the Bengal famine, and Indian Partition crucially informed Ghatak's artistic imagination. As he writes,

> We were born into a critical age. In our boyhood we have seen a Bengal, whole and glorious. Rabindranath, with his towering genius, was at the height of his literary creativity, while Bengali literature was experiencing a fresh blossoming with the works of the Kallol group, and the national movement had spread wide and deep into schools and colleges and the spirit of the youth. Rural Bengal, still reveling in its fairy tales, *panchalis*, and its thirteen festivals in twelve months, throbbed with the hope of a new spurt of life. This was the world that was shattered by the War, the Famine, and when the Congress and the Muslim League brought disaster to the country and tore it into two to snatch for it a fragmented independence. Communal riots engulfed the country. The waters of the Ganga and the Padma flowed crimson with the blood of warring brothers. All this was part of the experience that happened around us. Our dreams faded away. We crashed our faces, clinging to a crumbling Bengal, divested of all its

glory. What a Bengal remained, with poverty and immorality as our daily companions, with black-marketeers and dishonest politicians ruling the roost, and men doomed to horror and misery! ... I have not been able to break loose from this theme in all the films that I have made recently.[7]

Ritwik Ghatak assembles his narratives from the wreckage of violence left in the wake of World War II and the Partition. He was not the first Bengali filmmaker to turn to the Partition as the subject of his cinema; Nemai Ghosh's *Chinnamul* (1950), which offered Ghatak his first role as an actor and assistant director, portrayed the experience of Partition refugees. The film failed at the box office, and Nemai Ghosh left for Madras to work as a cameraman. Since Pakistan had a general ban on all Indian films, Ghatak's films were not screened in his birth city.[8]

The three films that I consider here, *Meghe Dhaka Tara, Komal Gandhar*, and *Subarnarekha*, often called Ghatak's Partition trilogy, discohere the unified narratives of Partition by pointing to mimetic doubles, symbolic concatenation between mythological and public woman, and sonic inversions that rupture the harmonizing closures of social realism. The films shuttle between the romantic pastoralism of the Bengal countryside and the urban squalor of modern life in post-Partition Bengal. Against the vista of a lost idyll, where all certitudes of family, friendship, and home have crumbled, appear twinlike orphans, a brother and a sister, tentatively holding hands. Ghatak dramatizes the relationship between the two Bengals through the metaphor of twins separated at birth. Undermining the idea of two coherent, independent nation-states of India and Pakistan, Ghatak points to the profusion of mimetic doubles in his films. For Ghatak, then, the promise and betrayal of mimetic kinship fuels the dark undercurrent of the antagonistic politics of the Partition.

Meghe Dhaka Tara (1960)

Ghatak's *Meghe Dhaka Tara* (The Cloud-Capped Star), is based on a story by Shaktipada Rajguru, a Bengali novelist who moved to West Bengal after the Partition. My analysis of the film focuses on two interrelated themes in Ghatak's Partition cinema: the idea of the public woman who, by entering the gendered precincts of the public sphere, played a pivotal role in establishing a sense of financial independence. I also consider the public woman as one half of a pair of twins, a recurrent concern in Ghatak's cinema, which enables him to use tropes of kinship to establish the affinity between person and place in Bengal.

The public woman

Born on the same day as the benevolent mother-goddess Jagaddhatri, Neeta mimetically embodies the generous and munificent daughter. The symbolism of the benevolent mother-goddess converges on the material particularity of Neeta, the film's central character. At once compassionate goddess and public woman, the iconic mother and the never-to-be-bride, Neeta's asexuality oscillates between competing representations of woman.

How do we unpack the discoherent images of mother-goddess and public woman? What particular cultural, social, and historical associations does this image evoke for its viewers? The religious and gendered iconography of the resistance to the Viceroy of India, Lord Curzon's attempt to partition Bengal in 1905 laid the groundwork for the Swadeshi anticolonial movement in Bengal. Jasodhara Bagchi observes the ways in which the Hindu imagery of Bengal as the three-eyed mother-goddess gained cultural legitimacy in the wake of the first Partition of Bengal in 1905 and provided the foundation for community divisiveness.[9] By narrating regional solidarity through particular cultural idioms, Bengal was invisibly structured as Hindu province. This further positioned non-Hindus as outsiders enfolded within a benevolent Hindu cosmogony. The naturalization of Bengal as Hindu region, reinforced by nation, community, and family, festered for a long time before 1947.

Ghatak reaches into this reservoir of images and mythologies, while simultaneously complicating them by aligning them with alternative tropes. After migrating to Calcutta as refugees from East Bengal, Neeta, the eldest daughter, provides for her erstwhile well-to-do but now-impoverished family. Like the goddess Jagaddhatri,

Neeta supports her beloved elder brother, a promising musician; her athletic younger brother; her seductive and conniving younger sister; her father, a former school teacher; and her mother, an embittered, devious woman.

Ghatak portrays the men in the family as particularly unmotivated; their languor oscillates from a depressive inertia to shrewd self-interest.[10] Ghatak etches out the effects of genteel poverty on the somatic rhythms of the men: The father finds nostalgic recourse in repeated literary references to Yeats and Shakespeare – his stuttering literary references feebly attempt to recover a sense of home in poetry. The father's loss of phallic authority is portrayed through four successive images: He is displaced from his home to a refugee camp; he loses his legs in an uncanny accident; he witnesses his son descend from his class/caste privilege and join ranks with working-class laborers, and he observes his daughter endure the depredations that her own family heaps on her. The Yeats stutter suddenly gives way to a Zola-esque non sequitur: "I accuse!" exclaims the father, pointing a finger at the camera. This diegetic rupture awaits its full elucidation until *Subarnarekha*, Ghatak's final film in the Partition trilogy, in which the protagonist, Iswar, turns the accusing finger toward himself and insists on his complicity in the perpetuation of injustice toward women in post-Partition Bengal.

The elder son, Shankar, neglects to provide for the family and instead focuses on his enduring love for music at a time when all else seems to be in flux. In addition, Neeta's boyfriend, Sanat, also leans on her income to support his scientific research. Unwittingly, each character exploits Neeta's labor power to serve his/her own ends. Neeta's labor and exploitation by her family eventually rob her of her very life, as she succumbs to terminal tuberculosis – a disease that Ghatak well knows was also referred to as "consumption." Neeta is consumed; her labor gradually depletes her as she expends her life energy in supporting her loved ones.[11] Her labor production causes wear and tear; her work, which keeps her family alive, consumes her.

The emasculation of these men inverts the gendered dynamics of patriarchal, middle-class Hindu society. This inversion of gendered authority creates a preposterous family, as it apparently endows Neeta with phallic authority. Ghatak's portrayal of preposterous domestic arrangements intervenes into nationalist discourses that imagined the nation itself as family.[12] Neeta's cannibalization by her family allows us to see how her family "employs" Neeta to repair their broken lives. In *Meghe Dhaka Tara*, however, the materialist critique is interrupted by archetypal images, most significantly that of the mother-goddess. Ghatak juxtaposes the archetypal images with gender inversions within the family to reinforce the distance between powerful female deities and their overwrought everyday counterparts. This convergence of archetype and gender role reversal demonstrates the contradictory demands placed on women in everyday life.

Several feminist scholars of Partition have warned against totalizing depictions of the sexual violence that marked women's bodies as bearers of community and tradition. Their important work has reminded us that the social dislocations produced in the wake of Partition also enabled some women to emerge into the public sphere as laborers who secured the main source of income for their families. For example, Jasodhara Bagchi notes, "The historic assertion of the refugee-woman as the tireless breadwinner changed the digits of feminine aspiration of the Bengali bhadramahila and altered the social landscape irrevocably."[13] Likewise, Urvashi Butalia observes, "Just as a whole generation of women were destroyed by Partition, so also Partition provided an opportunity for many to move into the public sphere in a hitherto unprecedented way."[14] In a similar vein, Tanika Sarkar notes, "Partition thus paradoxically intertwined great loss with new beginnings – a complex motion of history which is obscured in the conventional focus on the victimhood of women ... forced into new public and political roles and identities, they also came to possess spaces that had been denied to them in more secure and sheltered times."[15] Gargi Chakravartty details the experiences of refugees from East Bengal and echoes the voices of aforementioned critics when she writes, "Too often, women's experience of Partition becomes a story of loss and victimhood, of violence and oppression."[16] The contributions of these feminist scholars foregrounds the ways in which the cataclysmic event of the Partition also opened up many opportunities for women.

Recounting the stories of several refugee women from East Bengal who took on the responsibilities of financially supporting their families, Gargi Chakravartty writes,

> The economic responsibility had so far been with the male
> members; it was always assumed that sons were to be
> the bread-earners of the family. Now daughters began to
> shoulder the burden, facilitating a major breakthrough in
> the attitudes of a patriarchal society ... it was not a smooth
> transition. The older generation found it difficult to accept
> their daughters taking up office jobs and there was resistance;
> at most, family seniors would accept women working in the
> teaching profession.... Young girls from dislocated families
> of East Bengal were forced to ignore the social stigma and
> plunge into white-collar jobs; frequently, they went to college
> for graduation, not to groom themselves as future brides or
> housewives, but rather to qualify for jobs as clerks, typists,
> stenographers, sales girls etc.[17]

In Chakravartty's analysis, the post-Partition turmoil created the conditions for daughters to take the place of sons, consequently emancipating them from the weight of familial and cultural orthodoxy. Although Chakravartty's intervention affirms how the Partition enabled the emancipation of women from patriarchal strictures, her interviewees evince a less assured relationship to "liberation." For example, Hena Chowdhury, a migrant interviewee, holds the social and economic ruptures produced in the wake of the Partition accountable for her elder sister's inability to get married. As she puts it, "Partition was *responsible* even for this."[18] Likewise, Sabitri Chattopadhyaya, another migrant interviewee, reiterates a similar sentiment, "Yes, what I definitely lost out on was having a family of my own. Every woman desires, at some stage to set up a home with a husband, children and others. I was no different."[19] These comments suggest a complex negotiation with the idea of "the public woman": while averring that their emergence into the public sphere benefited them economically, in their own analysis these women suggest that becoming the breadwinner comes at the cost of family life.

Ghatak's cinema creatively intervenes into the binaristic paradigm of oppression/liberation by representing the subjections that inform Neeta's subjecthood. His portrayal of Neeta does not rehearse normative liberal ideas about inherent yearnings for agentive freedom; his depiction of the public woman does not resurrect her as the sovereign subject of liberal humanism who emerges from patriarchal shadows into the bright light of public life. Likewise, Ghatak portrays Neeta's mother in a complex manner; she is caught between her instinct toward self-preservation and the preservation of her family on the one hand, and her feelings for Neeta, which swing from shrewd manipulation to remorse.

In addition, the symbolic archetypes inform and illuminate the shifting subject positions within Ghatak's female characters. Several film scholars have observed the way in which the feminine principle in *Meghe Dhaka Tara* is split three ways: the cruel mother, the sensual sister, and the nourishing protagonist, Neeta. For example, Ashish Rajadhyaksha has noted:

> The woman protagonist is split in three ways. Going beyond Neeta, it extends to the other women as well, so that the mother takes on the cruel aspect, the one with the most tenacious grip on life. Geeta is the sensuous female – the woman, as C.G. Jung describes in the social anima, who "feels where a man thinks." Neeta, the third, is the nourishing force, the provider, the preserving, and nurturing heroine ... when a woman takes on the role of all three, she becomes a towering, super-human force, corresponding then with the enormously powerful archetype of the Great Mother, to use the term by Erich Neumann.[20]

However, an overemphasis of archetypal symbolism in the depiction of these female characters subdues Ghatak's sharp materialist critique. Reading Ghatak's characters entirely through archetypes reinforces stable interpretations and underestimates the critical force of his disjunctural depiction of post-Partition female subjectivity. In his portrayal of post-Partitioned female subjects, Ghatak concatenates archetypical symbolism with historical materialism. While drawing out archetypal symbolism within his female characters, Ghatak also insists on their everyday material travails. The complex and contradictory portrayals of these women do not allow them to petrify into altogether symbolic archetypes.

For instance, Ghatak's depiction of the mother does not ossify her into the "cruel archetype." Rather, he masterfully demonstrates that despite the mother's empathy toward Neeta, her circumstances have forced her to behave in a manner in which Neeta's aspirations must be sacrificed for the survival of the family. This is most clearly exemplified in the scene where the mother witnesses the younger sister seduce Neeta's fiancé. Momentarily, the mother's face signals her remorse for the heartbreak that this sororal betrayal portends for Neeta. In this manner, Ghatak eschews freezing his characters into archetypes by delineating subjectivity itself as relational and contradictory. Unlike the coherent and stable characters in social realism, Ghatak's characters constellate complex and discontinuous selves depending on the particular social circumstances.

The convergence of mythological abstraction and everyday particularity produces a discoherent subject, a thematic concern, which is formally reinforced by the noncontinuity of the editing. Through the discontinuous filmic narrative, Ghatak discards conventional, uniform, linear narrativization.[21] By constellating Hindu sacred mythology to the quotidian everyday, Ghatak offers us juxtapositions that rupture the unified liberal subject of social realism and shocks us out of our habituated and complacent modes of perception. Through destabilizing juxtapositions of sacred and secular tropes, Ghatak's disjunctural depictions expose not only the contradictoriness of post-Partition gendered subjectivity but also rupture the historical continuum and throw light on the heterogeneity and non-unitariness of the present.

In addition, Ghatak suggests that the story of Neeta is not unique. "Thousands of Nitas emerged in the lanes and bylanes of refugee colonies," writes Gargi Chakravartty. Ghatak connects Neeta's story with her double, an anonymous figure who uncannily conveys Neeta's gestus. As she walks to work in the sweltering heat, Shankar mistakes the stranger for his sister. Again, the closing image of the film depicts a Neeta-like woman on her way to work, when her slipper

snaps, rehearsing the identical opening scene when we see Neeta hob-
bling along with her broken slipper. In citing Neeta's gestus, Ghatak
eschews the romantic, individual hero, and depicts the proliferation
of similar public women. Neeta is inconceivable as a singular and
autonomous character, situated outside the frameworks of history,
society, and politics. In this way, Ghatak's film charts the banality
rather than the singularity of the gendered violations in post-Partition
Bengal.

Mimetic doubles

While the figure of Neeta constellates the prosaic clerical employee
with mother-goddess, Ghatak also takes pains to demonstrate her
twin-like kinship with her brother. Neeta's bond with her brother
is played out against the vital, natural landscape. Ghatak reinforces
the mimetic relationality between person and place by juxtaposing
the story of the siblings – here Neeta and her brother – with that
of the twin Bengals. Through natural rather than territorial tropes,
Ghatak establishes the nonsensuous similarity between person and
place. Clearly inspired by, and struggling with, Tagorean romanticism,
Ghatak depicts a lush, verdant riverine landscape that resounds with
music. Nature does not guarantee succor, however; the indifference
of the unmoving mountains in the final scene, for instance, depicts
the growing estrangement among kin; as Neeta's family gain prosper-
ity, they become increasingly indifferent to her suffering. Her family's
coldness toward her is mimetically reflected in the same mountains,
once a source of solace to her.

Music weaves person to place, and Ghatak's use of Tagore's
music, Rabindra Sangeet, is particularly appropriate to demonstrate
this sense of embeddedness and love for the countryside.[22] The musical structuration of songs within the Rabindra Sangeet repertoire
reinforces the narrative dialectic between structure and play: The
dhaung offers scope for improvisation but within the foundational
structure of melody and variations of musical flourish. Formally,
Tagore's Rabindra Sangeet drew inspiration not only from the high
classical traditions of *ragas* and *dhrupads*, but also from the music of
the Bauls, traveling folk performers from Bengal.[23] The folk music of

these mystic minstrels motivated Tagore. He appreciated the Bauls' intimacy with their gods, their syncretic religious practices, and their sense of play and ease as opposed to the reverential distance and orthodoxy of institutionalized religion.[24]

Lyrically, Baul folk music suffuses the filmic narrative with songs urging the goddess Durga to return home. According to Ghatak, "The traditional songs that circulate in Bengal at the time when Uma is supposed to return to her in-laws' home have been used as part of the music in *Meghe Dhaka Tara*, just as wedding songs are profusely scattered throughout *Komal Gandhar*. I desire a reunion of the two Bengals. Hence the film is replete with songs of union."[25] The terrain of kinship and home provides the ground on which to rhythmically reinforce thematic concerns with unions and partitions between people and places.

Meghe Dhaka Tara opens with a shot of a large tree and a gurgling brook. The elongated musical notes of the *meend* reinforce Shankar's indolence and set it against the energetic pace of his working sister, Neeta, as she walks briskly toward him. He sings and the notes of Rabindrasangeet fill the air, fusing music and nature, while lyrically introducing the imagery of the hills, a theme that is returned to in the film's closing scene, which we discussed earlier. Later, Shankar renders a haunting version of the popular *khayal* in *Miyan Ki Malhar*, "*Karim Naam Tero*," which forewarns of storms that lie ahead.[26] Shortly thereafter, Neeta's health begins to deteriorate. While the narrative charts Shankar's growth from his tentative *hansadhwani* at the beginning of the film to his robust, full-throated song at the end, we simultaneously witness Neeta's regression as she collapses from overwork and loses her voice – her very breath – as she succumbs to tuberculosis.[27]

Shankar's protest against Neeta's exploitation occurs just before the Rabindra Sangeet that brother and sister sing in unison. Invoking the image of the powerful storm, they sing, "The night the doors to my room came crashing down." The song interweaves erotic and religious imagery in the lyrics that call on its singer to "open out the emptiness of her home and life, and herald the arrival of the man she has waited for." The pathetic fallacy here augurs the impending storm in Neeta's

Figure 3.1 Neeta prepares to leave home. *Meghe Dhaka Tara* by Ritwik
Ghatak. Courtesy National Film Archives of India.

life. A photograph captures the image of Shankar and Neeta, twin figures holding hands, standing against the immense hills. The clouds
gather in the darkening storm outside, and the photograph crashes to
the floor as the *raga* swells. The song heightens their bond with each
other and estranges them from the rest of the family. The image of the
twins, captured in the photograph, reinforces the nonsensuous similitude between person and place, and emphasizes the mimetic relationality between the twins.

The Rabindra Sangeet evokes the mood of romantic pastoralism, but this is sonically undercut by the sound of whiplashes, an
aural refrain throughout the film. The musical scene closes with the
sound of a whiplash, an aural signifier that resembles the non-diegetic
sounds that signal Neeta's humiliation at the discovery of Sanat's infi-
delity. After discovering her sister and her boyfriend together, Neeta
rushes downstairs from his apartment to pulsing sounds such as the
whiplashes that we will hear later. She clutches her throat as if the
sound were choking her very breath.

Neeta's health deteriorates, and she is moved to a sanatorium in the outskirts of the city, near the hills. She hears news of her family's many accomplishments from her brother, who continues to visit her. The film ends with a heart-piercing, Munchian scream. "I want to live," cries out Neeta, and her voice resounds, booming back from the unmoving, indifferent hills – a destination she once dreamed of as a utopic home. If nature had once channeled the sacred energies of the cherished landscape, Neeta now inhabits a disenchanted world. No sonorous music resounds through the hills; only her own desperate voice ricochets back to her.

Ghatak's acerbic portrayal of the public woman, the female breadwinner of the family, locates the gendered violence of the Partition not in spectacular instances of overt sexual violence, but in the banal interstices between private and public life. Although the Partition did provide spaces for women to leave their homes, take up jobs, and support their families, it also robbed some of these women of their sexual desires. The portrait Ghatak paints of the public women who took on the burden of supporting their families punctures the humanist triumphalism that denies the familial, sexual costs that some of these women had to bear.

In addition, through Ghatak's use of cross-gender twins, *Meghe Dhaka Tara* illustrates the disparity that undergirds the relationship between the pair: The divergent fortunes of the cross-gender siblings ensure that the success of the brother is erected on the squandered hopes of the sister. The post-Partition life of the public woman does not halt gendered disparities. In the process, Ghatak makes public the ignominies of "the private" as the very terrain on which fierce competition ensues over material resources. Here, intense manipulations, subterfuges, and betrayal among kin reveals the impossibility of romanticizing any idea of home.

Komal Gandhar (1961)

Komal Gandhar (The Gandhar Sublime or E-Flat), Ghatak's most hopeful of the three films made on the Partition, was produced in 1961. The filmic narrative evokes traumatic memories of the 1943 Famine and the 1946 Noakhali riots through its portrayal of refugee migrations in the wake of Partition. In situating itself against these traumatic events that orphaned the two protagonists, the film returns to themes explored in *Meghe Dhaka Tara*: the public woman and non-sensuous similarity between person and place explored through twin protagonists. Ghatak reinforces his point about the Partition of the two Bengals by evoking the twin-like relationship between Bhrigu and Anasuya – both orphan figures – whose tentative union at the end of the film offers hope for a future that unites those who have been sundered by the border.

Theatre offers the exemplary paradigm in *Komal Gandhar* in which to situate Ghatak's political argument about the mimetic relationality between the two Bengals. Bhrigu and Anasuya belong to rival theatre groups but come together in an effort to make socially relevant art. Theatre and family, and theatre as family, are the tropes that Ghatak employs to make his case for imagining kinship across the border. Each of the films in Ghatak's Partition trilogy unfolds at the narrative intersection of art, grief, and history: in *Meghe Dhaka Tara*, the elder brother eventually gains recognition for his talent, but at the cost of his sister's life; in *Subarnarekha* (which we will examine in greater detail later) Abhiram writes fiction to capture the grief of the current historical moment while Seeta plays the *tanpura*. The turn to art to assuage grief in *Meghe Dhaka Tara* and *Subarnarekha* reveals artists who withdraw from the world in order to immerse themselves in their art. By contrast, *Komal Gandhar* uses the frame of theatre to suggest that it is not in withdrawal from society and into reflective art but rather in artistic sociality and political solidarity that the work of poesis must be undertaken.

Cultural production in general – and theatre in particular – was an important source of communitas for the refugees in West Bengal. The Indian People's Theatre Association (IPTA), the theatre branch attached to the Communist Party of India was a significant cultural organization with pan-Indian roots, and a critical resource that used dramatic means to raise questions about social justice. No longer confined to the four walls of a building, IPTA theatre activists vigorously sought nonelite, indigenous, and folk forms and eschewed the conventions of bourgeois proscenium theatre. As Jasodhara Bagchi and

Subhoranjan Dasgupta have observed, "The cultural movement of the IPTA was a direct response to the hunger and death of the people of Bengal in the 1943 famine, a perverse enterprise of the British government towards the war effort."[28] Gargi Chakravartty also notes:

> Theatre occupied a prominent space in the life of these colonies, thereby further enriching a general trend towards theatrical activity characteristic of the time, popularly known as Group Theatre movement.... Since the staging of Nabanna during the Bengal Famine period, IPTA workers, spread themselves far and wide breaking down the four walls of the auditoria. A large number of refugee women joined the Group Theatre Movement – cultural activities helped in nurturing a cultural identity, and second, economic need brought women towards theatres, clubs, jatras, and the cinema.[29]

Several schools, clubs, and *mandirs* sprouted within the refugee colonies and these social/institutional spaces offered some relief from the claustrophobia of the one-room houses. Cultural organizations surfaced even within homes. For example, arriving from Barishal in a refugee ship, Pritilata recalls her days in Shahidnagar Colony in the 1950s: "Shab Peyechhir Ashar (name of a Calcutta club) was very popular. We performed the Broto Chari Nritya (a kind of folk dance) there," and its message of social commitment, resonated through the lanes and bylanes of the colony.[30] Thus the cultural work not only reflected the concerns of the dispossessed but also supplied the frameworks within which refugees sought systems of social and emotional support.

An artist across many mediums, Ghatak wrote, performed in, directed, and produced numerous plays on the stage and in the streets for IPTA,. His significant influence with IPTA is evident in his play *Dalil* (Document), which was voted best production of the IPTA All-India conference in Bombay in 1953. Following differences with IPTA, Ghatak formed his own theatre group, Group Theatre, and staged his play *Sei Meye* in 1969 with patients from a mental asylum, where he had also resided for some time.

In *Komal Gandhar* Ghatak chronicles the ideological rift within IPTA, which ultimately led to its collapse. He exposes the petty politics that enter into and eventually disintegrate this cultural institution. A brief history on IPTA will help to situate some of the conflicts that Ghatak attempts to depict in his film. In 1942, a group of young artist-activists in Bombay and Calcutta formed an informal organization called the Indian People's Theatre Association. Recognizing theatre's potential to rouse people into political action, and given the political ferment of their times, the theatre activists began staging plays to mobilize popular opinion. Inspired by "the Little Theatre Groups in England, the 1930s Works Progress Administration (WPA) theater project in the United States, the Soviet theaters, and the strolling players in China who staged antifascist plays to protest Japanese exploitation," IPTA was cosmopolitan in its narratives, methods, and beliefs, while simultaneously drawing on indigenous theatre forms of the places where they traveled and performed.[31] By 1944, the IPTA had established regional presence in Malabar, Andhra Pradesh, United Provinces, Assam, Punjab, and Delhi.

Bijan Bhattacharya's *Nabanna* (Bountiful Harvest), directed by Sombhu Mitra (in which Ghatak assayed a role), indicts British colonial governance for the Bengal Famine and was critical in granting artistic and political legitimacy to IPTA. The subsequent plays took on various issues regarding social injustices at home and abroad: the war in Europe, the rise of fascism, increasing repression from British imperialism, and the heightened politics of the nationalist movement, in addition to speaking up against repressions faced by disenfranchised groups, including landless peasants and workers, among others. As Som Benegal puts it, "Whatever the origins of the I.P.T.A., it clearly directed its messages to the masses rather than to the bourgeoisie" and "took up issues of social abuse, religious bigotry, political oppression and economic exploitation."[32]

However, competing interests between those who valued creative experimentation on the one hand, and those who valued social justice through theatre on the other, began to splinter IPTA. The tensions between those who wanted to develop a more robust and vital artistic technique and perfect the formal craft of their theatre, and those who were suspicious of formal perfection at the cost of revolutionary content, eventually disintegrated IPTA.[33] Ghatak portrays this divisiveness in *Komal Gandhar*.

The film begins with a staging of *Dalil* (A Document), a play that Ghatak himself had written and directed in the 1950s. Bhrigu, the protagonist of *Komal Gandhar*, serves as artistic director to the theatre company, Nireeksha (Probe). *Dalil*, the play within the film, is set against the Partition of India in 1947 and centers on a family forced to leave its homeland in eastern Bengal. The film portrays the petty jealousies and competitiveness that cause Nireeksha and rival group Dakshinapath to part ways from a formerly single company. Anasuya, the star performer of Dakshinapath, does not subscribe to the petty quibbles of her fellow actors and decides to work with Nireeksha.

In *Komal Gandhar*, Anasuya portrays the consummate public woman: She is a theatre actress; an orphan; her fiancé resides in Germany; her aunt accuses her of associating with actors of poor reputation; her own fellow actors accuse her of "flirting" and warn Bhrigu to be careful of her. As in *Meghe Dhaka Tara*, here, too, Ghatak juxtaposes the public woman against mythological figures. If in *Meghe Dhaka Tara* the symbolism of Jagaddhatri, the benevolent daughter, abrades against the material, embodied travails of Neeta, then in *Komal Gandhar* Kalidasa's Sakuntala chafes against his female protagonist, Anasuya.[34] In this way, Ghatak concatenates mythology and history; the narrative account is interrupted by the mythological story of Sakuntala, and as in *Meghe Dhaka Tara*, the mythological elements rupture the continuum of linear historicism.

In Kalidasa's play Abhijñānaśākuntalam (Of Shakuntala Recognized by a Token), Sakuntala attempts to revive King Dusyanta's lapsed memory of her through a ring, a token that he presents her with before taking leave of Sakuntala and the forest. In *Komal Gandhar*, too, material objects serve as repositories of memory (*smara*) – thus the diary of Anasuya's mother and the gold medal of the grieving mother are handed over to Bhrigu, the surrogate son and the keeper of maternal memory. The mementos do not merely trace an alternate familial genealogy but also rupture the unitariness of the present by materially introducing an uncanny object that discloses the specters of the past. By accepting the precious possessions from Anasuya and the grieving mother, Bhrigu now serves as witness to the dispossessed dimensions of refugee subjectivity. Bereft of mother and son respectively, the refugee women appoint Bhrigu as surrogate brother and son through material tokens that disclose the precarity of self-possession.

In addition to the mythological trope of Sakuntala, the sound design incorporates many Baul marriage songs, interweaving mythology and folk narratives of unions and separations. As with Neeta in *Meghe Dhaka Tara*, Anasuya is not unique or singular: For example, her characteristic posture, her gestus in Brechtian terms, reminds a passing political activist of his dead sister.[35] Ghatak demonstrates that Anasuya is not a romantic heroic protagonist but is rather one among many whose life was disordered by political history. The semblance of his sister, which the passerby glimpses in Anasuya's gestus and comportment, reinforces the ways in which Ghatak connects Anasuya's story to other public women in post-Partition Bengal.

Interjecting the mythological story of Sakuntala into *Komal Gandhar* makes visible the thematic concerns of self-absorption and sociality within the larger context of art and politics. In an important moment in the film, Anasuya rehearses the scene from Kalidasa's acclaimed Sanskrit play in which Sakuntala prepares to leave the forest to join King Dusyanta, but the entire forest comes alive and clings to her, refusing to let her go. Even the deer tugs at Sakuntala's sari to prevent her from leaving home. Anasuya's attempts to perfect the scene frustrate Bhrigu, the director. He urges her to use her own "emotional memory" to arrive at the authentic affective register.[36] In a Stanislavskian vein, he urges Anasuya to rummage through her repository of traumatic memories and relive the pain of losing her home. Just as she is deep in thought, a little urchin repeats the scene in the play; he tugs at her sari, begging for alms. A later scene in the film again reinforces the juxtaposition of Sakuntala's story with that of Anasuya: She idly plays with the prop deer from the Sakuntala production while discussing her plans to leave home and join her fiancé, Samar.[37] The superimposed images of the mythological character and the public woman disintegrate the coherence of Anasuya as she is caught in the conflict of choosing between France to join her fiancé and leaving her home in Bengal.

In addition to counterposing myth and history, Ghatak returns to his evocation of sonorous nature and its mimetic constitution of the people in the region. Ghatak launches his critique of the narrow-mindedness of nationalist rhetoric that reduces the love of country to an acquisitive desire for territoriality. In a significant scene, the Nireeksha theatre group travels to Lalgola, a town by the Padma River. The players enjoy their break from rehearsals by the watching boats race along the glistening river. The boatsmen's songs, offered to the river goddess, fill the air. In opposition to the static, rooted, and territorial claims of identity, Ghatak looks to the fluid, shape-shifting form of the river as the mode through which to narrate his love for place.

In Ghatak's films, the return to expansive nature from the stultifying refugee camps in the city does not offer any comforting closures.[38] The sonic register consistently undercuts the pictorial plenitude with sounds of whiplashes, outside the diegetic frame. *Komal Gandhar*, translated into "E-Flat," suggests that the account is never fully conveyed by ocularcentric modes of apprehension. The cacophonous soundscape disallows any harmonizing romance of the Partition. Even as the narrative moves toward a tentative union, the sonic register abrades against any easy closure.

Bhrigu and Anasuya wander off and reminisce about their childhood in East Bengal, which lies just across the river. The two orphans share their profound grief: Bhrigu affirms his attachment to East Bengal, "Why should I leave? Leave my fertile land, the Padma River, why should I go?" Anasuya recalls, "My mother died during the Noakhali riots. She was like a flame." Later in the film Anasuya discloses that Bhrigu's spirit reminds her of her mother's. "She had your eyes, Bhrigu," recalls Anasuya to Bhrigu, suggesting that he is almost her mother's son, almost her twin.[39] The metaphor of joining and disjoining that runs through the film evokes the image of Ghatak's beloved Bengal – disjoined and out of joint. The silver, glimmering Padma River flows like a mirror that simultaneously cuts and reflects the two Bengals.

BHRIGU: This is a foreign country, across the river Padma. I can never go there. The rail track used to connect us, now it ends here abruptly and divides us from the other side.

74

Figure 3.2 Mimetic doubles: Bhrigu and Anasuya reflect the relationship between person and place. *Komal Gandhar* by Ritwik Ghatak. Courtesy National Film Archives of India.

ANASUYA: What happened to our Bengal?
BHRIGU: We had good lives, now we're suddenly destitute.
ANASUYA: I am so alone.

The camera pans to take in the vast sweep of the countryside and follows a railway line that is abruptly cut off as it reaches East Bengal. In the words of Ghatak, "When the camera suddenly comes to a halt at the dead end of a railway track, where the old road to East Bengal has been snapped off, it raises (towards the close of the film) a searing scream in Anasuya's heart."[40] In this scene the separation of the two Bengals triggers Anasuya's breakdown – her realization of how "alone" she is, how she longs for solace in togetherness. "East Bengal looks like a small green girl, smiling sweetly," she says, displaying tenderness for what was technically Pakistan, a country born from the violence of the Partition. Barely any words are spoken in this scene; the heavy silence conveys the depth of their melancholic grief for home.

Ghatak affirms that the union of the two Bengals cannot be located within a nationalist consciousness but rather within a regionalist one. It is the concrete sensuousness of *desh* (region), the familiar and beloved region that Ghatak yearns for, not the abstraction of nation. His contemporary, Satyajit Ray, also remarks that Ghatak is above all a Bengali filmmaker, an observation that does not provincialize Ghatak's cinema, but rather establishes Ghatak's love for the riverine place of his birth. Ghatak indicts the ways in which love for place is manipulatively inscribed as narrow nationalist aspiration for territoriality. He repeatedly portrays the sense of alienation among his protagonists as a consequence of being torn asunder from the life force of a dynamic embeddedness in which they lived prior to the Partition.

Unfortunately, the reception of *Komal Gandhar* confirmed the narrative of petty bickering that the film attempts to expose. Ghatak was deeply hurt when he discovered that his former friends sabotaged its screening.[41] The rumor that hired goons, ostensibly by both the Communist and Congress Parties, were planted among the audience to disrupt the screening by sobbing loudly during funny scenes and breaking into uproarious laughter at the serious ones, still circulates in Calcutta today. In the words of film critic Partha Chatterjee: "The audience was alienated and the viewer-ship fell dramatically after a promising run in the first week. The film had to be withdrawn. He, being the co-producer, had to share the burden of the financial loss. It broke him. His descent into alcohol began soon after."[42]

Subarnarekha (1965)

Subarnarekha, a film that juxtaposes urban squalor and Tagorean pastoralism, concludes Ghatak's Partition trilogy. Ghatak completed *Subarnarekha* in 1962 and released it in 1965. The film follows the fortunes of Iswar, the upright liberal Brahmo Samajist who, along with his little sister, Seeta, lives in a refugee colony. Iswar takes Abhiram, a destitute boy, under his wing after some hoodlums abduct his mother for illegal squatting in the refugee colony. When his friend Rambilas solicits Iswar's skills as manager for his iron foundry, Iswar decides to leave Navjivan colony in Calcutta for Chhatimpur in rural Bengal. His friend Harprasad, the leader of the refugee colony, is disappointed that Iswar's self-interest trumps his sense of social responsibility.

Years pass, and Abhiram and Seeta, who frolic along the banks of the Subarnarekha River like twin siblings, find that their fondness for each other has blossomed into romantic love. Abhiram turns down Iswar's advice to leave for Germany to train as an engineer. He chooses instead to leave for Calcutta with Seeta to eke out a living as a novelist. Against the wishes of her brother, Seeta turns down the marriage proposal already secured by Iswar and marries Abhiram instead. Iswar's intense, almost incestuous attachment to Seeta underpins his violent rejection of Abhiram as her potential spouse, but he masks his sexual jealousy by deploying prevalent rhetorics of caste inferiority.

Abhiram's artistic dreams do not come to fruition – his novels are deemed too nihilistic and depressing. Now working as a bus driver, Abhiram gets beaten to death by a mob after he accidentally kills a child. This leaves his wife, Seeta, and their child, Binu, destitute. Seeta takes to prostitution as a means to survive, but her first customer turns out to be her brother, Iswar, who lands at her door following a drunken evening with his friend Harprasad. Seeta kills herself. Iswar tries to convince the court that he is responsible for his sister's death but, much to his distress, is exculpated. The final scene depicts Iswar and Binu, Seeta's orphan son, walking together toward the Subarnarekha River, in a tentative search for home. As in his earlier films, *Subarnarekha* dramatizes the costs of territorial nationalism by demonstrating the violence of sundering what belongs together. The film displays the nonsensuous similitude between person and place, between twin Bengals.

Like the other characters in the trilogy, Ghatak etches out Brechtian protagonists: There are no singular, autonomous heroes in Ghatak's Partition oeuvre. Iswar is not the bildungsroman hero but rather one character among many, a refugee struggling to overcome the odds that history has placed against him. For instance, early in the film, we see Iswar as surrogate for the former manager at the iron foundry. In filling the vacant position, Iswar did not predict that his fortune would mimic that of his predecessor, whose mental stability comes undone in the wake of his daughter's elopement. Ghatak confirms the substitutability of his protagonists when he defends the plot of *Subarnarekha*: "Take for instance the brother's turning up at his prostitute sister's. If we keep in mind the narrative's thematic thrust, we realize that any prostitute the guy visited would still turn out to be his sister. Here that point has been expounded mechanically: the aim is to allude to the general through the particular."[43]

By dramatizing the divergent life choices that Iswar and his doppelgänger, Harprasad, make, as Partition refugees Ghatak exposes the competing pulls of liberal self-interest on the one hand and Marxist sociality on the other. How does one proceed with life after it has been rent asunder by traumatic historical events? Does one hold on to liberal self-interested motives or work with socialist aspirations to rebuild community? *Subarnarekha* displays the tension between liberal and Marxist normative aspirations through the themes of self-absorption and social relationality. The film opens with Harprasad's speech: "Life is not lived for oneself but for the other. The person who limits himself with his own interest is incapable of love."

The filmic narrative pivots around this tension between self-absorption and social responsibility as illustrated by the competing choices made by Iswar and his dark double, Harprasad. *Subarnarekha* suggests that neither position can offer any guarantee against further misfortune. The film traces how two men who chose different paths end up with similar fates. The choices are grounded in different ethical matrices – Iswar chooses by the logic of liberal self-interest, Harprasad is guided by the rhetorics of community activism. Both find that their loved ones – Iswar's sister and Harprasad's wife – commit suicide as a result of extreme poverty and desperation.

Here, too, Ghatak is discontented with telling a linear, historical story and takes pains to generate dialectical images through competing registers of history and mythology. Consider, for instance, a powerful scene early in the film: Two orphan children, Seeta and Abhiram, frolic along the banks of the river Subarnarekha, amid the abandoned ruins of an aerodrome. Playing in the middle of the material remainders of recent historical events of World War II, the children innocently turn the wreckage into their playground, turning the site of ruin and destruction into their generative playing field. Ghatak describes the scene: "A little boy and a little girl, fascinated with

78

wonder and lost amidst the ruins of that aerodrome, have gone searching for their forgotten past.... The two innocent creatures would not
know that it is several such ruins of aerodromes that *lie behind the
disaster that looms over them.* Still they play in the midst of destruction and ruin. How frightening their innocence is!"[44]

As Seeta walks away from the abandoned airstrip, she runs
into a *bahurupi*, dressed as Kali, the destructive goddess.[45] Terrified,
she runs away. By juxtaposing the incongruous figure of the *bahurupi* against the banality of war detritus, Ghatak offers us a flash of
illumination: we dread the *bahurupi* performer, while we normalize
destructive technologies of state violence. According to Ghatak, "I
sought the Bohurupee out.... In the film I have drawn on this theme of
Mahakala in several ways to underscore the hollow values of modern
life rent asunder from its moorings in the puranic tradition."[46]

In addition to the sudden cinematic rupture created by the figure of the *bahurupi*, Ghatak also layers the social realist account of
the character Seeta with the archetypal resonances of the mythological
Seeta. Just as the archetype of Jagaddhatri layers over the character of
Neeta in *Meghe Dhaka Tara,* and the story of Sakuntala informs the
character of Anasuya in *Komal Gandhar,* here the narrative of the
mythological Seeta underlies the story of the historical character of
Seeta. Each film delivers its moment of shudder: Neeta's scream, "I
want to live," which resounds in the hills surrounding the sanatorium; Anasuya's sudden breakdown at the Padma River; and Seeta's
brutal suicide. All three expose the power of violent abstractions, con-
stellated through a sacred-secular topos, as they converge on the body
of the public woman.

Evoking the multiple displacements suffered by the mythological Seeta, Ghatak also points to the modern abstractions that
perpetuate violence against women. He portrays the inability of the
liberal justice system to indict a society that continues to brutal-
ize its women. Iswar desperately pleads guilty to the court, but his
plea is turned down. He is unable to convince the court of his role in
the dehumanization of women. Ghatak demonstrates the continuity
between Seeta's suicide and Iswar's trial and reveals the complicity of
the justice system in the cruelty toward women.

The convergence of modern and mythological abstractions on the female is exemplified in the scene where little Seeta, on her arrival at the iron foundry, first hears the story of the mythological Seeta. Ironically, the former manager, whose own life story portends that of Iswar, narrates the story of Seeta's gendered displacements. The convergence between the character and the mythological figure is brought to its culmination at the end of the film, when, on recognizing her brother as her first customer, Seeta commits suicide. Seeta's death at the threshold of prostitution evokes the many accusations that the mythological Seeta suffered after her abduction by Ravana. In addition, as Erin O'Donnell has pointed out, Seeta's story is shadowed by the Sati mythology in the Puranic tradition.[47] Here Daksha, intoxicated by the heady perfumes of a magic garland, makes sexual advances toward his own daughter, Seeta. Ghatak exposes the precarity of kinship in his depiction of the incestuous undercurrents between Iswar, the inebriated brother, and his sister, now a prostitute. The dominant national account that narrates the nation as family and conversely posits the family as the building block for the nation comes undone. The shadow of incest falls on all three films but is most explicitly dramatized in *Subarnarekha*. Through the specter of incest, Ghatak not only reveals the rule-bound cultural dimensions of normative kinship but also exposes kinship as fragile, precarious, and susceptible to social rearrangements. Ghatak puts the reigning heterosexist imaginaries that figure nation as mother into crisis by making vulnerable the norms that structure kinship.

Secular violence

For Ghatak, modern war is the telos of instrumental rationality: "The ruins ... lie behind the disaster that looms over them." It is this preposterous logic of the "before-behind" that Ghatak explores in a narrative that refuses the linear teleology of progressivist historical narratives. The preposterous here is akin to what Harprasad refers to as the *bibhatsa rasa*, the *rasa*, or pleasure, of disgust. Much like the Benjaminian "angel of history," the before-behind offers up a vista of time, abrading against what Benedict Anderson has described as the "simultaneous empty homogeneous time of the nation."[48]

By foregrounding the detritus of war, Ghatak exposes the ways in which state violence has been normalized in modern society. Ghatak makes Harprasad the most articulate critic of modern society's moral bankruptcy. In a scene toward the end of the film, Iswar and Harprasad indulge in a drunken binge; the men refer to alcohol as regenerative *amruth*, sacred nectar. In his inebriated state, Harprasad remarks: "The way is like a sharp razor's edge. That's what the sages tell us. They didn't see the atom bomb. Never. They haven't seen the war, haven't seen famine. Haven't seen the riots, haven't seen the country divided. The hymn for worshipping the sun is unnecessary."[49] This scene signals the preposterous modern world through a number of sonic reversals: the *malhar raga*, suggestive of generative monsoons, plays against the downpour in the filth and gloom of Calcutta; a classical Hindustani Khayal melody plays in the midst of gambling; Sanskrit *shlokas* are recited in the nightclub; and finally the sonic juxtaposition of Patricia from Federico Fellini's *La Dolce Vita* when Iswar arrives at his sister's doorstep against the squalor of her life; the discoherence of image and sound produces a shudder of horror, which culminates in the expressionist portrayal of Seeta's suicide.

The partitions between the sonic and visual juxtapositions sensuously alert us to the multiple disorientations produced in the wake of the Partition. In the words of Ghatak, "Literally in *Subranarekha* the problem that I have taken up is that of the refugees. But when I use this word, 'refugee,' or displaced person, I do not mean only the evacuees of Bangladesh. In these times all of us have lost our roots and are displaced; that's my statement. To elevate the term 'displaced' from merely the geographic to the more generic sense has been my intention."[50] Ghatak illustrates the many ways in which these two men have lost their material and moral ground. The mimetic figures of Iswar, Harprasad, and the former manager are deterritorialized by the loss of the women in their lives. In the absence of these women, they no longer recognize themselves.

Figure 3.3 Kinship in crisis. *Subarnarekha* by Ritwik Ghatak. Courtesy
National Film Archives of India.

Ghatak carefully etches out the powerful bond between Iswar
and Seeta early in his film. In an intensely intimate scene between the
two siblings, Iswar tells Seeta that she reminds him of their mother:
"Your style of scolding reminds me of her," he says, "the same stiff
neck, same frown, same walk even. Sometimes, I get startled. I feel
like I am being scolded by my mother." Seeta strokes Iswar's hair, "I
am your mother." Iswar raises her chin, her slender head poised upon
his fingers, "You won't leave me like our mother did?" he asks. Seeta
remains silent. This scene, at once erotic, incestuous, and intimate,
offers a moment to witness the ways in which the self is composed
like a palimpsest, full of traces left by others. Her decision to marry
Abhiram against the wishes of her brother, then, literally pulls the
ground from under his feet. Her departure from his life leaves Iswar
forlorn, disoriented, and orphaned. He stumbles through a preposterous world, one that leads him, at the end of the film, to seek out the
sexual services of his sister.

Against the ravages of an impoverished migrant life and the vortex of gloom and destruction, the glimmering Subarnarekha River serves as a utopic idyll. When they arrive from the refugee colony, Nabajeevan, to the iron foundry, the assistant remarks to little Seeta that beyond the Subarnarekha is a beautiful land with big butterflies. Iswar chides the assistant for telling lies. Nevertheless, this idyllic image of an imagined home across the river impresses itself on Seeta's mind. The desolate orphans summon the memory of the Subarnarekha to help them get through the depredations of life. Their utopic idea of home, a desperate fiction, is rooted not in territory but in the imagination, and it is summoned through the power of music.

As with his earlier films, Ghatak juxtaposes the disenchantment of urban life against the embeddedness of person and place in rural Bengal.[51] Seeta's early Krishna kirtan songs narrate the aching desire for a reunion between the twin-like Radha and Krishna and metaphorically evoke the twin Bengals separated by an artificial border.[52] Seeta, a trained musician, sits out in the fields playing on her *tanpura* and singing songs of Krishna kirtan. The songs that Seeta sings evoke the unmarried, non-hierarchical relationship between Radha and Krishna, a playful and joyous relationship, where roles are reversed and re-reversed in celebration and delightful abandon. Here there is no hard dividing line between the one and the other, "there is an implied interchangeability and flow."[53] Set against a horizon of hills and rivers, Seeta's love song to her twin, full of desire and yearning, transforms to a desultory tune in the slums of Calcutta where she sings, plaintively, to entice customers.

The Rabindra Sangeet offers a repeated refrain in the film. Seeta sings the song *"Aaj dhaaner khetey"* as a happy and carefree child, and later she sings the song to her own son, Binu. After the death of his father, Seeta comforts her son and assures him that they will move to a new home:

BINU: Where's the new house?
SEETA: When I was your age, a person showed it to me. The winding river, and blue, blue hills; up above the butterflies flutter around and sing songs.

83

BINU: Have you been there?
SEETA: No, I've only seen it from afar.
BINU: I will go to Subarnarekha.

Iswar is tormented because he is unable to rid the song from his head and is taken aback when Binu breaks into the same song after his mother's death. As Chidananda Dasgupta has observed, "Time and again, Ghatak's films take us to the brink of despair, and retrieve us – often with a Tagore song."[54] Through the sonic register, Ghatak exposes the ways in which the past suffuses the present: Seeta lingers in Binu's song as a ghostly presence, flickering between memory and specter. Ghatak also takes this a step further, however, and like Tagore, seems to ask, "Who are you in the deep recesses of my inner being?" "Who am I," he seems to ask, "if I am composed of traces of you?"

The lingering traces of the nonidentical, persisting in gestus, in expression, and in music points to a proliferation of specters that undoes the autonomous, sovereign subjects of the Partition. The spectral traces confound not only the progressivism of historical time but also the rational confidence in the absolute autonomy of partitioned subjects. Ghatak evokes porous and indistinct boundaries between the past and the present, between the self and the other. The dissolution of borders separating partitioned subjects affirms the enigmatic traces of the nonidentical that compose the self. In each of his Partition films, Ghatak explores the ways in which grief disperses the boundedness of the sovereign self.

As they walk toward the distant hills, enveloped in fog, Binu asks Iswar, his uncle, "Mother used to say that big, colorful butterflies play among the flowers by the Subarnarekha River. Is it true?" The story has come full circle. Iswar, however, has shifted from an understanding of mimesis as falsehood to an understanding of the sustaining power of mimetic homes in the imagination. "Yes, it is true," he affirms to his young nephew. Truth is released from the prison house of rational empiricism; the film charts Iswar's growth by revealing his shifting conceptions of truth from a Brahmo-Samajist rationalist idea of truth to a passionate appeal for a juridical acknowledgment of truth to a more supple understanding of truth – one that recognizes the power of the imagination as a force for truth. The Subarnarekha beckons the two orphans, the weary uncle and the hopeful boy, and they walk toward it in their search for home. In each of his Partition films, Ghatak offers an idea of home, rooted not in territoriality, but in the powerful terrain of the imagination.

4　The poetics and politics of accommodation

> The world will endure even when I am gone, Someone will
> remain who bears my likeness.
>
> Nasir Kazmi

Mohan Rakesh's short story "The Owner of Rubble" begins with a
melancholy moment.[1] Abdul Gani, a frail and elderly man from
Lahore, steps off the bus from Lahore with tear-stained eyes and a
toothless smile. After seven years, he is again in his beloved home-
town, Amritsar. He looks around him; Amritsar, "a place of wonder
and surprise," is both familiar and strange.[2] His gaze, illumined by
his memory, caresses the contours of his cherished city – the same
bustling marketplace, a new cinema, a vanished neighborhood. It was
seven years ago, in 1947, on a hurried and manic night, that Gani took
flight from home. Where was it now?

　　Searching for his home in a city of strangers, Gani comes upon
a crying child. Her elder sister, in an effort to placate the child says,
"Stop crying, you little devil! If you don't that Muslim will catch you
and take you away!"[3] This remark, at once banal and bigoted, triggers memories of Partition when thousands of women and children
were abducted.[4] The sister's strategy to silence the child digs deep
into the traumatic repository of the Partition. Soon, a rumor circulates that a Muslim was trying to kidnap a child. Women and children
rush indoors, quite literally rendering Gani the outsider. Unmindful
of these quotidian partitions, Gani tentatively hobbles along to find

Kazmi, "Daem abad rahegi duniya/Hum na honge koi hamsa hoga," in
Generations of Ghazals.

86

his home. He arrives, guided by memory and strangers, at a heap of stone and ash. His home was burned down during the Partition riots.

In an uncanny moment, Gani turns questioningly to Raka, a local hoodlum, lying regally by the rubble. Raka is startled. Does the old fool know that Raka killed his family, that he deployed the rhetoric of religion in order to acquire Gani's newly constructed house? Unfortunately for Raka, someone set the house on fire, and now Raka's plans, too, smolder in the rubble.

The very windows that were shut as the screams of Gani's son and his family echoed in the streets are now pried open to witness the confrontation between victim and perpetrator. The silent witnesses at the windows watch keenly as Gani intuitively looks away from Raka. He stoops down to examine the remains of his home, standing beneath the charred frame of the door, at the cusp of an inside and outside, ironically symbolizing the breakdown of the border separating the home from the world.

"The Owner of Rubble" converges on home as both concrete and conceptual ground to consider how displaced people such as Gani inhabit a disjunctive temporality, neither securely at home in the new nation nor fully severed from the old. The story illuminates the polarization of the neighborhood into insiders and outsiders and interrogates the forms of sociality that Partition disrupted and engendered. The real or potential radical severance from place offers a moment to consider home not only as a site of stability and refuge but also as one fraught with betrayal and cruelty. The repressions inherent in the making of national identity compel minority and refugee subjects on either side of the border to confront the unhomeliness of home.[5]

Although Muslims, Sikhs, and Hindus were the primary players in the dramas of the Partition, it is instructive to consider the role played by other religious minorities. For example, Bapsi Sidhwa's novel *Ice-Candy Man* explores the ways in which the minority community of Parsis in Lahore negotiated the ethnic violence during the Partition; the Parsi child narrator, Lenny, unwittingly colludes in the capture of Ayah.[6] Likewise, Manto's short story "Mozel" reveals the sartorial disguises that were assumed to confound religious identities; here, a Christian woman puts herself at risk to assist her Sikh friend during the riots.[7] These narrations illustrate that Parsi and Christian minority communities, among others, often served as witnesses and sometimes as active collaborators who facilitated or thwarted the designs of perpetrators.

In this chapter, I specifically address the ways in which Hindu and Muslim minority communities configured questions of displacement, national belonging, and gender. By looking at two performance texts, M.S. Sathyu's film *Garm Hawa* (1973) and Asghar Wajahat's play *Jis Lahore Ne Dekhiya* (1988), I argue that home, property, and the idea of accommodation provide an urgent lens through which to consider the anxieties regarding belonging in the partitioned subcontinent.[8] These texts demonstrate that the dialectical tension between nation and migration is negotiated along the vectors of region, religion, and gender. I explore how mimetic doubleness disturbs the symmetries of insider/outsider and unsettles the spatial and social binary divisions of the Partition, illustrated in Mohan Rakesh's "The Owner of Rubble."

Dominant narrative constructions of the nation foreground the "natural" link of person to place. This troubled the incorporation of refugees into India and Pakistan and cast the minorities as potential migrants with divided allegiances. The trope of roots, uprootedness, transplantation, hybridity, and other botanical metaphors pervade Partition discourse.[9] Liisa Malkki argues that, through the abundance of botanical metaphors, the relationship of people to place is naturalized in discursive and representational practices. Everyday discourses construct the nation, as well as culture, as inherently rooted in place, reflecting "a sedentarist metaphysics" in scholarly and in everyday, thinking.[10] Because of these sedentarist habits of thought, displacement itself is constructed as aberrational, with uprootedness connoting a pathological condition signaling a loss of moral character.

In the case of Partition refugees – despite the state's efforts mounted to rehabilitate displaced people – dominant representations in the public sphere continued to cast them as threatening orderly civic life. For example, Jawaharlal Nehru, the first prime minister of India, expressed his sadness at the revival of increasing communalization in postcolonial India thus: "All of us seem to be getting *infected* with the refugee mentality or worse still the RSS mentality. That is a curious finale to our careers."[11] M.K. Gandhi also spoke extensively about the "shortcomings" of refugees and rebuked their errant ways, including their proclivities to the black market, petty thieving, bribery, and acts of violence and chided their failure to be "sober, responsible and industrious citizens."[12]

As figures of national incorporation or abjection, refugees and minorities were uneasily accommodated in dominant nationalist narratives. Whereas the refugees' iterative constitution as citizens in the new nation-state required a permanent displacement from their homes, minorities were often viewed as potential immigrants. Religion and region played a key role in the formation of citizenry: The assimilation of Hindus and Sikhs into India was less thorny than was that of Muslims, whose motivations for staying in India were deemed suspect. The parallel was also true: A Muslim's choice to stay back in Pakistan was considered obvious, but a Hindu's choice to stay in Pakistan posed much more of a problem.

The new nation-state of Pakistan created in 1947 consisted of two geographic masses of land – West and East Pakistan, separated by many hundreds of miles of Indian territory. The overwhelming ethnic, cultural, and linguistic differences between the "two Pakistans" undermined the myth of Muslims constituting one nation. The alienation and bitterness of the Muslims of Bengal fostered a secessionist movement in Bangladesh, led by the Awami League, agitating for East Pakistan's autonomy. On March 25, 1971, General Yahya Khan, president of Pakistan, launched an attack on Bangladesh. On December 3, 1971, Indira Gandhi, the Indian prime minister, launched a full-scale intervention to crush West Pakistan and secure Bangladeshi independence. On December 16, the Pakistani regime agreed to an unconditional surrender, and Bangladesh was established as an independent nation-state under the Awami leader Sheikh Mujib ur Rahman

Garm Hawa, made in the year following this major war between India and Pakistan, is a meditation on the 1947 Partition. The proximity of the 1971 war once again brought to the surface questions of refugees, minorities, gendered violence, and incipient nation formations. The 1971 war confirmed that the Muslims did not constitute "a nation" and made apparent the bigotry toward Bengalis in West Pakistan. Made in the wake of the 1971 war, the film enables a consideration of the fraught negotiations of those who must choose either to live in their homeland as minority subjects or leave as refugees for a new nation-state. In many ways, depicting the 1947 Partition also enables Sathyu to reflect on the questions that arose in response to the 1971 war; refugee migration and gendered violence were central to the upheavals in both 1947 and 1971.

Gender and minority in *Garm Hawa*

M.S. Sathyu's debut film, *Garm Hawa* (Hot Winds), was released in 1973. *Garm Hawa* captures the conflicted negotiations that Muslims, who chose to stay back in India as minority subjects, experienced during Partition. The filmic narrative politicizes the geography of the local community in Agra by examining the classed and gendered tensions of post-Partition Muslim communities in India.

Garm Hawa is based on an unpublished short story written by controversial Urdu writer Ismat Chugtai, an important feminist voice of the Progressive Writers' Association (PWA). The PWA, established in 1937, was a leading literary organization that wielded considerable influence during India's independence struggle. Kaifi Azmi, who adapted the story for the screen, was also a prominent figure in the PWA, and Indian People's Theatre Association (IPTA). "I was born in enslaved India, have lived in independent secular India, and God willing, I will die in socialist India," declared Azmi, who fervently held on to a Nehruvian vision of a socialist and secular nation.[13] IPTA (which I discussed in Chapter 3) was formed five years after the PWA and was also a left-wing cultural organization that fostered artistic responses to the political issues of the day. Founded in Bombay in 1942, IPTA was dynamically engaged in the anticolonial movement. The director, M.S. Sathyu, was affiliated with IPTA and continues to be involved in theatre, film, and cultural activism.

Garm Hawa imbibed the formal and aesthetic features of PWA and IPTA, especially its advocacy for social change through the genre of social realism. *Garm Hawa* deviated from dominant portrayals of Muslims in the "Muslim social" genre of Hindi cinema such as *Mughal-e-Azam* and *Pakeezah*, which employed lyric realism to evoke and sometimes mourn, in nostalgic tones and in heightened verse, the passing of the rich poetic and expressive traditions of Urdu from public life.[14] Unlike the images of cultured leisure that the "Muslim socials" proffered, *Garm Hawa* crafted its artistic idiom from the everyday, the marketplace, the banal world of commerce and daily cares.

Garm Hawa was shot entirely on location in Agra. The film was held up for eight months by the Censor Board, which feared that *Garm Hawa*, in the political climate of the 1971 war, would evoke memories of sectarian violence and trigger communal tensions. After some deliberation, the film was released to high commercial and critical acclaim. The film steered clear of the violence of the Partition and instead focused on the question of migration – real and imagined – that haunted the nation's Muslim minorities. Ironically, the very film that was expected to provoke communal tensions was eventually awarded the National Award for Best Film on National Integration.

The film explores a Muslim family's experience of Partition and examines their ambivalence about whether to stay in India as minority subjects or migrate to Pakistan as *muhajirs*, the term for Muslim refugees in Pakistan. The plot revolves around Salim Mirza (played by veteran Balraj Sahni), a well-to-do middle-aged shoe manufacturer in Agra, whose family has been in the leather business for generations. Thus far, his business has prospered because of his diligence, compounded by the fact that high-caste Hindus consider touching leather inauspicious and have stayed away from the business.[15] Post-Partition India, however, rewrote professional mores in north India, and several upper-caste migrant populations rapidly took to the trade in order to find means to survive, disordering earlier forms of communities through their lack of adherence to caste proprieties. The desperation that many high-caste migrants experienced forced them into occupations that were traditionally considered inferior to their caste. The Partition altered the caste-dictated professional landscape of the new nation-state and rendered the traditional occupations of certain castes and classes open to eager and desperate migrants. *Garm Hawa* illustrates how this changing professional physiognomy deals a blow to Mirza's business and consequently to his family as well.

In circumstances exceedingly hostile to Indian Muslims, Mirza's elder brother, Halim – ostensibly a fierce advocate of the Muslim League – secretly leaves for Pakistan with his wife and son, Kazim.[16] Halim Mirza, unlike his brother, is portrayed as an opportunist who took to his heels, reneging on his allegiance to Indian Muslims. His performance of zealous patriotism is constantly foregrounded in the film as artifice and as theatre – for example, his declamatory speeches, punctuated by the ringing sounds of applause. Through various nondiegetic techniques, the film highlights the constant theatrics of his behavior. His departure is read as a betrayal of India's Muslims, who are left to fend for themselves in a dire and forbidding political climate. The understanding remains, however, that Halim's son, Kazim, once settled, will return to marry Salim's daughter, Amina, with whom Kazim has been in a romantic relationship.

Garm Hawa explores how the specter of real and imagined migrations haunts the Muslim minority subject. Salim's eldest son, Bakr, leaves for Pakistan in frustration when he encounters unrelenting professional discrimination against Muslims. His youngest son, Sikander, a fresh, first-rate graduate, cannot find a job, as Muslims are viewed suspiciously as potential migrants to Pakistan. The wedding of his beloved daughter, Amina, to Kazim, who sneaks across the border to India, is called off when the police arrest and deport him.[17] After her failed courtship with Kazim, Amina gets romantically involved with Shamshad (Mirza's sister's son, whose father skips the border to escape his debts). He, too, eventually, leaves for Pakistan and marries another woman. Amina, in abject despair, commits suicide.

To make matters worse, Salim Mirza gets embroiled in a minor scuffle as a result of which he gets injured and his factory is set on fire. Hounded by other traders and accused of being a Pakistani spy, Mirza finally decides to migrate to Pakistan. On the way to the station, the family's *tanga* (horse-drawn carriage) is obstructed by a huge procession of young activists. In the final scenes of the film, Mirza decides to stay on in India and fight for secularism and class equality by joining the protesting masses. He gets off the *tanga*, hands the house keys to his wife, and joins the protest.

The film opens with a series of photographs of key political figures: Gandhi, Jinnah, Nehru, and Mountbatten, interspersed with images of migrating masses on trains, ships, and *kafilas* (foot convoys). The relay of photographic images concludes with a profile of Gandhi as the picture "falls" – in three brisk, abrupt frames – to the gunshots that shatter the image. The aural soundscape evokes unions and leave-takings through wedding songs on the one hand and sounds of trains on the other.

The opening image depicts the figure of Salim Mirza standing, unswervingly, against the backdrop of a train that slowly begins to move. After visually establishing the dialectic between stillness and motion, nation and migration, the opening dialogues underscore this theme. "Why are these trees uprooted?" asks the driver of the cycle rickshaw that is taking Mirza home. "These hot winds" (*garm hawa*), "they will uproot even the sturdiest trees," he responds. "Even the remaining few will soon succumb to its pressure." The "hot winds" signal the gathering momentum of strident ethnic nationalisms. The image of the train captures the imminence of massive dislocation, and its haunting, aural reverberations return, intermittently, to punctuate the film. Ironically subverting the colonialist image of the train as the purveyor of the industrial modernity that united the length and breadth of the diverse nation, the Partition transformed its image into a foreboding emissary, an uncanny reminder of the "gifts" of slaughtered bodies sent across in trains by Muslims in Pakistan and Hindus and Sikhs in India.

The plot revolves around Salim Mirza, an upright Muslim citizen, and portrays the material and emotional hardships that he endures in partitioned India. As a patriotic Indian citizen, Mirza is committed to its secular ideal and is reluctant to leave. The film, however, reveals the ambivalent ways in which Muslim men are configured as national subjects. In the filial metaphors that equate the nation with the mother, the Indian son emerges invisibly structured as Hindu and upper caste. Relegated to the status of minority citizen, the Muslim male subject emerges not as the natural son of the nation but rather as the minority subject who needs the protection of the state.

In *Garm Hawa*, the figure of Salim Mirza, patriot yet pariah, represents both the outcaste son and the minority citizen who requires the paternalistic support of the state. Capturing the prevailing ambivalence towards the Muslim patriot, *Garm Hawa* dialogically refracts the dominant political rhetoric surrounding Muslims at that time. Muslims in post-Partition India were frequently exhorted to prove their patriotism. Pandey recounts an occasion when "the renowned Socialist leader, Dr. Ram Manohar Lohia, speaking at a public meeting in Delhi on 11 October 1947, urged [India's Muslims] to ... 'surrender arms and ... be loyal citizens of India, ready to fight, if need be, against Pakistan or any other country.'"[18] Likewise, Govind Ballabh Pant, Congress chief minister of Uttar Pradesh, in a speech to Indian Muslims again underlined their need to perform their loyalties to the Indian nation-state, as their status as Muslims marked them out as a vexed category: "Indian Muslims should 'realize clearly' what loyalty to the nation would mean if Pakistan invaded India," he declared. "Every Muslim in India would be required to shed his blood fighting the Pakistani hordes and each one should search his heart now, and decide whether he should migrate to Pakistan or not."[19] Gandhi also echoed the fears of the changeability of Muslim allegiance: "They must understand that if they are to live with the Hindus as brothers they must be loyal to the Indian Union, not to Pakistan."[20]

Whereas public discourse surrounding the question of Muslim allegiance to the Indian nation positioned the minority as potential refugee with dual national fidelities, *Garm Hawa* explores the ambivalence toward Muslims that laced both professional and private attitudes. Through clever filmic technique, M.S. Sathyu plays into and manipulates the audience's sense of us and them, majority and minority positions, in the post-Partition state. Interrupting conventional realist identification with the protagonist, Sathyu instead sets up a mimetic relationality between the spectator and the invisible, empowered citizen.

At three key points in the film, the audience is positioned uncomfortably as the empowered, "natural" son of the nation. In the first such moment, Salim Mirza goes to take a loan from the Punjab National Bank. Rather than showing Salim Mirza's dialogue with the official, the camera positions the film audience in the banker's position: Salim Mirza pleads to *us*. By suturing the gaze of the spectator to that of the privileged Indian citizen, Sathyu achieves a remarkable tension, positioning the audience to see, even to enact, the quotidian workings of discriminatory practices against minorities. This technique is repeated when Salim Mirza interviews to move into a new house; here, we occupy the position of the landlord. Finally, we are identified with the interviewer during Sikander's job interview, in which he is told, "Why don't you go to Pakistan? It'll be easy for you people there."

By rendering invisible the empowered positions of the banker/landlord/employer (privileged through their positioning as Hindu, upper-caste, male subjects) and fusing the audience's perspective with that of the decision makers, Sathyu compels his audience to mimetically inhabit the position of the privileged citizen and evaluate his own complicity in the financial, territorial, and professional disempowerment of the minority citizen. In all three cases, the ideal national subject undemocratically denies the Muslim his legal rights by rehearsing the conceptual slippage of Muslim from minority citizen to potential refugee. Forcing the audience to mimetically occupy these positions of power, Sathyu exposes "our" complicity in the routine discriminations that Muslims encounter in their everyday lives.

If Muslim men in India trouble the logic of the nation as family, then Muslim women were simply invisible in the emergent national imaginaries. *Garm Hawa* presents a poignant account of the ways in which Muslim women negotiate their relationship to place through patrilocal kinship. Sathyu's depiction of the three women – grandmother Daadi, mother, and daughter Amina – and their relationship to home is a telling indictment of the gendered entitlements of the new nations in making.

Consider, for instance, the grandmother's attachment to her home. The home, for Daadi, is not merely a place of residence for the living but, more importantly, an enclosure that entombs the dead. When Daadi first hears about the possibility of being evacuated from their property she cries out in alarm, "Your father's bones are buried here. I won't leave." Likewise, when the family moves out of the house, Daadi hides in the lumber room to avoid leaving. As she is physically lifted and carried away from her mansion, she cries, "How am I going to face him on Judgment Day?" The film depicts the violence of internal migrations where one does not need to travel across the border to become displaced. For Daadi, leaving home is tantamount to abandoning her husband, a violent act of betrayal and desertion. Daadi is unable to reconcile such a powerful relationship to home with the instrumentalist logic of "evacuee" property.

Daadi rejects the empiricist logic of the state's intervention into their family property: "Who is going to make me leave my *haveli* [house]? I only gave birth to two sons. Who is the third *haqdar* [claimant]?" Daadi looks both backward at her spectral husband and forward to her sons as the legitimate owners of her property. When the Mirzas finally move to their cramped new house, Daadi occupies the upstairs room so she can look at the *haveli* from there.[21] As she gets more frail and sickly, Daadi insists on visiting her beloved *haveli* one final time. A *doli* (bridal palanquin) carries her to her home, and sounds of wedding music accompany her arrival and rehearse the scene of her wedding. Once on the soil of her former floor, Daadi's wistful gaze caresses the contours of her *haveli*, the aural soundscape teeming with voices from her past. Then, suddenly, she dies, and the soundscape resounds with the screeching sound of a train.

Daadi's relationship to her home signals the competing notions of property at play in conceptions of accommodation, ownership, and belonging. Her relationship to her *haveli* is mediated through her husband and sons. Women's dependent status on men not only made patrilocal residence normative for citizenship, but also made women themselves figure as movable property.[22] Vazira Zamindar explains the predicament:

> Women were not entitled to autonomous citizenship because Article 5 of the citizenship laws by which their "domicile" was vested in that of their father or husband. Because permits were issued to both individuals and households, women,

96

often incorporated in households, moved between the two states without directly engaging contestations of citizenship. However, with the onset of the passport system [in 1952] when women applied as individuals for passports their legal status as dependants became of importance.[23]

If Daadi is physically displaced from her *haveli* as a result of the "evacuee" clause, for Amina home itself is the scene of her displacement. *Garm Hawa* depicts the mimetic relationality between Daadi and Amina: Amina figures as Daadi's double –her deformed shadow. The sound of the impetuous train indexing the real death of Daadi also portends the social death of Amina as a rejected bride. This scene of Daadi's homecoming in a *doli* is deliberately juxtaposed with the subsequent scene where Shamshad leaves for Pakistan on the train. The juxtaposition of Daadi's arrival at her home and Shamshad's departure to Pakistan also presages Amina's failure to be a bride and signifies her social and personal estimation as a failed woman. It is no coincidence, then, that most of Amina's interaction with all characters in the film revolves around the question of her wedding. Similarly, the scene of Amina's burial invokes Daadi's plaintive voice: "Everyone is leaving. No one even wants to carry a fistful of earth for my burial." The corresponding image reveals Salim Mirza's fist slowly pouring soil onto her grave. Salim Mirza buries his daughter, while his mother's words reverberate in his memory; the mimetic doubling disperses the unity of the funeral scene.

If the relationship between Daadi and her property is conserved through her role as wife and mother, then Amina, through her failure to inhabit either of these roles, is uneasily accommodated within normative patriarchal frameworks. She finds herself "excessive," an idea elaborated during the scene in which the family moves to a smaller house, and the mother asks Amina and Sikander to share a room. Amina quarrels that the house is too small, in response to which Sikander quips, "The house is not too small; you are too much." Sikander's innocent teasing raises the unpleasant reality that within the Muslim Personal Law in India – in both Hanafi and Shia law – women receive half the share of their male brothers, so Amina as an unmarried woman within the parental home drains her family's resources. A mounting sense of unhomeliness haunts Amina, who suddenly exceeds her shrinking world and finds herself displaced while at home.

The escalating unhomeliness comes to a crisis when Amina realizes that Shamshad, too, has betrayed her. The film does not vilify her fiancés – each is revealed as caught within the particular political exigencies of his time. Indeed, Kazim and Shamshad appear twin-like, almost substitutable. For Amina, however, the repeated betrayal by her fiancés – who are, significantly, also her cousins – constitute a humiliation that she is unable to endure. The betrayal by kin slips through the cracks of the grand official narratives of the need to avenge the violated women of Partition. These ignominies, enacted within domestic spaces, point to the crisis in the stability of kinship, the terrain where the antagonistic politics of the Partition was played out. The clandestine betrayals by men from the same family destabilize the secure bonds of kinship and undermine the homology between nation and family.

In a particularly poignant scene, Amina wears her bridal clothes and ornaments, which often constituted the dowry and a significant portion of women's movable property.[24] She gazes at her own reflection in the mirror. Shamshad, wearing the groom's headdress, approaches from behind. The mirror momentarily unifies Amina and Shamshad displaying the spectral traces of loved ones across the border that compose Amina's sense of coherent selfhood. She turns to look at him but he vanishes.

The uncanny doubleness of the image, which dissolves as she turns around to face Shamshad, evokes the spectre of Daadi's dead husband; the spectral traces of those not immediately present constitute the selfhood of both women. This particular topography of the self, composed of enigmatic, spectral traces of the other, undermines the bureaucratic, institutional mechanisms by which Partition sought to institute and reify national difference. Amina slits her wrist with a blade. The blood encircles her wrist like the red bridal bangles that, like wounds, drain her of her very life, collapsing her wedding with her death.

Figure 4.1 Amina turns back to look at her beloved who vanishes from the mirror. *Garm Hawa* by M.S. Sathyu.

Amina's death is triggered by the romantic betrayals that disable her from embodying given notions of gendered ethnic ideologies. This is in contrast to both Mirza and Sikander, who love their nation and choose, despite the odds, to struggle for its secular-socialist ideals. Amina's conjugal rejection by both men indexes her social death, disabling any identification with the nation. If the Muslim woman's relationship to nation is configured via her conjugal relationships, then Amina is literally unaccommodated within the new nation.

The sense of unhomeliness, experienced by the minority community of Muslims who persevere in India nonetheless, also produces alternative elaborations of community. Where the filial metaphor must construct the Muslim as the interloper, Sathyu illuminates other modes of sociality, animated by the restless energy of the young, disenfranchised citizens. Whereas Mirza continually declines to join activists in rallying for government support for jobs, equality, and food, his son, Sikander, considers it pivotal to support and enlist in such protests. Sikander forms his own community of friends, consisting of other disillusioned youth; they coordinate protests against the state, animating the new forms of sociality. At the end of his tether, Mirza finally relents and agrees to go to Pakistan. The film visually captures his anguish as he resolves to leave home: The scene takes long shots of Salim against his beloved Agra, the Taj Mahal, and his front door – images that nostalgically romanticize Salim's sense of belonging. When the Mirzas are in a *tanga* riding the dusty, crowded streets of Agra as they leave for the station, they run into hordes of protestors clamoring for better employment, better wages, and food. Sikander longs to join this crowd and enlist in their struggle against structural inequities rather than leave the country. Having forged relationships with a larger community, Sikander and his friends strive to fulfill the thwarted promises of a secular and socialist nation-state. He looks meaningfully at his father, who encourages him to join his friends. As Sikander gets off the *tanga* to join the crowd, we hear the feeble murmurings of his mother, calling out his name. Salim Mirza looks out into the crowds with a wistful sadness and then gathers himself together and says, "I am sick and tired of a life spent in isolation." Choosing the life of activist relationality over a wounded solipsism, Mirza climbs down from the *tanga* and asks the driver to return to his house. Again, we hear his wife's incredulous sigh, "Oh, Allah!" Salim Mirza hands the keys back to his wife and we see a shot of her fist unfurl to take the keys. Salim chooses to stay back, build coalitions, and fight to reclaim his right to be at home in the new nation. Although both Salim and his wife are constructed as imperfect national subjects, the film idealizes Salim's patriotism, while it disapproves of his wife's desire to leave.

The film concludes as Mirza walks into the crowd of thronging protestors to the poetic verse of Kaifi Azmi:

Jo door se karten hain toofan ka nazaara
Unke liye toofan yahan bhi hai, wahan bhi
Mil jaaoge dhara mein to ban jaaoge dhara
Yeh waqt ka ailaan wahan bhi hai, yahaan bhi.

The poem evokes the image of a stream joining the river and suggests that individuals should dissolve their narrow self-interests for the greater goals and aspirations of nation-building. This utopia of socialist solidarities reiterates the theme of the dissolution of borders separating the self from society (when you merge into the stream, you become the stream) even as it reminds its audiences that the scattering of showers and the portending storm darken the unpartitioned sky on both sides of the territorial border.

The film poetically and performatively suggests the power of counterpublics to bring to fruition the squandered hopes of national independence. The film closes on a socialist, Nehruvian vision of brotherhood, where the Muslim minority subject joins hands with other workers to strive and rebuild an imagined community. Mirza rejects the isolating and disempowering image of a wounded minority; he asserts his rights as a citizen over his rights as a member of a religious minority, a choice vindicated by the National Award that the film received.

Whereas the nation unfurls itself as an imagined community that beckons Salim and Sikander, to Salim's wife it only represents a repressive institutional force, invading her personal life through its coercive strategies. Although applauding Salim's difficult decision to stay back and struggle through activist relationality, the film suggests how such a conception of the public is denied to his wife. His choice to embrace coalitional groups to struggle for his vision of a secular democratic nation consigns her to the gendered privations of the domestic sphere. The public world of political activism is not open to her, and she returns home with dashed hopes of leaving for Pakistan.

Her life is enclosed within the house, and the image of the fingers enclosing the keys especially marks the ways in which both nation and home reverberate as authoritarian and policing institutions for her. She is completely fractured in this final scene, first through her feeble, disembodied protesting voice, and then through a close-up of her hand. The minority woman is not securely accommodated within the national imaginary; she appears only as a trace of her male kin. *Garm Hawa* illustrates the gendered inequities that constitute the Muslim minority's experience of national modernity, which, even as it offered possibilities of coalitional solidarity to the ethnic other, remained conservative in its treatment of the gendered experiences of religious subalternity.

Of routes, roots, and refugees in *Lahore*

We are all ... equal citizens of one state.... Hindus would
[soon] cease to be Hindus and Muslims would cease to be
Muslims, not in the religious sense. Because that is the
personal faith of each individual, but in the political sense as
citizens of the state.

M.A.K. Jinnah[25]

Expressing his inclusivist idea of Pakistan in his inaugural
speech, Jinnah addressed the Constituent Assembly on August 11,
1947, just days before the independence and formation of Pakistan. It
is unclear whether Jinnah invokes this secular ideal in his speech in
order to quell the mounting religious violence across the borders; to
suggest that the grounds of nationhood should not determine the mode
of its governance; to secure Muslim economic, cultural, and political
interests without espousing a priori virtues of an Islamic state; or if
he had influenced religious loyalties to secure a powerful position of
leadership. Whatever his motives in urging secular public practice, the
Pakistani nation that the two-nation theory gave birth to continued to
raise the specter of the illegitimacy of non-Muslims in Pakistan.

Asghar Wajahat wrote *Jis Lahore Ne Dekhiya* in 1988, in the
wake of the sweeping changes associated with General Zia-ul-Haq's
Islamist brand of politics. Zia was profoundly influenced by his family's migration from Jullundhar to Peshawar. At an international
Islamic conference, the president declared: "I will tell you what Islam
and Pakistan mean to me. It is a vision of my mother struggling on,
tired, with all her worldly possessions in her hands, when she crossed
the border into Pakistan."[26] By the time Zia took over from Zulfikar
Bhutto the position of president through a military coup in 1977, the
ground was already prepared for aggressive institutional redefinitions
for what kind of Islamic practice was appropriate for Pakistan.[27]

General Zia's policies attempted to strengthen Pakistan's
Muslim identity by legally disempowering non-Muslim minorities.
In 1984, a series of judicial reforms entrenched the second-class citizenship of minorities: not only were non-Muslims barred from giving
evidence against Muslims in newly established Islamic courts (sha-
ria courts), but any evidence supplied by a religious minority would

count for only half that submitted by a Muslim.[28] The very next year, a separate electoral system was restored, which denied non-Muslims the right to vote in territorially demarcated constituencies, curtailing the rights of religious minorities to only elect representatives of their respective communities. In addition, the changes in the public education system, including changes in textbooks, prepared the ground for a systematic ideological shift in normalizing the Sunni Muslim as the normative Pakistani.[29] General Zia's presidency also witnessed the formation of the Muhajir Qaumi Mahaj (Refugee People's Movement), launched to protect Muhajirs who, on the ground of ethnicity, were discriminated against for educational and employment benefits. The incendiary tensions resulted not only from Sindhi-Muhajir opposition but also from Sindhi fear of others who had moved into the province, including Baloch, Pakhtuns, and Punjabis.

Wajahat's play emerges at a moment when a culture of anti-minoritarianism entrenches itself through legal-institutional apparatuses of state and when *muhajirs* seek institutional and political channels to express their frustrations at being denied their political rights due to their ethnic difference. At this heightened political conjuncture when the accommodation of minorities and refugees in Pakistan was hotly debated, Wajahat's play makes an eloquent argument for the promise of an alternative imagined community.

When Asghar Wajahat wrote his play in 1988, a full fifteen years had lapsed since the release of *Garm Hawa*, and much had changed in India as well. Most noticeably, the Nehruvian dream of a socialist and secular India, so powerfully captured in the final scene of *Garm Hawa*, had begun to crumble. The late 1970s witnessed the uneasy manipulation of religious symbols in electoral politics. The notion of democracy was reduced to electoral politics. Nehru's daughter and political successor, Indira Gandhi, subtly played into religious sentiments as an electioneering strategy to consolidate a Congress majority in national politics. In the words of Sunil Khilnani, "Indira Gandhi had appeared to be the biggest threat to democracy but, in fact, the effect of her rule was to throw open the state to popular demands and to brand the idea of electoral democracy indelibly on the Indian political imagination."[30]

Several new political actors entered the fray as representatives of communities, thus reifying collective identifications on political grounds. Conflicts arose between social groups whose identities could be activated for political ends. The alarming rise to ascendancy of the Hindu right in the 1980s was not an atavistic response but was produced as a result of the particular modes of representation that the state employed. The rise of the Hindu right on the one hand, and the coalitions formed between various "backward" and lower-caste groups on the other hand, indicated the political emergence of community identities. In the years between *Garm Hawa* and *Lahore*, these community identities were reified in political arenas and exerted a tenacious hold over the political imagination of the nation. These community identities, invoking the rhetoric of antiquity, in fact demonstrated that they were products of national modernity, not remnants of the past.

Beginning in the late 1980s, passionate identity politics increasingly pervaded public life. Conflict between the state and society also increased. Several of these community groups accused the state of appeasing its political minorities. The Hindu nationalists castigated the state's pseudo-secularist policy of interfering with Hindu religious practices while upholding the Muslim Personal Law. For example, in 1985 the Supreme Court broke with legal precedents and under Criminal Penal Code granted Shah Bano, a divorced elderly Muslim woman, maintenance from her husband. A year later, this decision was annulled because Congress feared alienating its Muslim voters. The verdict was repealed on grounds that the case must be adjudicated according to the special provisions stipulated in the Muslim Personal Law.[31] Again, in 1990, upper-caste youths condemned state protectionism toward lower- and backward-caste communities by implementing the Mandal Commission recommendations. Further, regional movements demanding greater rights to self-determination also held the state responsible for its partisan allocation of resources and unwarranted meddling within regional affairs. It is important to place these multiple grievances within the shifting frameworks of the Indian state, which witnessed the growing size of the electorate, competing demands on state-controlled resources, and the brisk rise of democratic politics.[32]

I met Asghar Wajahat in March 2002, when the pogroms against Muslims in Gujarat had just broken out. Fifty-eight Hindus burned alive when a train in Godhra, Gujarat, was set on fire, allegedly by Muslims. This atrocity was followed by systematic violence against Muslims in the state of Gujarat. Wajahat is a playwright and novelist, as well as a professor of Hindi literature in Jamia Millia Islamia University in Delhi. His fifth play, *Lahore*, has already seen more than 500 productions in Hindi, Marathi, and Urdu, and has played to packed houses in Delhi, Bombay, Chandigarh, Karachi, and Washington, DC, and most recently in Palo Alto, California.[33] The well-known film director Govind Nihalani plans to make a film version of the play.

Whereas Wajahat had explored issues of Hindu-Muslim tensions in his fiction, *Lahore* was his first attempt at tackling the Partition. He alleged that the frequent and shrewd appropriation of the Partition by right-wing organizations in both India and Pakistan rehearsed the founding fictions of Islam and Hinduism as two incommensurable national communities. Wajahat's contemplative musings on his experience as a Muslim minority in India reflected both his sense of humor and irony, something that resonates in his play, *Lahore*, as well.

Asghar Wajahat wrote this trilingual play in Hindi, Urdu, and Punjabi to explore what he calls "the vacuum" in people's lives when they are forcibly uprooted from their homes. In his words, "People can never forget their home."[34] Both "evacuee" and "vacuum" share the etymological reference to vacating, or taking leave. It is no wonder, then, that *Lahore* explores both the material repercussions of being an evacuee while still at home and the affective force of a vacuum that fills the life of the refugee.

Whereas *Garm Hawa* examines the construction of the Muslim minority subject as potential refugee, *Lahore* examines the heterogeneous experiences of Muslim subjects in Pakistan. *Jis Lahore Nai Dekhya O Jamya Nai*, the full title of Wajahat's play, is a Punjabi proverb that translates into, "The one who has not seen Lahore has not lived at all." The phrase is spoken by Mai, the only Hindu left in Lahore, a city still reeling from the violence of Partition. In *Lahore*, Wajahat stages the encounter of Mai with a Muslim family from

Lucknow, India, during Partition, to whom Mai's house is mistakenly allotted. The contestation over home that ensues between both parties is the ground on which the plot unfolds and, in the process, brings to crisis notions about belonging and its relationship to property, community, gender, and nation.

Mirza's family – consisting of his wife Begum, their son Javed, and daughter Tanno – arrives from their home in Lucknow to a palatial *haveli* in Lahore, after spending several intervening months at a refugee camp. The Custodial Office in Pakistan deems Mai's *haveli* an evacuee property and allots the house to the Mirzas. On exploring their new home, they unexpectedly chance upon an old woman living in the house, who claims that the mansion belongs to her. The question of property figures centrally in these discussions of home and belonging. In an effort to throw out the old woman, Mirza contacts the Custodial Office, only to find it rife with corruption and bigotry. The officers rebuff him and warn him that he stands to lose the house if he continues to aggravate them.

The Mirzas are desperate to get her out of their house, but despite all kinds of machinations on their part, she refuses to leave. The transformative moment in the altercation occurs when Daadima begins to see the semblance of her granddaughter, Radha, in Mirza's daughter, Tanno. Wajahat depicts the gradual affective trajectory that the Mirzas chart, from plotting Mai's murder, to "winning her over" through an instrumentalist display of affection, to genuine concern over her safety and well-being. Mai's consistent efforts to orient and assist the new refugees in Lahore steadily earn her their favor and trust. The Mirzas traverse the full spectrum when, on Mai's death, Mirza performs the role of elder son and sets fire to her funeral pyre.

The Maulvi, the local Muslim priest, also participates in the funeral. A local Punjabi thug, Pahalwaan, a "son of the soil," so to speak, cannot tolerate this and bristles at the chanting of Hindu prayers by Muslims. The play closes as three masked men enter the Maulvi's place of worship and murder him to the disembodied wails of women, anticipating funeral laments. Unlike the hopeful closing in *Garm Hawa*, which affirms the power of the Nehruvian socialist imaginary, *Lahore* ends on a more sinister note. The different endings

themselves index the changed political scenario in which the Partition
was being recast and suggest the rise in identity politics in both India
and Pakistan in the intervening fifteen years.

Wajahat charts a trajectory where the Partition's hard, religious
polarity between Hindus/Muslim yields to fashion a new filial economy founded on an ethic of hospitality. Wajahat uses accommodation
as a material, political, and philosophical signifier to raise questions
about home, refuge, and belonging for minorities and refugees in
post-Partition Lahore. The question of hospitality, of the ethical proximity between the host and the hostage, is dramatized within the larger social dramas of the Partition and is a theme that we will return to
in Chapter 6 on Kashmir.

Wajahat's depiction of a diverse community of Muslims, each
with their own conceptions of Islam, powerfully destabilizes the mythology of the two-nation theory. Wajahat undermines the myth of the
autonomous religious subjects of Partition through his formal invocation of Nasir Kazmi's *ghazals*, which function to suture the scenes in
the play. The dissolution of hardened religious identities augurs the
emergence of alternative arrangements of sociality. The dispersal of
the crystallized, bounded religious subject reveals the heterogeneity
of subjects who inhabit a spectrum of religious positions. Moreover,
the mimetic relationality between Hindus and Muslims in this play
reveals the persistence of the ineffable trace of the other in the constitution of the self, undoing any absolute binary polarities between
religious groups.

Heterogeneous Muslim nation

Arguments for Pakistan ranged across a wide spectrum: Whereas
elite Muslims from Central Provinces attempted to restore some of
the political power lost to the Muslims after the 1847 rebellion, the
impoverished Muslim peasants desired economic emancipation from
the repressive demands of the dominant *zamindari* system of rural
Bengal's Hindu landowners, and still others, mostly from northwest
India, were drawn to idea of a "viable safe haven" for Islam in India.

Lahore powerfully destabilizes the mythology of a monolithic, unified Muslim "nation" by foregrounding multiple ways

of embodying Muslim-ness. By highlighting the perspectives of Muslims, differently situated through vectors of class, region, and sect among others, Wajahat offers a palimpsestic picture of Lahore in 1947 through the lens of major redefinitions of Pakistani religious identity during General Zia's regime. Reading 1947 through debates that increasingly define Pakistan through narrow sectarian constructions allows Wajahat to critique the untenability of rhetorics that claimed unity and uniformity among Muslims within the subcontinent. The question of Islam, then, is central to the idea of national belonging. In this play, Pahalwaan (the indigenous Punjabi Muslim), the Maulvi (Islamic religious scholar), Nasir (refugee from Ambala), and the Mirzas (refugees from Lucknow) offer competing representations of Islam, illustrating that Muslims did not constitute a homogeneous community.

The Mirzas arrive in Lahore from Lucknow, a city burgeoning with Urdu literary activity and especially well known for the Progressive Writers Association. The character of Nasir, the poet from Ambala, charts a different trajectory of migration, however. In fact, the majority of Muslim refugees migrated from East to West Punjab in the wake of the worst kind of brutality, and effectively evoked the image of the persecuted Muslim fleeing to safety from the terror of religious violence. Whereas the Punjabi migrants were more easily absorbed as a result of their regional knowledge, language, geography, and culture, their Urdu-speaking counterparts, especially from the Central Provinces, exhibited a melancholic nostalgia for the world they left behind.

Wajahat deliberately sketched the Maulvi as a generous and humane scholar with an expansive understanding of Islam to counter the stereotype of Muslim priests as parochial, retrogressive, and playing into communal passions. The figure of the Maulvi recalls Mushirul Hasan's attempt to recuperate the diverse efforts made by religious leaders to counter the demands for a separate Muslim nation. Hasan has reminded us, "Their role should not be written off or relegated to a historian's footnote."[35] With just a handful of characters, Wajahat portrays a diverse Muslim world differentiated by region, sect, and class among other vectors of belonging. Wajahat places this panoply of characters around the figure of Mai, a solitary Hindu widow turned hostage in her own home.

The symbolic tension between host and hostage gains additional power from the prevailing discourse of the "hostage theory" of religious minorities within both nations, which mimetically tied the treatment of Muslim minorities in India to the treatment meted out to Hindus in Pakistan. According to this logic, Muslim refugees in Pakistan had to be patient with Hindus, for aggression on their part could risk the safety of their Muslim counterparts in India. This formulation made Muslims in Pakistan responsible for the well-being of Indian Muslims. This was not merely sentimental rhetoric as many of the *muhajirs* had in fact left their friends and family behind. As Vazira Zamindar puts it, "To make an argument for Pakistan's duty towards Muslims in India, the diversity of Muslims who remained in India was harnessed to the cause of Pakistan."[36]

On the other hand, in India, Home Minister Vallabhai Patel responded to concerns about the ill-treatment of "non-Muslims" in Pakistan thus: "It is a rather difficult matter, because the present position is not quite settled, but the non-Muslims coming from Pakistan here are treated as our nationals, as they have left Pakistan with the intention of settling down here."[37] Therefore, the official position in India on Hindus and Sikhs left behind in Pakistan was ambiguous: They were only partially inscribed as Pakistani national subjects, their patriotic sentiments being compromised by their religious beliefs.

As in *Garm Hawa*, the interarticulation of soil and self in *Lahore* enunciates a profound physical and psychic dislocation enacted on the increasingly deterritorialized refugee. The imagery of roots abounds in this play through metaphors of renewed mappings of place and identity. For example, Mirza expresses his initial disenchantment with Lahore when he claims, "Nothing can replace what we've left behind ... do you see any fragrant creepers of the queen of the night here?" He soon alters his opinion, however, and even intercepts his wife's longing for their home by saying, "These are strange times. Such nostalgia will get us nowhere. We have to grow roots here for our children's sake."[38] Mirza's counsel to grow roots in Lahore demonstrates that home is not only reconstructed through a nostalgic past but also imagined through a projected futurity. Mirza's comment reveals that roots can be manufactured and interrogates the naturalization of national rootedness. The scene evinces some of the anxieties that *muhajirs* faced about rhetorics that privileged locality and roots as absolute signifiers of national belonging.

For the *muhajirs*, the parallel with the Prophet's *hijrat* (exodus) offered a powerful moral discourse of the founding of Pakistan through their heroic sacrifice, thus compensating their lack of roots by committing to a project whose definitions of a "natural" Muslim community would soon be challenged. *Muhajirs*, Muslim refugees from India, sought to establish themselves as the "authentic" Pakistanis by comparing their migration to the archetypal Muslim *hijrat* from Mecca to Medina led by Prophet Mohammed to establish the first Islamic community in seventh-century Arabia. According to *muhajirs*, Muslim minorities fleeing India rehearsed a modern account of that historic event; they made heroic sacrifices and endured suffering and hardship, much like their historic counterparts. They argued that *muhajirs* had been at the forefront of the Partition movement and had made considerable *qurbani*, or sacrifice, for the establishment of Pakistan. Thus the *muhajirs* powerfully deployed the Judeo-Quranic myth of *hijrat*, or migration, to make an argument for accommodation within the new Pakistani nation. It is within this sense of moral entitlement that we must place the Mirzas' sense of frustration and exasperation with Mai's insistence on staying in her house.

The juxtaposition of Mai, a Hindu mother, against a Muslim motherland also undermines the genealogical claims of national rootedness. The corporal presence of Mai, the Hindu owner of the house, forks a disidentification between mother and motherland. Mai gradually begins to serve as the surrogate mother for the disenfranchised, migrant Muslim community.[39] The idea of the surrogate mother, rather than the symbolic mother, enables us to think beyond the question of ontology and presence, and toward an ethics of proximity. Surrogation allows us to think of the mimetic semblance that lingers and disorders the boundedness of an autonomous self. This "performance genealogy," as Joseph Roach puts it, complicates the ontological certainty of natural national rootedness.[40]

The incongruity of Hindu mother and Muslim motherland dramatically refigures the topography of the national family. It also ironizes the metaphor of the nation itself as an all-encompassing genealogical tree naturalizing the national lineage through organic images.[41] The genealogical family tree evokes the notion of temporal continuity of essence and territorial rootedness. *Lahore* illustrates the gradual way in which Mai becomes the surrogate mother for the refugees in Lahore. Through its anomalous depiction of a universal Hindu mother against a Muslim motherland, *Lahore* disrupts the naturalizing rhetoric of the genealogy of national essence.

The stalemate between the Mirzas and Mai, the Muslims and the Hindu, begins to unravel when Tanno, the Mirzas' teenage daughter, calls out to Mai as "Daadima," or grandmother. As if in a dream, Mai descends from the stairs and gazes at Tanno and sees in her the spectre of her granddaughter, Radha. The semblance of Radha, the trace of her granddaughter, lingers in the address of Tanno. The scene precipitates a rearrangement of the social relations within the house; the substitution of Tanno for Mai's absent granddaughter, Radha, lost to her in the upheaval of the Partition, preempts the importance of surrogation in rearranging sociality in the wake of the Partition.

The scene preempts the denouement, when on her death, the specter of Mai assembles an alternative family. What ethical appeal does the corpse of a Hindu woman make to the Muslim community? How does this urgent sense of ethical responsibility toward a corpse reveal the enigmatic ways in which the self is summoned by the address of the other? Putting oneself in the place of the other – it is this empathic substitutability that we find again toward the end of the play when Mirza plays the role of Hindu son in the cremation rites for Mai.[42]

In the penultimate scene in the play, Wajahat dramatically captures the empathic substitutability at the heart of ethical practice. The stage is softly lit, and the spectral figures bearing the dead body of Mai are barely discernible. The stage grows brighter and the entire male cast of the play, all Muslim, become perceptible in Mai's funeral procession. Slowly, they begin to chant the accompanying funeral mantra, *"Ram naamsatyahai"* (the word of Ram is truth). The funeral

Figure 4.2 Mai turns to the call of "Daadima," or grandmother. *Jinnay Lahore Nahin Vekhya* by Sheema Kirmani. Photographer: S. Thyagarajan, Theatre Archives: Natarang Pratishthan.

procession crosses the platform and again the stage plunges into darkness. Mirza enacts the role of Mai's son in this ritual ceremony, and the Muslim community participates in performing the last rites of her Hindu funeral.

Theatre, more than any other expressive practice, draws its force from the mimetic relationship of substitution, of taking the place of the other, or as Levinas has reminded us, as the "otherwise than being" at the basis of proximity. The staging of the funeral scene mounts a vivid challenge to the idea of national essentialisms through an embodiment of religious difference. The brief scene captures a moment when religious polarities are displaced through a series of surrogations that reconfigures the ethical terrain of accommodation. This scene suggests the importance of shifting from a politics of signification to the ethical terrain of mimetic substitution. The ethic of substitutability – the idea that the one evacuated will be replaced by another – that the mother will be given a dignified burial, if not by her son, then by his surrogate, rearranges the terrain of identity politics to ethical practices of responsibility. This is the trajectory the play follows; how far we have come from the exclusive identity politics of accommodation at the beginning, to the end where we see the force of responsibility of one toward the other.

Nasir's *Ghazals*

Lahore recreates the polyphonic linguistic landscape of Lahore by juxtaposing Hindi, Urdu, and Punjabi. The soundscape of Lahore reverberates not only with the three languages, it also throbs with the alternating texture of Pahalwaan's patriotic clamor on the one hand and the melancholy *ghazals* of Nasir on the other. Nasir Kazmi's poetry evokes a deep sense of solitude and is in sharp contrast to the pounding rhythms of group passions invoked in Pahalwaan's jingoistic slogans. These two distinctly different rhythms of exilic solitude and communal ardor sonically interrupt one another.

Nasir's poetry functions as an intertext in this play and relativizes the authorial voice through the incorporation of another voice into the text. Wajahat claims that he wrote very few lines for the poet and took most of them from Nasir's poetry and interviews.[43] The interweaving of two authorial registers, the use of three different languages, and the competing worldviews of Nasir, Pahalwaan, the Mirzas, and the Maulvi complicate the uniformity of "the Muslim voice" and challenge the monological authority of the two-nation theory.

Wajahat uses the *ghazals* of the historical poet Nasir Kazmi to suture the narrative.[44] The *ghazal*, an ancient poetic verse form, derives from the Arabian panegyric *qasida* from the sixth century AD. A poetic form consisting of rhyming couplets and a refrain, the *ghazal* traveled to South Asia in the twelfth century under the influence of the new Islamic Sultanate courts and Sufi mystics. Although prominently written in Persian and Urdu verse, today *ghazals* are written in a variety of South Asian languages.[45]

In India, the *ghazal* belonged to the high literary traditions of the Indo-Muslim elite, the fortunes of which dwindled in the aftermath of the 1857 War of Independence. Suddenly demoted and charged

with accusations of stultifying self-indulgence, the *ghazal* was sin-
gled out for exemplifying Muslim decadence. In the words of Frances
Pritchett, "The rebellion of 1857, together with its brutal, destructive, and long-lasting aftermath, marked the real end of aristocratic
Muslim culture in North India."[46]

Despite their intensely personal content, *ghazals* were often
sung at *mushairas*, or symposia where poets gather to perform their
works. Indeed, Nasir's poetry was only published in one book collection (in addition to appearing in magazines). His fans mostly knew
him through the cultural practice of *mushairas*, where the poet publicly recited his poems. As C.M. Naim has observed, "In Urdu society,
poetry is the most public form of literature. Mushairas, or public readings of poetry, are still extremely popular, just as the habit of quoting
poetry in everyday speech is as strong as ever."[47]

In his book *Ravishing DisUnitites*, Agha Shahid Ali describes
the centrality of the audience in the co-constitution of the *ghazal*'s
poetic articulation:

> The audience waits to see what the poet will do with the
> scheme established in the opening couplet ... when the
> poet recites the first line of a couplet, the audience recites it
> back to him, and then the poet repeats it, and the audience
> again follows suit. This back and forth creates an immensely
> seductive tension because everyone is waiting to see how the
> suspense will be resolved in terms of the scheme established
> in the opening couplet; that is, the first line of every
> succeeding couplet sets the reader (or listener) up so that the
> second line amplifies, surprises, explodes ... the audience is so
> primed, so roused by this time that it would break in with the
> poet at the end.[48]

Not only is the audience incorporated within the apparently dyadic
address, but the spectral traces of former *ghazal* poets also haunt the
verse. Kenneth Bryant suggests that intertextuality is key to understanding the multiple textual traces in the *ghazal*. According to him,
the tradition of *ghazals* itself is "a kind of text ... not the product
of a single recitation, nor of a single poet; rather, it is an on-going

collaborative endeavor. But like the *ghazal*, this second text is also a serial or at least a cumulative, recitation."[49]

What can Wajahat's use of Nasir's *ghazal* poetry tell us about the Partition? Consider, for instance, this Kazmi poem that appears in the play:

> Flowers are separated from their fragrance, this time.
> O friends, what sort of air is this, this time.
> Petals cry, beat their heads;
> there has been a general massacre of flowers, this time.
> Who should I show the wound of devotion?
> There's a lack of sincerity in the city, this time.
> Those were the outsiders, but my friends.
> I need a favour from the dear ones, this time.
> Friends have parted many a time, but;
> a novel scar has bloomed, this time.
> I don't feel like listening to the clamour of spring, Nasir.
> I've heard something else, this time.[50]

In Kazmi's verse, the predictable expression of romantic love through tropes of nature is upturned. Twisting the conventional motifs of anguished separation and rapturous union, Kazmi offers metaphors that strain the imagination: How do you partition a flower from its fragrance? How do you unite the call of spring with murderous screams? Capturing the violence of partition through sensuous evocations of smell and sound, Kazmi suggests that the Partition sundered those who belong together; conversely it conjoined that which should be kept apart. What kind of preposterous spring is this? Was this the promised generative nation? Wounds, not flowers, blossom in this spring –wounds inflicted by too little faith, and too few friends. This spring is indeed different, the poet cautions, because flowers die and death flowers.

The *ghazals* express powerful emotions of love – even torment – at the separation of the poet from the one he loves.[51] In his lucid analysis of the lyric poetry of Faiz Ahmed Faiz, Aamir Mufti notes the ways in which the *ghazals* resist a "reification of self and other" and "disconcert the self with the recognition of the sameness

of the other, without collapsing the distinction between them."⁵²
Similarly, Nasir Kazmi's poems evince the suffering of being torn
from oneself, of the absolute noncoinciding, diachronic presence of
the other held within the self. For example, in another *ghazal* Nasir
Kazmi writes: "A voice repeatedly reminds my heart: I'm not separate
from you, listen carefully." The *ghazal* is predicated on this mimetic
doubleness – of the otherness of the self.

For the listener the pleasure resides not only in the poetic
ingenuity within the rigid structure of the meter but also in the gen-
tle oscillation between experience and expectation: between the
haunting memory of former such *ghazals* and the imaginative vari-
ation on an established theme. The doubleness of the *ghazal* incorporates the audience into its address. The *ghazal*'s rhyme scheme
augurs by aural semblance what might be coming and incites the
audience to participate in the completion of the verse. The repetition and refrain withhold gratification, tantalizingly inviting the
audience to complete what the poet has begun. So, while the content of the *ghazal* is intensely personal and addressed to a lover, it
simultaneously constitutes the audience as witness to that address.
Likewise, the formal reversion in the final lines of the poem from the
first to the third person suggests the torsion of the self, the turning
away of the self from the self. The poet is now witness to the fissure
within the self and comments in the third person on the constitution
of the self through its address to the other. It is the simultaneously
private and public character of the *ghazal*, its location at the interstices of solipsistic immersion and audience relationality that gives it
its power.

The *ghazal*'s formal discoherence, its thematically independent
couplets held together by mesmerizing aural semblance, resists hermeneutic exegesis and disclosure. In its form itself the *ghazal* reveals
how two apparently incompatible ideas can be brought together poetically, without one subsuming the other. Formally, the *ghazals* poetically illustrate the possibility of holding incommensurable logics in
a way that augments the beauty and sonority of the verse. Its haunting melodies elude and displace the urge to pin down, analyze, and
make meaning of the poetry; despite the sometimes obdurate opacity

of the *ghazal*, its nonteleological structure, we sense the fullness of its haunting eloquence and lyrical power.

The doubleness contained within the *ghazal*'s poetic form undermines the rhetoric of sovereign religious and national subjects produced by the polarizing discourses of the Partition. Disordering the binary partitions through which the nation is organized, Wajahat reveals the indelible trace of the other in the making of the self. The formal discoherence of the *ghazal* and its composition through the address of the other suggests an ethical mode of accommodation.

Whereas in 1973 *Garm Hawa* could proffer an image of social-ist solidarity, in 1988, Wajahat reminds us that these fragile visions of alternative communities are too easily snuffed out. Both perform-ances, however, do provide alternative notions of community. *Garm Hawa*'s affirmative closing with the image of socialist solidarities and *Lahore*'s image of Muslims in a Hindu funeral procession provide images to reimagine new forms of political community. These alterna-tive visions of community reconstitute polarized versions of us/them. By illuminating fragile moments, when a vision of a counterpublic emerges, *Garm Hawa* and *Lahore* fashion new forms of solidarity on the ghosts of violently sundered communities.

These narrations illustrate the ways in which the kinds of loss and suffering experienced during Partition and its multiple violations contribute to the making of new kinds of subjectivities, new versions of self and other, new homes in the world. But these new homes in the world, too, are built on gendered notions of exclusion. While offering new homes and new communities for some disenfranchised citizens, M.S. Sathyu and Asghar Wajahat obscure the violence and repressions in the routine and quotidian structurings of home. Like all homes, they constitute bonds of nurture and support for some but also represent conditions of repression and control for others. Although liberating to the disenfranchised male subjects, these masculine solidarities con-tinue to produce newer legitimations and prohibitions for the women in these narratives. It is crucial, then, to heed Gyan Pandey's counsel to "recover a different kind of 'national' past, recalling not suicide and murder ['sacrifice' and 'war'] and the eternally fixed collective sub-ject, but labour and creativity, and varied, internally differentiated communities, made up of thinking, acting, changing and fallible human beings...and on that basis, struggle to build other kinds of political community in the future, more self-consciously historical and more self-consciously accommodating."[53] The precarious image of alternative imaginings of community, predicated on mimetic doubleness, enlarges our idea of accommodation but reminds us that emergent communities are often extensions of homes, offering both their refuge as well as their terror.

While *Garm Hawa* and *Lahore* consider the gendered political economy of property and explore the ways in which the borders of private and public worlds separate women from the imaginaries of national belonging, Chapter 5 addresses the various ways in which women circulate *as* property of family, community, and nation. Here, the borders separating self and society are both confounded and reconstituted as gendered violence transforms women's bodies into political artifacts. We shall now turn to the question of gendered violence that constituted the experience of Partition for its survivors.

5   Somatic texts and the gender of partition

I am also of human kind
I am the sign of that injury,
The symbol of that accident,
Which, in the clash of changing times,
Inevitably hit my mother's forehead.

Amrita Pritam

The Partition's gendered violence against men and women took on an uncanny mimetic dimension. Not only were members of communities responding mimetically to violence done across the border, but the nation-states, too, participated in this scenario of mimetic violence. As I argued in Chapter 4, the bureaucratic institutionalization of "the hostage theory" tied the treatment of minorities in one country to the treatment meted out to their counterparts in the other country. Likewise, the recovery of abducted women followed a similar mimetic logic: Each nation agreed that the exchange of abducted women across the border must be equal in number.

The Abducted Persons Bill, moved through the Indian Parliament on December 31, 1949, defines an abducted person as "a male child under the age of sixteen years or a female of whatever age who is, or immediately before the 1st day of March 1947, was, a Muslim and who, on or after that day and before the 1st day of January 1949, had become separated from his or her family and is found living with or

---

Amrita Pritam, "The Scar," trans. Harbans Singh, in Amrita Pritam, *The Skeleton and Other Writings*, ed. Khushwant Singh, 76.

under the control of any other individual or family, and in the latter case includes a child born to any such female after the said date."[1] The bill reveals the paternalism of the Indian state and reinforces the homology between family and nation.

Troped on the figure of the woman, "national honor" was hotly contested in the Constituent Assembly debates. The debates evince a particular anxiety about the fertility and the reproductive capacities of the recovered women. Consider, for example, Minister of Transport Shri N. Gopalaswami Ayyangar's argument while introducing the Abducted Persons (Recovery and Restoration) Act of 1949: "While in India we have recovered women of all ages and so forth, in Pakistan they had recovered for us only old women or little children."[2] The recovery project devolved around a specious enumerative calculus that fetishized fertility while exchanging (and often forcibly recovering) populations of abducted women.

The sexual violence during the Partition was enacted on the bodies of the women of Hindu, Muslim, and Sikh communities.[3] Official numbers of women abducted during Partition are 50,000 Muslim women in India and 33,000 Hindu and Sikh women in Pakistan. Numbers here, as Gyanendra Pandey reminds us, hardly work in the cold and sober register of bureaucratic accounting. Rather, the constative "fact" of numbers is deployed for its performative force, to make a claim for a mimetic exchange of women across the border.

The multiple forms of sexual violence against women included rape; mutilation; forced conversion; honor killings; sexual mutilation; inscription of religious insignia on their bodies; parading them naked in sacred spaces such as temples, mosques, and *gurdwaras*; and cutting their breasts off, symbolically severing their role as potential nurturers as well as emphasizing to other men that these women were "hand-me-downs." Sometimes families traded their women in exchange for freedom; at other times women were urged to take their own lives in order to protect communal "honor." Many women simply disappeared.

The symbolic elevation of woman as the repository of culture and tradition ironically positioned real women as targets of violent assertions of family, community, and nation. The mimetic rivalry

120

between advocates of community and nation converged on women. The female body served as the terrain through which to exchange dramatic acts of violence. The gendered violence of the Partition thus positioned women between symbolic abstraction and embodiment. How is the body hailed, renewed, sustained, threatened, and constituted through modes of address? If the subject is constituted through the address of the other, how does mimetic relationality undermine the idea of sovereign subjects?

In the context of the Partition, women's bodies circulated as texts, thus complicating the binary between language and embodiment. As tokens of exchange between opposing members of community and nation, female bodies served as somatic texts. The violence of the Partition attempts to deploy women's bodies as signs within a patriarchal representational economy through which men from opposing communities/nations communicate to each other. The violent inscription of female body as somatic text, however, produces its own excess.

In this chapter, I argue that Kirti Jain's 2001 production, *Aur Kitne Tukde*, depicts the hieroglyphic circulation of female bodies in a mimetic dialogue between men from opposing communities and nations. Marking female bodies through specific acts of gendered violence constitutes a mode of transcription to communicate with other men who will encounter this body. The relationship between embodiment and discourse is complicated in a scenario where bodies themselves circulate as texts.

I conclude my discussion of women as somatic texts in Jain's play by reading it against gendered violence on men. In particular, I consider Manto' short poem "Sorry," a scene from Khushwant Singh's *Train to Pakistan*, and Bhisham Sahni's short story "Pali." The relatively fewer fictional and representational accounts of Partition that focus on male sexual objectification are replete with accounts of mistaken religious identity and the centrality of the circumcised penis as index of religious difference. Whereas Jain's play allows a sustained engagement with different kinds of violence (conversion, abduction, rape, martyrdom, forcible recovery) that produced 'woman' through competing discourses of family, community, and nation, the narrations of Manto, Singh, and Sahni play on the fact of circumcision inscribed on male genitalia that could incite or forestall injury. Eliding inquiries into how male bodies were sexually marked and mobilized participate in displacing the focus onto the violated female body. Repressing scenes of emasculation and memories of masculine humiliation serves to ensure the heterosexual machismo of nationalist projects by deflecting the gaze away from injured male bodies. To begin, let us turn to Kirti Jain's *Aur Kitne Tukde*.

Aur Kitne Tukde

Kirti Jain's *Aur Kitne Tukde* (How Many More Fragments) intervenes into existing accounts of gendered violence that narrate the ways in which the Partition radically altered the lives of numerous women.[4] The play premiered at the National School of Drama (NSD) in New Delhi on March 29, 2001, and was written by B. Gauri and conceived and directed by Kirti Jain. Kirti Jain teaches modern Indian theatre at the National School of Drama in New Delhi and is also the recipient of the best play award for *Subarnalata* from the Sahitya Kala Academy, a state-funded organization for the promotion of arts. B. Gauri is a graduate of the National School of Drama and former student of Kirti Jain.

After its premier at the NSD, *Aur Kitne Tukde* was subsequently performed in several cities, including Mumbai in 2001, Chandigarh in 2001, and Lahore in 2005. It was also staged at the Asian Women Directors Theatre Festival in New Delhi in 2003, alongside two feminist productions, Maya Rao's *A Deeper Fried Jam* and Anuradha Kapur's *Antigone Project*. In conjunction with these feminist performances that condemn the recent pogroms against Muslims in Gujarat, *Aur Kitne Tukde* reminds us that memories of the 1947 Partition do not remain impervious to revision but are shaped by contemporary events, such as the recent violence against the minorities –most notably Delhi in 1984, Bombay in 1992–1993, and Gujarat in 2002. The reemergence of the Partition in public discourse at a historic moment when the nation witnesses an alarming increase in hate crimes directed against minorities reveals the ways in which the Partition refuses to circumscribe itself as a bounded historical event thus both eluding and exceeding a sense of narrative closure. The memory of the Partition crucially persists in shaping community and public life in India.

Aur Kitne Tukde dramatizes the appropriation of female bodies through acts of rape, abduction, branding, forcible conversion, and martyrdom. The play stages the gendered violence of the Partition at the intersection of somatic materiality and discursive abstraction: Saadia is abducted, raped, and renamed and converted to Hinduism; Vimla suffers rape and mutilation before she becomes a social worker, who then "recovers" other women; Zahida is forcibly evicted from her new loving home with Kirtar Singh and remarries a Muslim in Pakistan; Harnam Kaur tries, but fails, to become a martyr, as a result her son disowns her through the expressive silence in his oral testimony. Exploring the four fragmentary narratives that structure *Aur Kitne Tukde*, I examine the ways in which embodied acts of sexual violence, conversion, martyrdom, and state violence transform bodies into somatic texts.

Chagrined by a poster she encountered daily on her way to work, Kirti Jain recalls that the idea for this play first emerged from her exasperation at the poster's message, which declared: "*Stri ka Samman, Rastra ka Samman*" (the honor of the woman is the honor of the Nation). Jain locates her critique of the sexual violence of the Partition at the conjuncture of the symbolic abstraction of woman as repository of national honor and the everyday material violations that women experience. *Aur Kitne Tukde* probes how gendered ideologies construct women not only as site for the articulation of abstract discourses of community and nation but also as targets of these violent imaginings.

Inspired by Urvashi Butalia's collection of oral histories, *The Other Side of Silence*, Kirti Jain began her own explorations into the multiple and contradictory genealogies of violence around Partition. Jain acknowledges her debt to the significant contributions of Veena Das, Ritu Menon, Kamla Bhasin, and Urvashi Butalia, who have addressed the question of gendered violence during Partition. These feminist Partition scholars attempt to redress the bias in Partition historiography that speaks of the epochal event in terms of its political causes and disregards the violent ruptures it produced in the lives of more than 12 million people. Their scholarship emphasizes the experiences of everyday citizens in order to critique political history as well as find a way of writing it differently.

Aur Kitne Tukde crafts its narrative by blurring generic boundaries between fiction, oral narratives, and official historical accounts. Kirti Jain creatively appropriates history and fiction and transforms them into a self-conscious narration of the gendered brutalities during the Partition. By theatricalizing the discursive protocols of history, oral narrative, and fiction, Jain intimates the role of artifice and mimetic construction in each of these genres. Ultimately, her fragmentary narrative dramatizes the oral historian's project to "restore these voices to history."[5] By foregrounding the artifice in its narration, however, Jain circumvents the problem of presenting the subaltern subject's voice as pure presence. Rosalind O'Hanlon's warning to subaltern studies historians of resurrecting an "essential subaltern consciousness" is especially pertinent in this context.[6] It is important to heed her counsel that in recovering marginal voices lost to history, the subaltern studies historian is in danger of recuperating the classic, unified, self-constituting, subject-agent of liberal humanism.

Likewise, Joan Scott warns against constructing a prediscursive foundational category of experience by speaking of individuals who "have experience," rather than speaking of subjects who are "constituted by experience."[7] While critiquing such accounts of transparency, she says, "[They] take as self-evident the identities of those whose experience is being documented and thus naturalize their differences. When experience is taken as the origin of knowledge, the vision of the individual subject (the person who had the experience or the historian who recounts it) becomes the bedrock of evidence upon which explanation is built."[8]

The plot-driven oral narratives in Butalia's collection attempt to excavate the "experience" of violence that people encountered during the Partition. Jain's project is somewhat different: She explores how gendered selfhoods (as victims, survivors, martyrs, perpetrators) are performatively produced through iterative discourses of family, community, and nation. Jain circumvents the liberal humanism that sometimes structures oral histories by refracting "presence" through mediated narrations. Jain complicates experience by foregrounding the discursive production of sexed, religious, and ethnic subjects. By intermixing genres, Jain destabilizes the fixed and autonomous subjects of history and oral narratives: They no longer provide unmediated access to the real by means of their experiences. Thus, despite the overwhelming associations of live theatre to somatic and affective immediacy, Jain avoids a "metaphysics of presence" by emphasizing the performative production of the gendered Partition subject.

Aur Kitne Tukde was fashioned from two oral histories of Damyanti Sahgal and Basant Kaur (all names in *The Other Side of Silence* are pseudonyms), one newspaper account of Zainab and Buta Singh, and one dramatized version of Jamila Hashmi's short story "The Exile." The play thus consists of four fragments: The stories of four women who survived Partition and narrate their experiences of fragmented nations, homes, and lives. "Fragment," then, in this context, signifies official history as a "broken piece" masquerading as the indisputable grand narrative.[9] It also points to the "broken peace," which returns to rupture and challenge orthodox historiography's claim to unified, totalizing narratives. The title of the play, *Aur Kitne Tukde*, reinforces the centrality of fragmentation not only within the formal dramatic structure but points also to the fragmentary nature of memory explored in the various pieces that constitute this play.

The play begins with a brisk Punjabi folk dance, with many actors taking the stage and transforming it through their spirited dance and song to springtime in Punjab. The music, dance, and movements are strongly evocative of the festive season of Basant when the burnished mustard fields blaze in the sun and Punjabis hold feasts and kite-flying competitions, and take part in community singing and dancing. A festival enjoyed by both Hindu and Muslim communities, Basant triggers a different memory – one that sensuously evokes the joy of comingling and play.

The dance slowly transforms into theatre exercises that quickly flow into each other. The first exercise consists of walking briskly in space, usually played in order to energize and orient the actors to their shifting relationship to other actors and to the space;

the second consists of mirroring exercises, used to train actors in precise observation. The theatre games are also carefully chosen to signify multiply in this context: Walking briskly in space, careful not to collide into other actors recalls the confusion, urgency, and panic of the itinerant wanderings that many displaced people experienced. The second game consists of mirroring exercises in which one person stands in front of the other, carefully mirroring the other person's movements.

The theatre exercises reinforce the theme of mimetic relationality, a theme that resurfaces in the shrill polemics of the exchange and recovery of abducted women between the two nation-states. Evoking the image of mimetic doubles also ironically serves to undo the rhetorics of bounded and autonomous subjects of the nation-states of India and Pakistan. By framing the traumatic narrations of the four characters with theatre exercises, *Aur Kitne Tukde* flouts the conventions of traditional realistic theatre and frames the play as a self-conscious narrative that foregrounds the artifice of its creation. In this way, *Aur Kitne Tukde* represents the affective power of the survivor's experience at the same time that it highlights the discursive production of experience.

Conversion: between the body and the soul

The Punjabi folk dancing melding into theatre exercises and raucous games concludes to the shrill laughter of one of the players. She collapses, breathless, on a *charpoy*, or a string-bed. The character is Saadia, and the Saadia narrative derives from Jamila Hashmi's short story "The Exile."[10] Through imaginative narrative strategies, Hashmi's story dialogically engages with prevailing political rhetoric that mobilizes the myth of Sita. In "The Exile," the unnamed Muslim narrator is abducted and forcibly married to a Hindu man. She visits the Ramlila with him and their children and recalls her carefree youth in pre-Partition India. Every year, crowds gather to see the performance of Ramlila; Sita weeps as she endures her exile, and Ravana's effigy burns as Rama vanquishes him.[11] The narrator recasts the epic with herself as Sita, her brother as Rama, and her Hindu abductor as Ravana.

The short story refracts dominant political rhetoric in India at the time, which cast Muslims as marauding Ravanas. The widespread political rhetoric in India during the Partition further inscribed female bodies by casting all abducted women as mythical Sitas. The invocation of the Hindu goddess in this context invisibly structured all abducted women as Hindu, requiring protection from Muslim abductors classified as the demon Ravana.[12] For example, during the passing of the Recovery Act, Professor Shibban Lal Saxena (Uttar Pradesh general) appropriated the rhetoric of the *Ramayana*, casting the Indian state as ambiguously secular:

> Even now the Ramayana and the Mahabharata are revered.
> For the sake of one woman, who was taken away by Ravana,
> the whole nation took up arms and went to war. And here,
> there are thousands and the way they have been treated.... If
> there is any sore point or distressful fact to which we cannot
> be reconciled under any circumstances, it is the question of
> the abduction and non-restoration of Hindu women ... as
> descendants of Ram, we have to bring back every Sita that is
> alive![13]

In this manner, political rhetoric drew on an available repertoire of orientalist clichés that configured the Muslim as sexually excessive and inscribed an ideology of state protectionism that necessitated Hindu patriarchal control over female sexuality.

Several newspapers took up the issue with gusto. *The Organiser*, an RSS-run newspaper, carried a story on its front page:

> For the honor of Sita, Sri Rama warred against and destroyed
> Ravana ... today when tens of hundreds of Hindu women are
> spending sorrowful days and unthinkable nights in Pakistan,
> the first free government has nothing but a whimper for
> them.[14]

Pandit Thakurdas Bhargava, another key figure in the Constituent Assembly debates who vociferously argued against the forcible recovery of women, also invokes the mythical analogy and rewrites Hindu epic as "our own history," insidiously establishing the newly independent nation as a Hindu nation predicated on the erasure of multiple histories of Muslims, Christians, Sikhs, Jews, and Parsees:

> We all know our own history, of what happened at the time of Shri Ram when Sita was abducted. Here where thousands of girls are concerned, we cannot forget this. We can forget all the properties, we can forget every other thing but this cannot be forgotten.[15]

By rearranging the terrain of religious identification, Jamila Hashmi suggests the ways in which the proximal, neighborly relations between Hindus and Muslims are reconfigured into an intractable oppositional binary through the Partition's identity politics.

The narrator drifts through an apparently illusory world; the village Sargraon appears like a dollhouse: "They don't seem to be real. Sargraon too is nothing more than a shadowy village. Everything around me is illusory."[16] Although her present world is distant and unreal to her, her memories of the past are vivid: the betrayal of friends, the burning cities, worn-out people on the move, the image of her father's body lying in a gutter in a pool of blood, her mother's heart pierced by a gleaming spear. The narrator inhabits a heterotemporal universe that accommodates multiple, discontinuous worlds. Historicist accountings that seek to cohere this unruly heterotemporality into a univocal, linear, ordered narrative of the movement of the convert from Muslim Saadia to Hindu Sumangala elide the spectral profusion of dispossessed selves that inhere in the "now."

The story heaves between the carnivelesque Ramlila fair and its underbelly – the gruesome bodies on display in the violence of the Partition. The giant, carnival idols of Ramlila refract the "real" bodies with gaping mouths, protruding eyes, and swollen faces. "The Exile" locates the violence of the Partition at the conjuncture of symbolic abstractions and somatic brutalities.

The narrator's discontinuous identification with Sita reiterates the ways in which she is constituted through her relational ties to people, places, festivals, and stories. The mimetic relationality here reveals her as always already haunted by a spectral alterity. "The Exile" presents a narrative subject who is constituted at the cusp of

128

the dominant discursive realm of Hindu gods, festivals, and cultural practices on the one hand, and her particular experiences of Muslim gendered subjectivity on the other.

Let us return to the character Saadia in *Aur Kitne Tukde*. In their adaptation of the short story, Kirti Jain and B. Gauri depict the ways in which the body is threatened, sustained, and renewed through forms of address. Beginning with the perlocutionary force of a threat, Raghuvir, Saadia's abductor and future husband, exposes the vulnerability of Saadia's body to multiple speech acts that follow. When Raghuvir's mother renames her Sumangala, she offers her both the promise of a renewed existence through a discursive address, as well as a warning to terminate her past life. Saadia reinvents herself as a Hindu wife, and contends with competing inscriptions on her body, while dwelling in a nonsynchronous, heterotemporal world.

Saadia uses the charpoy to visually recreate the time and space of her carefree days prior to Partition, as she plays on her balcony, swings around the merry-go-rounds with her brother, and recollects the home she left behind during the Partition riots. As she languishes in her nostalgia, Raghuvir, her vulgar and boorish abductor, enters the stage. He intimidates Saadia with the threat of violence – the threat itself a bodily act – auguring a temporal horizon of ominous futurity. She acquiesces and goes along with him.[17]

Saadia abruptly returns to her sordid present time and space and recoils from her spirited former self into a terrorized and apprehensive woman. The very space her body traversed, in spinning and leaping as she reenacted her former life, suddenly shrinks. Not only the physical space but the conceptual distance she charts through her imagination and her memories also swiftly withers as she enacts her abduction.

We travel back in time as the two characters reenact the abduction. Raghuvir brings her to his house and throws her at his mother's feet as his definitive triumph.[18] His mother, although disappointed with Raghuvir, does not challenge or thwart his abduction. Jain highlights the subtle ways in which several people passively contributed to the violations of the Partition. In order to resignify Raghuvir's abduction into a socially acceptable relationship, his

Figure 5.1 Saadia hides under the string-bed. *Aur Kitne Tukde* by Kirti Jain. Photographer: S. Thyagarajan, Theatre Archives: Natarang Pratishthan.

mother refashions the abducted Saadia as a Hindu bride and changes her name to Sumangala. By marrying her abductor (like so many other women during the Partition), Saadia confirms the bourgeois respectability that marriage conferred on abducted women. While Partition scholars have attended to the ways in which women were repatriated into their "original homes" through flexible kinship relations, Jain examines the ways in which the violent crimes of perpetrators against women were obscured or resignified; converting and marrying these abducted women offered a means for the perpetrators to rewrite their own violent past.

The scene allows us to consider the dislocations that forcible marriage and conversions produce in the social and spiritual, public and private lives of those unwillingly converted. Forcible conversion to another religion marks a violent appropriation of a woman's body through the rhetoric of her soul.[19] The template of conversion, while staking a claim on the soul, does so through the conduit of the body. Jain reminds us of the clandestine and quotidian ways in which

Hindus convert Muslims; Saadia's conversion to Hinduism screens the transgression of her own son, retroactively resignifying and legitimizing his criminal behavior. The dominant perception of converting the "ethnic others" as an act of conquest is mobilized in this context, where private shame masquerades as ethnic chauvinism. The scene ends with Saadia, bewildered and trying to absorb the radical transformation of her sexual, social, and religious identity in one swift move from Muslim daughter to Hindu wife.

The Saadia segment sets up a crucial question that resonates through the entire play: How is the body sustained and threatened through modes of address? The scene where the abductor's mother renames Saadia into Sumangala is a particularly potent demonstration of linguistic agency. The illocutionary speech act of naming works multiply: It resignifies her son's abduction by framing it within respectable bourgeois norms of marriage; it confers Saadia with the possibility of a renewed social existence. As we have already noted, Saadia is reluctant to return to her family because she fears that she would have no place at home as a raped and abducted woman. She worries that she would be a scourge on her family; indeed, she may even be considered socially dead to her family.[20] In this context, the act of renaming offers her the very terms through which the recognition of existence becomes possible. The act of naming, however, also terminates her prior life: The speech act while situating her within an alternative world simultaneously dislocates Saadia. By erasing her former life through forcible marriage and conversion to another religion, the abductor's mother deterritorializes Saadia a second time.

Further, Saadia decides not to return home when a Recovery officer appears at her door to restore abducted women to their original homes. She chooses to renounce her previous identity in that crucial moment when return was a distinct possibility; this overdetermined "choice" is fraught with considerations of her own safety, her concern about how/if her family would accept her, her relationship to her daughter, and her daughter's relationship with her family. This vignette reveals the multiple, competing identifications that one negotiates, some of which become politically and affectively significant at certain times. Saadia chooses to remain with her abductor, but her decision is shot through with contradictions and complicated claims to agency.

This segment makes vivid that binaries of domination and subordination are unable to capture the complicated sense of agency Saadia displays in this scene. Dominant understandings of feminist agency assume a particular liberal humanist account, with freedom and choice as the telos for women resisting the orthodoxy of family and community on the one hand, and the sexual violence at the hands of the ethnic other on the other hand. Caught within a domination/subordination paradigm, prevailing liberal conceptions of agency make it difficult for feminist social workers to recognize that these women *do* act when they decide not to leave their abductors. The Saadia segment reveals how conditions of oppression engender and enable certain capacities for action, which may not be captured through teleological accounts that reduce and collapse agency into resistance.[21]

Sexual violence

The second character we meet in the play is drawn from the account given by Damyanti Sahgal (pseudonym) in Urvashi Butalia's collection of oral histories, *The Other Side of Silence*. In the play, Vimla is an elderly social worker, and her job consists of recovering abducted women and restoring them to their homes. Whereas Saadia's narrative inhabits a nonsynchronous time, Vimla's story zigs and zags backward and forward through recollection, interview, and dialogue. We learn early that Vimla's father turned her away when she returned home because as a raped woman she was now "socially dead" to her family. The affirmative representation of a Partition rape survivor redresses masculinist narratives that present rape as the terminus of gendered subjecthood.

In the most graphic scene of the play, Vimla recalls the neighborhood on fire on the night she was raped. She recalls precise details: She boards a train to Kulu; before her train reached its destination in Amritsar, the train stops and the lights go out. A disembodied male voice impersonates the train stationmaster: "Everybody close your windows!" A chilling, unvoiced terror seizes the travelers on the train. The lights abruptly go off. The train creaks up to the station and comes to a halt. All of a sudden, disembodied noises of crowds, panic, and mayhem flood the empty stage, aurally indicating the surge of perpetrators who burst into the train. Stricken with fear, Vimla observes five armed men ahead of her. Their eyes fall on her. They move toward her. Now on the floor of the stage, Vimla reenacts the scene as ominous sounds of turmoil, commotion, and fear encircle her. She struggles to hide, but they clamber upon her. She thrashes about, struggles, scratches with her nails, kicks, and screams. Drawing out his sword, the aggravated rapist swiftly disciplines her spirited resistance. Covering her mutilated breasts in her arms, Vimla recalls, "He disfigured the most beautiful part of my body."

Vimla explicitly critiques the problematic claim that equates national honor with female bodies. Drawing attention to the radical particularity of violated bodies, she protests: "For me it was not the nation that was cut up – it was my body. I wasn't unique in this. Many, many women's bodies were torn and their flesh lacerated to bear the signs of religious insignia. Our dignity paid the price for the nation's honor." How do we distinguish between the dignity of the particular person and the honor of the abstract nation? Resisting the rhetorics that reduce the particular person's heterogeneous and complex subjecthood to instrumentalist symbolization, Vimla powerfully exposes the subsumption of the particular to the universal as a form of violence. As the symbolic repository of familial, community, and national honor, the female body was denied its somatic, nonfungible particularity. The concreteness of Vimla's experience exceeds the competing abstractions that various social groups impose on her.

Vimla's outcry illustrates the instrumentality of rape, abduction, and sexual violence as a way to emasculate men from other communities; their inability to protect their women kin signaled the effeminization of their male counterparts. During war, the symbolic concept of woman as nation instigates practices of sexual violence against women. As the symbolic mother of the nation, the woman metaphorically and literally regenerates the nation, compelling the enemies to seize the female womb, which signifies the occupied territory. The act of rape functions symbolically as a means to pollute the generative source of the national family. Therefore, war rape appropriates women's reproductive power to prevent progeny or sully progeny and to inscribe female bodies with messages to men from the opposing camp. Thus the body of the woman becomes the filter through which races/nations/religions intermingle, confirming the instability of these categories. This is why policing female sexuality becomes crucial as a way to ensure the purity of ethnic and national identities.

Aur Kitne Tukde makes dramatic the visual force of sexual violence through which Vimla's body was turned into a somatic text in a dialogue conducted between male enemies. Narrating her traumatic memory in a solo scene, Vimla shifts her position from violated object to authorial activist. Vimla's narrative concludes not with the masculinist telos of rape but rather with the image of Vimla as an agential social worker. Jain subverts the narrative determinism that surrounds dominant literary representations of rape by undermining the classic trajectory that situates the "rape" at the climax of the narrative.[22] Having rejected the bourgeois respectability that marriage conferred on several raped women during the Partition, Vimla's post-rape narrative rewrites the patriarchal narrative of the social death of raped women. Moving toward economic and social independence, Vimla affirms that even an epochal event as disruptive as Partition did create possibilities for some women.

As Chapter 3 on Bengal Partition pointed out, the Partition afforded many women the opportunity to move out of the domestic sphere and inhabit other social spaces. Vimla's character affirms that this cataclysmic rupture enlarged social spaces for some women. Partition altered traditional seclusion and marriage practices by affording educational mobility and employment for girls and women. Because of the breakup of the family structure, these women had to be economically independent, bolstering their sense of self-worth. Sometimes, families exploited the economic productivity of the women, as we have already seen in the case of Ghatak's film *Meghe Dhaka Tara*. Bibi Inder Kaul, the first principal of a new college in Amritsar who migrated from Karachi, says, "I had spread my wings.... Partition gave me the opportunity to get out of the four walls of my house … I feel Partition forced many people into taking the initiative and finding their own feet."

Despite the humanizing sentimentalism in Vimla's scenes with her father and sister, this fragment allows us to glimpse the multiple possibilities that became available to some of these women as traditional familial and social structures were altered by the Partition. Jain undercuts the melodramatic framing of this scene by displaying complex identifications of Vimla not as abject victim, but as a post-rape survivor and then as a resolute social worker, intent on recovering abducted women. It is in this professional role that her path crosses that of Zahida, the next character to whom we now turn.

Illocutionary force of law

In this fragment, Jain draws on the well-known Zainab–Buta Singh tragedy of a Sikh husband and a Muslim wife who lived in India after Partition. The iconic story of Buta Singh's impetuous love that disdained the boundaries of nations and religions has been the subject of films such as the Bollywood blockbuster *Gaddar* as well as Gurdas Mann's *Shaheed-e-Mohabbat*.[23] Urvashi Butalia reconstructs this story from newspaper articles and other sources. Zainab (Zaahida), a young Muslim woman, was abducted when her family was on the move to newly created Pakistan. These scenes in *Aur Kitne Tukde* are, for the most part, conventional chronological dramatizations. When the Abducted Persons Act was enforced, Zaahida was forcibly sent back to her family in Pakistan in spite of the fact that she had settled into a loving relationship with Kirtar Singh. The state, by fashioning itself as the guarantor of rights, claimed to protect its "injured" citizens through its democratic largesse. The episode of Zaahida and Kirtar Singh explores the violence perpetrated by the state in forcibly recovering women who had rehabilitated themselves in their new environment.

The state's annulment of the marriages and forcible restoration of the abducted women to their parental homes infantilizes the women and treats them as property to be restored to their fathers. As the Saadia fragment makes visible, these women had a difficult "choice" to make: Stay with and attempt to begin anew a life with their abductors or return as social outcasts to their parental homes. Many of these women acclimatized themselves to a new life; to be forcibly restored to their parental home denied the complicated agency these women exercised in reassembling their lives. The combined efforts of both the Indian and the Pakistani governments to recover abducted women and restore them to their original homes were met with spirited opposition from many of the abducted women themselves.

In its attempt to regain reproductive and symbolic control over women, the state in this episode is represented as a callous perpetrator of gendered inequities. Zaahida's opening scene shows her leaving home with her family and bidding farewell to her lover. This scene is deliberately juxtaposed against the subsequent one in which we see her again, with her back to the audience. Finishing her *namaz* prayer, Zaahida demonstrates that she has not renounced her faith after her marriage to a Sikh man. Kirtar Singh, her husband, walks into the frame, and their ensuing conversation depicts a happily married couple with two daughters from the marriage. An officer interrupts this scene and informs them that he is from the Recovery Operation and orders Zaahida to return to her family in Pakistan. When both husband and wife argue and plead to stay together in India, Vimla, as a social worker for the Recovery Operation, enters the scene. She persuades Zaahida to visit her family in Pakistan and personally vouches for her return to India and to Kirtar Singh. Zaahida protests, but they both soon realize that she cannot flout the state's interdiction. As Zaahida is forced out of her own home amid tears and protestations, Kirtar Singh vows to bring her back.

Jain disaggregates an abstract, disembodied, translocal understanding of the state through the iterative, particular practices of a woman social worker, who just a few scenes earlier, sharply criticizes the state's investment in "woman's honor." Nevertheless, the state is experienced here through the labor of Vimla, herself a contradictory recruit – at once a liberal champion of women's rights and a critic of masculinist discourses of community and nation. In portraying Vimla as an active social worker, forcibly recovering abducted women, Jain highlights Vimla's implication in the state project of recovering and restoring abducted women. For example, a prominent social worker

Figure 5.2 A scene of forcible recovery. *Aur Kitne Tukde* by Kirti Jain.
Photographer: S. Thyagarajan, Theatre Archives: Natarang Pratishthan.

Shrimati Durgabai rationalizes her decision to discount the recovered
women's opposition to their project. She says:

> May I ask: Are they really happy? Is the reconciliation true?
> Can there be a permanent reconciliation in such cases? Is
> it not out of helplessness, there being no alternative that
> the woman consents or is forced to enter into that sort of
> alliance with a person who is no more than the murderer of
> her husband, her father, her brother? Can she really be happy
> with that man? Is this woman welcomed in the family of the
> abductor?[24]

As we have already seen in the case of Vimla, there were many
instances of so-called recovered women being turned away by their
own family who considered them a social stigma.[25] For many of the
concerned families, these violated women openly signified familial
shame. However, the ruses of kinship circumvented familial dishonor
through various strategies, including marriage to men considered less

desirable because of caste, disability, and age differences. In the case of Saadia, we have already seen the covert strategies through which she was assimilated into the abductor's family. Flexible practices of kinship, as Veena Das argues, accommodated and absorbed the blows to familial honor, whereas the state practiced a far more rigid system of purity and honor by categorically defining abducted women as those residing with men of the opposing ethnic group. In her words, "The heterogeneity of strategic practices in the family allowed desire to flow even in relations defined by power, whereas in the order of the state, identity had to be so firmly fixed that the flow of desire could not be allowed to run."[26]

Das goes on to argue that recovering women endowed the state with new kinds of disciplinary power and concurrently produced citizens who actively legitimized the paternalist and protectionist role of the state toward its women. She contends, "By creating a new legal category, 'abducted person,' which brought such women squarely within the disciplinary power of the state, an alliance was forged between social work as a profession and the state as *parens patriae*, making official kinship norms of purity and honour much more rigid by transforming them into the law of the state."[27]

These female bodies were thus reappropriated by the state to signify the nation's paternal largesse. Mobilizing these bodies, the newly formed nation-state fashioned itself as the secular parent protecting its injured subjects. By demonstrating little interest in ascertaining whether the abducted women desired to return to their original families, the Parliament Bill manifestly illustrated the newly independent nation's paternalism. The Abducted Persons Act, by appointing a tribunal, divested these women of their legal rights to choose where they wanted to stay and with whom thus excluding women from the nation's fraternal imaginary.

In the final scene, we return to Kirtar Singh, who, after having endured many hardships, finally arrives in Pakistan. The spotlights cast two pools of light enfolding Kirtar Singh and Zaahida. Kirtar animatedly makes his case to the judge and recounts that he readily changed his religion from Sikhism to Islam in order to enter Pakistan. He transformed himself from Kirtar Singh to Jamil Ahmed. In the process, he shaved off his beard and removed his turban, thus removing all markers of his Sikh identity.

In her black burka, Zaahida remains motionless in the pool of light – almost stone-like, unyielding in her silence. Seized by panic, Kirtar Singh concurrently addresses both the judge and Zaahida in fits and starts. As he makes his case, he explains how she was forced to leave, despite many remonstrations. He entreats the judge: "The creation of Hindustan means nothing to me if my Zaahida does not return to her home. I only need your signature to take her back." Kirtar rushes over into her spot and drapes her with a vivid blue scarf – her favorite color – symbolically reenacting the *chaddar* (wedding) ceremony. Zaahida frostily stares back at him. The aloof, disembodied voice of the judge booms in the darkness: "Do you want to go with this man?" "I am a married woman," responds Zaahida, "I don't know this person." The illocutionary force of her denial of Kirtar Singh in the court transforms the constative fiat of legal testimony into a powerful performative speech act. The repeatedly dislocated Zaahida wounds Kirtar through her testimony; the force of her denial deterritorializes him.

This is an especially interesting moment in the play as the audience wonders: Which Zaahida is the authentic one? The one we see with Kirtar Singh at the beginning of the segment or the one who stands in court? Was she acting then, or is she acting now? And what does it mean that both instances of "acting" are situated within the theatrical frame? By pushing performance to the fore, Jain avoids excavating questions of meaning, truth, and intention behind these performances. The Zaahida segment forces the audience to consider the discomfiting idea that the "authentic self" itself may be the effect rather than the source of social performance.

Furthermore, Zaahida's body is variously appropriated and marked, first as a Muslim woman in her black burka, then resignified as a Sikh bride. As Zaahida stands on stage with the blue scarf superimposed on her black burka, the struggle between competing transcriptions of the same body, through sartorial means, is visually ratified. The competing double inscription on Zaahida's body, at once embodied and abstract, repeatedly appropriated for various masculinist agendas.[28]

Dressed in Muslim attire with a Muslim beard and a rumi cap, Kirtar Singh has, under duress, refashioned himself as Jamil Ahmed. The only moment in the play during which we see male bodies perform a fluid religious and national identity, the change in his social identity is conveyed through sartorial as well as somatic registers. Once again, Jain fractures the body as an organic, natural object having a fixed or innate faith and exemplifies the many ways in which political violence (of both the state and ethnic groups) attempts to inscribe and fix bodies as ethnic and gendered. Jain demonstrates how Kirtar's body, through its fluid fashionings, confounds ethnic and national purities.

By forcibly recovering abducted women, the state entrenches them as property of their communities while simultaneously taking away their citizen rights through coerced relocations across borders.[29] In highlighting the violence of the recovery project, Kirti Jain exposes the paternalism of the state and its attempts to fix these women as Muslim/Hindu. Jain's retelling of this story foregrounds the violence of the state in annexing the protean religious identifications and installing bureaucratic notions of ethnic taxonomies.

Discourses of martyrdom

The final character we meet, Harnam Kaur, is drawn from Butalia's oral history of a survivor of Thoa Khalsa, a village in Punjab. In March 1947, more than ninety Sikh women committed mass suicide by jumping into a well in order to avoid sexual violence. This fragment illustrates that women not only suffered violence at the hands of men from different ethnic groups but also from internalized patriarchal notions of honor from within their own communities and families.[30]

This particular segment begins with children (played by adults) playing around a slide. Suddenly, they decide to enact the legendary event of women jumping into the well. One by one, they climb to the top of the ladder and then slide into the well with exaggerated cries. One at a time, they all "die," and it is now Harnam's turn. Excitedly, she, too, goes up the ladder and glides down. She reaches the floor and says, "Oh! But I didn't die!" The children tease her and say she didn't try hard enough. She tries again, reaches the bottom and says, "But I am still alive!"

The lights slowly change as the children's game gradually transforms into an adult world. Now the taunts that come are no longer from children. "You are a shame to our honor. You are a stain on our martyrdom!" Harnam Kaur, now a real adult, climbs the ladder and tries again to kill herself. She reaches the bottom of the floor, and startled, she says, "Again, I did not die." There were too many bodies in the well by then and not enough water. She survived. Lying in the darkened well with dead bodies around her, she recalls: "When I realized I was alive, a tiny part of me was relieved. But I resolved to kill myself. I tried again. I failed. I remembered trivial details: the money I tried to save, my quarrel with Santosh. Had I known I was going to die, I'd have apologized. I jumped into the well a third time. But I still didn't die."

Jain's suggestion that Harnam Kaur was relieved to find herself alive interrupts dominant narratives of martyrdom, where all women acted out of their "own free will" to become martyrs. By pointing to the social pressures she faced in that moment, Jain exposes the complexities of recovering the "free will" of women whose subjectivities are discursively shaped through masculinist notions of honor. The women who committed mass suicide were faced with the difficult decision of choosing between torture, ignominy, ostracism, or death. The liberal fixation on freedom of choice as agential panacea obscures the complexities of the discursive fields of power within which historical actors are enmeshed.

On finding herself alive, Harnam Kaur was relieved. In trying to kill herself, then, Jain suggests, Harnam Kaur was capitulating to community pressure and subduing her own impulse to live. Jain points out that it is important to attend to these small signs of resistance that intercept hegemonic constructions of the gendered martyr. Harnam Kaur did not want to die, but her feebly protesting voice is hastily recuperated into larger masculinist narratives of sacrifice and martyrdom.[31]

A few intervening scenes later, we return to Harnam in a secluded spotlight, sitting a few yards away from her adult son, Jeet.

The thick darkness separates them and accentuates the divisions that Partition produced even within intimate, domestic spaces. Harnam laments that Jeet harbors a sense of resentment toward his mother. In a contrasting affect, Jeet proudly recalls for the audience the night of his sister's death. He admires his father: "It takes a lot for a man to kill the one he loves so dearly. But he did them [the women he killed] a favour." Harnam Kaur mocks Jeet's naive internalization of the dominant rhetoric of martyrdom: "Are you sure your sister really wanted to die? Or did she die because she was too afraid to resist?" These moments reveal the ambivalence in such relationships where filial love is interlaced with shame and rage. In creating an articulate and spirited Harnam Kaur, who bitterly challenges the rhetoric of martyrdom, Jain foregrounds the dissonant voices that unsettle discourses of heroic sacrifice.

Harnam Kaur walks back into her spot and thumps down metal tumblers as she lays out her son's meal. The quotidian domestic object uncannily resembles the well from which she survived. Suddenly, she is surrounded by miniature wells thoroughly deforming the domestic space itself. *Aur Kitne Tukde* captures the ambivalence of fraught filial affection: Jeet is caught between the immediacy of his concern for his mother and sister; on the other hand, he is powerfully interpellated by abstract discourses of heroic martyrdom.

Jain draws on oral narratives of Bir Bahadur in Butalia's collection to create the character of Jeet. Bir Bahadur's interviews were distinctly different from his mother's: They were infused with his own personal opinions, his analyses, his confident voice. Bir Bahadur's account incorporated his understanding of why these events had come to such a pass. Of his mother's survival, this is what he had to say: "The well filled up completely; one woman, whose name is Basant Kaur, six children born of her womb died in that well, but she survived. She jumped in four times, but the well had filled up, she would jump in, then come out, then jump in again, she would look at her children, at herself, till today, she is alive."[32]

But why does Bir Bahadur not acknowledge that Basant Kaur was his mother? How does his denial of his mother shape his and her sense of self? In the earlier fragments, we considered the ways in

Figure 5.3 Harnam Kaur – the failed martyr. *Aur Kitne Tukde* by Kirti Jain. Photographer: S. Thyagarajan, Theatre Archives: Natarang Pratishthan.

which subjects come into being through modes of linguistic address, that acquire their rhetorical force through the invocation of sedimented, citational conventions. Here, we consider silence itself as an eloquent speech act. To what extent is her subjectivity constituted by the denial of language, in particular by withholding the appellation of martyr? Butalia observes that nowhere in his interview does Bir Bahadur admit that the woman he talks about is in fact his mother. Although he dwells on his sister's brave death at the hands of his father, Bahadur simply erases his affiliation with his mother, whose persistent presence in his life disturbs the narrative of familial honor that Bahadur wants to assemble.

Basant Kaur, the woman on whom Harnam Kaur's character is based, was in her mid-sixties when Butalia interviewed her. She recounts to Butalia how she had attempted to drown herself in her village well in Thoa Khalsa when the women decided to kill themselves, en masse. But she did not die. She recalls: "I had some jewelry on me, things in my ears, on my wrists, and I had fourteen rupees on me. I took all that and threw it into the well, and then I jumped in, but it's like when you put rotis into a tandoor, and if it is too full, the ones near the top they don't cook, they have to be taken out. So the well filled up and we could not drown."[33] Note how the precision of recall (14 rupees) combines with the affective vacuum in Basant Kaur's narrative memory. Her oral narrative was plot-driven, lingering over minute, accurate details, breathlessly recalling a blow-by-blow account of "what happened." In surrendering to the details of the storyline, however, she does not betray the least emotion and withholds any analysis of the event.

Basant Kaur analogizes her survival by using metaphors from her everyday life. Using frameworks of trauma theories, one could argue that by gaining narrative control over her traumatic experience, Basant Kaur retrospectively attempts to gain mastery over that event.[34] As is apparent in her oral narrative, Kaur simply cannot accommodate this experience within her prior structures of knowledge and experience. The extraordinariness of this experience is narrated through the use of quotidian metaphors that reveal the inassimilability of this traumatic experience within her existing analytical categories.

Reading oral narratives through the interpretive frameworks of trauma theorists points to the inadequacies of language to articulate both the force and the incomprehensibility of the violence of the Partition. Theories of trauma generated from specific analyses of the Holocaust take for granted the a priori, coherent subject, attempting, through inadequate language, to represent a shattering event. How can we attend to the shattering force of language itself, the agential power of language to constitute the subject, and so take into account the reluctance – even impossibility – of the survivor's speech, as traumatic negotiations with the (de)composition of one's own sense of self?[35]

Cathy Caruth suggests that the repetitions and incursions of the traumatic event into everyday life illustrates precisely the way this violent event was not known in the first instance; the repetitious compulsions haunt the survivor, who retroactively seeks to prepare herself from the shock of this experience. What returns to haunt the victim is not only the reality of the violent event but also the reality of the way that its violence has not yet been fully known. In the words of Cathy Caruth, "The phenomenon of trauma, urgently demands historical awareness and yet denies our usual modes of access to it ... the trauma seems to evoke the difficult truth of a history that is constituted by the very incomprehensibility of its occurrence."[36] According to theories of trauma, the violent event is an affront to reason; our very ability to comprehend it prevents its assimilation within rational schemes of knowledge. However, it is important to remain vigilant of the way in which "rationality" itself gets naturalized in such an understanding of traumatic experience. The violence of the Partition does not affront rationality, rather it is a product of bureaucratic, institutional rationality.

Using the interpretive framework of ordinary language philosophy, and the insights of Wittgenstein in particular, Veena Das alerts us to the ways in which traumatic memories radically reshape everyday life. As she puts it, "The event attaches itself with its tentacles into everyday life and folds itself into the recesses of the ordinary."[37] Domesticating her experience with the phrase "rotis in a tandoor," Basant Kaur not only makes ordinary the extraordinary violence of Thoa Khalsa, she also reveals the deformations of the domestic sphere itself, as the trace of failed death radically animates her social relations with her kin.

Veena Das uses the distinction between speech and voice to point to the ways in which women may have rehearsed these accounts to such an extent that they are almost automatic, pure speech, without the animating presence of "voice." Das remarks that when these women narrated their experiences of Partition, they often encountered an obdurate "zone of silence."[38] They deployed language in a way that elided specifically brutal experiences or else lapsed into highly metaphoric descriptions of these traumatic events. This "voicelessness" – when words become "frozen, numb, without life"– presupposes for Das the subject who speaks or remains mute.[39] Likewise, Butalia observes that when she urged people to remember the events during Partition, she was confronted with an impasse: "Having begun to excavate memory, words would suddenly fail speech as memory encountered something too painful often too frightening to allow it to enter speech. How can I describe this, there are no words to do so."[40] In these accounts, the woman who speaks or fails to speak precedes the speech in question. But what are the ways in which survivors of the Partition are constituted through the very terms offered to them through the discursive address of others?

Never having experienced anything like this before, Basant Kaur does not have the analytical categories to process the violent experience at Thoa Khalsa. Instead, she uses the interpretive frameworks that are available to her, drawn from her everyday experience of domestic life. In the rendition of this event, however, Basant Kaur reconstitutes her own shattered subjectivity. The domestic miniaturizing of traumatic experience through the mimetic doubles of the unleavened bread and the tumblers ensures that the past is not past, that its memory has snaked its way into her uncanny everyday existence. A spectral doubleness oscillates between traumatic history and the domestic everyday life, reminding us that there was no closure of this violent event: The Partition persists in shaping the most banal parts of our life.

The play concludes with each character: Saadia, Vimla, Zaahida, and Harnam Kaur appear on stage, encircled in a pool of light. Looking at the ways in which subjectivity is constituted, shattered, and reassembled through linguistic address allows us to see the powerful ways in which these agents are enmeshed within discursive fields of power. Such an analysis enables us to stay vigilant of recuperating the a priori sovereign subject of liberal humanism and attends to the everyday tactics through which these women negotiate the persistent legacy of the Partition in their lives.

The foregoing instances demonstrate the ways in which female bodies circulated as somatic texts in a dialogue between masculinist parties. Kirti Jain foregrounds corporeal appropriations and reads the body as a parchment for discontinuous and sometimes overlapping patriarchal discourses of family, community, and nation. What remain absent in many fictional as well as oral accounts of Partition in the public sphere are the multiple cases of sexual dismemberment, castration, and other sexual violations perpetrated on male bodies.[41] This elision from artistic as well as historical memory serves to displace

146

attention from the emasculated male body, thereby upholding it as virile and robust, ready to assume the tasks of nation-building. It is to this question that we shall now turn.

Ethnic masculinity: Manto, Singh, and Sahni

Consider, to begin with, Saadat Hasan Manto's text "Sorry":[42]

> The knife
> Ripped through the stomach
> Reached down to the penis.
> The cord of the pyjama was cut.
> The man with the knife
> Exclaimed
> With surprise,
> As if he was reading the kalma to ward off evil,
> "Chi, chi, chi...I made a mistake."

The telos of gruesome violence culminates in a "mistake." The killer is no thinking agent, rather the knife acts, and he merely wields the active weapon. Succinctly and vividly evoking the unthinking "banality of evil," the killer is identified simply as "the man with the knife." And he has unwittingly murdered one of his own. This knowledge is confirmed when he gazes on the circumcised penis – an exceedingly potent marker of religious difference during the Partition riots. Whereas sartorial practices could perform and confound religious identity for men and women, male genitals were turned into touchstones of religious difference. Manto derisively suggests that an extra piece of flesh was all that could ultimately distinguish a Muslim from a Hindu.[43]

The murderer, in the face of this blunder, reflexively intones the habitual cadences of the *kalma*, the Muslim prayer invoking divine forgiveness. Chanted like a prayer, "Chi, chi, chi," the sonorous repetition registers the killer's habituated and glib techniques of self-management in the face of his systematic cruelty. The anticlimactic ending coalesces his mechanical violence with his equally mechanical invocation of religion to grant him clemency. The scene points not only to the ambiguity that surrounded religious identity, which produced multiple miscalculations and intra-community violence of the Partition. Manto also incisively sketches out the cold, surgical precision of the murderer. Rather than any empathetic remorse for his mistake, the killer's staccato conclusion suggests his irritation at his inefficiency. The brisk meter and economy of the poem formally convey the routine calculations and terse efficiency of the Partition violence thus undermining prevalent theories about people who were caught up in irrational acts of violence.

Manto's fiction is a landmark in modern Urdu literature, but during his lifetime he endured a great deal of hostile criticism. In the two decades of his literary career, from 1933 to 1955 (when he died from alcohol-related disease), Manto created a host of unforgettable characters, including political activists, prostitutes, and lower-class and outcaste figures. Much of his work, however, provoked conservative critics and aroused bitter controversy. Even his literary friends from the Progressive Writers' Association (PWA) spurned *Siyah Hashye*, his first collection of literary sketches on the Partition.

Manto, the most caustic chronicler of the Partition, writes with anti-sentimental cynicism, sardonic wit, and deep contempt for middle-class, bourgeois values. Manto left Bombay in India for Lahore, now in Pakistan, in January 1948. The Partition of British India profoundly altered his writing. Manto returns obsessively to the ruptures that the Partition produced in the everyday lives of its survivors. His bare, staccato lines shorn of all sentimentalism reveal the scene of violence in its most spare, even banal, moments. To many of his critics, the experience of Partition changed his fiction for the worse. Hurt by the derogatory remarks of his critics and friends from the PWA, he responded thus:

> I tried to retrieve from this man-made sea of blood, pearls
> of a rare hue, by writing about the single-minded dedication
> with which men had killed men, about the remorse felt by
> some of them, about the tears shed by murderers who could
> not understand why they still had some human feelings
> left.... It caused me great pain when some of my literary
> friends made cruel fun of my book, denouncing me as an

irresponsible carrier of tales, a jokester, a nuisance, a cynic and a reactionary.[44]

Later, in a speech given to college students in Lahore, Manto defended himself against charges of excessive violence in his Partition stories: "If you are not familiar with the time period we are passing through, read my stories. If you cannot bear these stories, that means this is an unbearable time."[45]

Manto builds the suspenseful account in his characteristic style – he layers detail on particular detail, taking his reader through familiar humanizing gestures. Then, just as the reader almost automatically predicts the likely turn the story will take, Manto unexpectedly pierces the film of sentimentalism with an anticlimactic inversion.[46] Manto's power lies in his ability to draw his reader into the story, inviting us to tarry awhile in a predictably gruesome scenario, the familiarity of which evokes either a sentimental catharsis, or worse, a sense of moral apathy. Then, suddenly startling his reader, Manto catches her off guard, inverting her expectation, producing a momentary shudder.[47] Peeling away the reader's horizon of expectation, the shudder enables her to glimpse the horror of the Partition.[48] The dislocating force of Manto's stories affectively rehearses the loss of footing, the sudden deterritorialization the survivors experienced, and reveals the precariousness of claims to the certitudes of religious identity.

Let us now turn to a scene from Khushwant Singh's *Train to Pakistan* in which the ethnically ambiguous Iqbal, the derided *babu* figure, has returned from England to Mano Majra to participate – albeit belatedly – in anticolonial nationalist politics. The scene is set at a time when the placid village is suddenly heaving with the Partition's religious and political tensions. The sub-inspector has mistakenly arrested Iqbal and now, in order to rectify his error, insists on ascertaining Iqbal's religious identity. He orders Iqbal to take off his clothes. Iqbal feels humiliated but acquiesces and slowly undresses in front of the inspector:

> The pajamas fall in a heap around his ankles. He was naked save for the handcuffs on his wrists. He stepped out to let the

policemen examine them. "No, that is not necessary," broke
in the sub-inspector. "I have seen all I wanted to see." ...
He ordered the constables to take the prisoners to the police
station. He went back to the rest house to report his discovery
to the magistrate. There was an obsequious smile on his
face. "... He says he has been sent by the People's party. But
I am sure he is a Muslim Leaguer. They are much the same.
We would have had to arrest him in any case if he was up to
mischief so near the border. We can charge him with something
or other later." "How do you know he is a Muslim leaguer?"
The sub-inspector smiled confidently. "I had him stripped."[49]

The conundrum of his religious identity, according to the sub-inspector, is inscribed on his genitals and concealed beneath his pants.
Therefore, taking the pants off will unzip his secret and indubitably
prove to which religious community he belongs. The "dis-covering"
of Iqbal's ethnic identity, through a scopophilic examination of his
genitals, however, proves erroneous. Iqbal is a circumcised Sikh, who
has discarded the sartorial and somatic markers of his Sikh identity:
He neither wears his hair long tied in a turban, nor does he have a
beard, wear the traditional *kada* – the silver bracelet – or carry his
small silver sword, the *kirpan*. After releasing him, the sub-inspector
is cavalier about his error in judgment:

> You can make fun of me if you like ... if you had fallen into
> the hands of a Sikh mob, they would not have listened to your
> arguments. They would have stripped you to find out whether
> or not you were circumcised. That is the only test they have
> these days for a person who has not got long hair and a beard.
> Then they kill you. You should be grateful to me.[50]

The sub-inspector reads Iqbal's body as a somatic text, on which is
inscribed "the fact" of his religious identity. He resignifies his mistake of conflating/collapsing Iqbal's religious identity with his circumcised penis into an account of Iqbal's deliverance enabled by the
sub-inspector. It was hardly his fault that Iqbal had shed the visible
markers of his religious identity.

150

In the radically altered environment of Partition violence, confirming one's religious identity through genital markers either secured or imperiled conditions of survival. However, even this acid test of religious affiliation did not prove immutable, as men frequently circumcised themselves, for reasons of personal choice as well as exigency. The unstable texts inscribed on male bodies in both stories points to the difficulty of discerning between Hindus, Muslims, and Sikhs. The rhetoric of truth, evidence, and ocular proofs attempts to access the inner truth of the victim's religious interiority but are consistently confounded by the somatic surface. By inverting the topology of the self, both Manto and Singh suggest that ethnicity may be produced through somatic practices that are inscribed on the surface materiality of bodies.

Examining men's genitalia as evidence of religious identity was not unusual; it was the most commonplace way of ascertaining difference or identity. Nevertheless, the mode of detecting the religious identity through the exposure of genitalia itself emasculated the victim. The process of ascertaining the fact of religious identity effeminized and made vulnerable the exposed body. The lingering gaze of the persecutor on the male genitals of the potential victim also offers up for speculation the ambivalent moments of homoerotic and/or homosocial pleasures. Absolutist theories of religious hatred are unable to accommodate the polyvocality of such ambivalent moments. The scopophilic pleasure of gazing on scenes of violence may derive from righteous ire or erotic stimulation. The public exposure of genitals is, of course, meant to shame the victim but also produce, through spectatorial practices, a slippage between the pleasures of indignation and those of desire.

Bhisham Sahni's short story "Pali" also explores the intimate violence within domestic spaces. The story recounts the terror of Pali, a four-year-old Hindu boy, who gets lost during his family's journey in a *kafila* (column of pedestrian travelers) from Pakistan to India. A Muslim couple, Shakur and Zenab, observing that he is lost, brings him to their own village, and begins to look after him as their own son. However, the local Maulvi (priest) hears about the presence of a Hindu boy and stipulates that he be converted into a Muslim if the family desires to keep him. Although the formal ritual of conversion was a nuisance to Zenab, she agrees and is relieved that the Maulvi did not insist that she relinquish Pali. Converting Pali to Islam consists of the ritual act of circumcision as well as reading the *kalma* (Muslim prayers.) Pali's circumcision enacts his rite of passage from a Hindu to a Muslim, and he is renamed Altaf. For four years, Altaf continued to lead a carefree and happy childhood with his Muslim parents.

Meanwhile, his biological parents, Manohar Lal and Kaushalya, are desperate to recover him, having also lost their newborn daughter during the riots that descended on the traveling *kafilas*. After several attempts, Manohar Lal finally confronts Altaf's new parents in the presence of legal counselors and state representatives, and after much negotiation takes Pali with him to India. Manohar's wife is overjoyed to see Pali, and his presence gradually revives her. During the celebration of his return, Pali suddenly leaves the guests to do his evening *namaz*, to the dismay of the guests present. The Hindu priest is outraged at this act and takes him aside and rebukes him: "We won't allow you to do such silly things in this house … those Musallas have planted the poison of fanaticism in his mind. And at such a tender age." Saying this, the priest orders that a barber be sent for to perform the boy's *mundan* ceremony (Brahman hair-shaving ritual.) Pali is terrified as the barber shaves off his hair to Hindu chants, and sobs, under his breath, "*Ammiji, abbaji.*" Finally, a tuft of hair is left in the middle of his cropped head. Pali is bathed, given new clothes, and the sacred Brahman thread is tied around him as he chants his name five times.

This scene illustrates how religious, caste, and national belonging is repeatedly inscribed on Pali's body, producing him variously as an upper-caste, Hindu, Indian male. Pali himself is terrorized as competing ethnic texts are inscribed on his body to render it "authentic," even as the habitual customs of intoning the *namaz* and calling out for his *ammiji* have not left their residual traces on his embodied memory. Pali's "kinesthetic imagination" reveals the persistence of embodied memory as a "mneumonic reserve."[51] The community inscribes ritual acts of circumcision or hair shaving on male bodies within intimate, domestic spaces. These somatic practices seal their male child within an ethnic group and produce him as an "authentic" member of the community. Religious authenticity then is produced through somatic inscriptions on the body.

The story illustrates the ways in which religious identity is produced through somatic and sartorial practices; the iterative citationality of embodied practices produces religious authenticity. Competing somatic practices attempt to fix shifting social identity by inscribing gender and religious and caste ideologies on Pali's body. The story also illustrates how ostensibly predetermined, invariant, and essential categories of gender, caste, and religion are discursively produced through the surface politics of the body.

In the foregoing instances we see that although male bodies are inscribed in order to somatically produce the fact of religious identity, the emasculating process of "dis-covering" the truth of one's religion unsettles the victim's gendered identifications; the performative force of sexual threat hovers over female bodies, which situates the gendered self in a vulnerable relationship to the destabilizing force of linguistic and somatic speech acts. The body, in these illustrations, emerges as a somatic text, produced through acts of violence, mobilized by competing or collusive masculinist discourses of family, community, and nation. The fluidity of social identity is annexed in the violent fixing of bodies as specifically gendered and ethnic. The narration by Kirti Jain and Manto, Singh, and Sahni foregrounds corporeal appropriations and read the body as a parchment for discrete, discontinuous, and sometimes overlapping patriarchal discourses of family, community, and nation.

6 Kashmir: hospitality and the "unfinished business" of partition

> Every particle of my Kashmir is hospitable
> Even the stones along the way gave me water.
>
> Mohammad Din Fauq

I was apprehensive when I arrived in Kashmir in mid-June 2010. Just days before my arrival, a young boy, Tufail Mattoo, had been shot dead by security forces for protesting against the killing of three Kashmiri youths in a "fake encounter" on the Line of Control in the Machil sector, the details of which had been published on May 29, 2010.[1] A day after my arrival, the Central Reserve Police Forces, paramilitary police under central government control, brutally thrashed Rafiq Bangroo; the young boy was in the hospital, gasping for life. For the next few days, there was an eerie calm in the Kashmir valley. If he died, there would undoubtedly be more protests, more police violence, more dead boys. I was nervous; the name stayed on my mind: Rafiq Bangroo.

I was in Kashmir to research and watch Bhand Pather, Kashmiri folk performers who travel from place to place with their extensive repertoires. An improvisational form, Bhand Pather – literally "actor's play" – incorporates dance, Sufi music, and puppetry, in addition to dramatic dialogues. The Bhands perform in a variety of spaces, which include terraced maize fields, shrine courtyards, and on the streets. In contradistinction to the Partition's exclusionary narratives of national belonging, the Bhand Pather illuminates a model of sociality that draws

Adabi Duniya, 6.19, special issue on Kashmir (March–April 1966): 190–191, as quoted in Ayesha Jalal, *Self and Sovereignty: Individual and Community in South Asian Islam since 1850* (London: Routledge, 2000), 353.

on and intermixes multiple cultural traditions. The Bhand Pather performances, from their music to their stories, disorder the discourses of religious polarities that were foundational to the two-nation theory. On my arrival in Kashmir, however, the "syncretic" theatre of the Bhand Pather seemed anachronistic in the wider political context of the Kashmir valley.

On my drive from the airport in Srinagar to Akingam, the village in the Anantnag district of Kashmir where one of the most active Bhand communities lived and performed, the sheer numbers of military personnel in the region alarmed me. Roughly 500,000 armed forces had been deployed to the Kashmir valley, more than the combined numbers in Afghanistan and Iraq.[2] We encountered military checkpoints every few miles along our 40-mile journey to Akingam. Along the way, my genial companions tried to lighten me up: Look at the scenery; isn't Kashmir beautiful? I looked out the window: The majestic mountains, the river winding through the valleys, the clear blue sky, the lush green paddy fields, the fragrant chinar trees – yes, Kashmir was indeed beautiful. The paradisial beauty of Kashmir has been deeply ingrained in the imagination of every Indian through copious media representations. Training eyes on the legendary beauty of Kashmir, however, required keeping Kashmiris outside the frame; if they enter at all, it is through the image of the beautiful and radiant Kashmiri woman, synecdochic for the valley itself. The aestheticization of Kashmir is predicated on a violence of percepticide, of cultivating the art of looking away from its brutalized people.[3]

In this chapter, I consider contemporary Bhand performance in the context of the political violence in the valley. Where are the Bhand Pather performers situated in the dramas of nationhood, in the antagonistic conflict between the Kashmiri freedom seekers and the heavy-handed Indian military in Kashmir? What cultural, social, and spiritual resources do the performances of the Bhand Pather offer to the people of Kashmir? Can suffering and grief generate a renewed commitment to public and civic life and fuel an urgent sense of community?

This chapter situates Bhand performance in the valley between the vectors of antagonistic regional politics on the one hand, and aesthetic practices on the other. Bhand performances combine satire and spirituality to counter the mimetic territorial rivalry between India and Pakistan. The trope of hospitality within Bhand aesthetic philosophy offers a crucial means of negotiating the unrelenting violence in Kashmir; I argue that the idea of hospitality is central to the artistic and social philosophy of Bhand theatre, which advocates an ethical mode of living with religious and cultural difference. After a discussion of the historical and cultural contours of this folk theatre, I situate Bhand performance within the historical context of political violence in the valley. Finally, I turn to the performance of *Badshah Pather*, a recent Bhand adaptation of Shakespeare's *King Lear*.

Satire and critique in *Bhand Pather*

I was excited to watch Bhand Pather, one of the oldest extant folk theatres on the subcontinent. The first references to the Bhand Pather are found in Bharata's *Natyashastra* (written sometime between 200 BC and AD 200). The reign of the medieval king Zain-ul-Abidin, referred to as Badshah (1420–1470), in the fifteenth century is often identified in these accounts as a time of great flourishing for the arts in general and for the Bhand Pather in particular. Zain-ul-Abidin called back to Kashmir the Brahmins who had fled to India (in the wake of his father Sikander's rule, the sultan of Kashmir). He liberally patronized Brahmanical learning; he even had various books, such as the *Puranas* and *Mimansa*, among others, brought in from various distant lands and distributed them to the learned.[4]

That cultural practices in Kashmir complicate and disorder the categorical production of Hindu and Muslim as separate, bounded, hermetically sealed religious traditions is made manifest in the *chok* dance, performed by the Bhand actors. Once a year, in honor of the goddess Shiva Bhagvati, the Muslim Bhands perform a special ritual dance in a Hindu temple in the foothills of the Akingam area. As theatre director M.K. Raina observes: "An extremely superstitious people the Bhands perform this particular *chok* at this temple and nowhere else."[5] The religious devotion that the Muslim performers bring to their ritual dance in the Hindu temple reveals neither mere lip service to the constitutional ideals of secularism nor a grudging charity that "tolerates" religious difference. By embodying religious difference, the Muslim performers interrupt the religious polarities that provided the basis of the two-nation theory. The *chok* performance confounds the modern polarities of religion in the provocative unruliness of cultural practices. This ritual dance mounts a robust challenge to the religious essentialisms of the arguments for Partition; the Muslim Bhand dancers capture a moment when religious boundaries are blurred in a vivid intermingling of multiple cultural practices.

Several theatre critics have noted the syncretism of the Bhand Pather, which is often said to exemplify the spirit of Kashmiriyat in the valley. In the words of Kashmiri theatre critic Javaid Bhat, "Nothing defines the limits and promises of Kashmiriyat better than the Bhand Pather ... the traveling theatre lends itself for a study of the shifting landscape of the inter-communal relationships, and ... offers a non-idealized version of Kashmiriyat.... Bhand Pather underlines not merely the shared cultural space and the interweaving of everyday Hinduism and Islam but demonstrates practically the sharp differences as well. And yet illustrates how despite such differences it is not impossible to live together."[6] This notion of Kashmiriyat was obviously not static but was shaped through dynamic interactions with regional, religious, national, and other forms of belonging.

In her recent book *Languages of Belonging*, Chitralekha Zutshi interrogates the notion of Kashmiriyat as a discourse of interethnic harmony, and she examines instead how such a discourse worked to repress crucial internal differences and contradictions of religion, sect, caste, class, region, language, and ethnicity. She considers, for example, the ways in which the ostensibly secular and nationalist National Conference deployed to paper the homogenizing discourse of Kashmiriyat over the widespread discontent within Kashmiri society, particularly among Muslims of the valley. The concept of Kashmiriyat was a neat way to propagate the idea of a peaceful coexistence of religious communities while obscuring the question of economic, material, and social differences among them. Zutshi warns against an uncritical acceptance of Kashmiriyat, "refracted through rose-tinted glasses, in which Kashmir appears as a unique region where religious communities lived in harmony since time immemorial and differences in religion did not translate into acrimonious conflict until external intervention."[7] Zutshi historicizes the complex and shifting terrain of Hindu-Muslim negotiations and in the process examines the material implications of a discourse on Kashmiriyat.

Zutshi's work is important in guarding against romantic recuperations of Kashmir as a utopic "paradise on earth" with tranquil interethnic relations, but it is also crucial not to discount the affective power of a shifting discourse on Kashmiriyat. Although the politics on the ground did not always correspond to the philosophy of Kashmiriyat, as Zutshi has argued, it still does not void the affective power of Kashmiriyat as an imaginative and aspirational force that crucially informs narratives of Kashmiri identity. Kashmiriyat continues to exert an enormous power in the Kashmiri political imagination, one that is still summoned to imagine a utopic blueprint for its future.

In the Bhand Pather performances, Kashmiriyat emerges as a "structure of feeling" that foregrounds the necessary embeddedness of social life. In direct contrast to the prevailing rhetorics of freedom that subscribe to bounded notions of collectivity such as Pakistan's religious nationalist argument and India's secular nationalist argument, the Bhand Pather evinces an alternative vision of community.

On my arrival in Akingam in the late afternoon, I had the opportunity to watch some of the plays from the traditional Bhand repertoire. This was quite typical for Bhand performances, which are usually held before or after afternoon prayers; evening performances are rare, given the political unrest in the region. The performances often begin with invocations, conclude with blessings, and when performed in shrine courtyards, the actors seek the intercession of the saint of the particular shrine. Thus, even if the content is not overtly religious, the performances are often framed by religious practices.

Humor is vital to Bhand Pather; in fact, the word "Bhand" itself derives from the Sanskrit *band*, meaning "joke," and the spirit of comedy infuses this folk theatre.[8] The *pather* dramatizes the conflict between those caught in asymmetrical relationships of power. The Bhand Pather repertoire includes plays such as *Aarim Pather*, on vegetable growers; *Grees-Pather*, on peasants; *Watal-Pather*, on dalits; *Bakerwal-Pather*, on the Bakerwals – a nomadic tribe of

Kashmir; *Buhri-Pather*, on Bohris, or traders; *Raze Pather*, on kings; *Gosain-Pather*, on Hindu-hermits; *Angrez-Pather*, on British colonial rulers; *Hanz-Pather*, on fishermen; and many more. Here I consider two specific *pather* to draw out some of the larger political and social implications of their subversive humor: *Shikargah* and *Darza Pather*.

Shikargah, a dramatic sketch that portrays the relationship between humans and animals, is rendered through the use of masks and animal costumes. *Shikargah* begins with a depiction of a disturbance within the mountainous abode of Shiva. Here, the Muslim Bhand dressed as the Hindu god Shiva flees from his abode. A foreign hunter from the royal court enters the scene and harasses the local forest dweller when he warns him of a lion that has been roaming the forests. What ensues is the typical hilarity of talking at cross-purposes and the absurd brutality of the foreign hunter. The delicate balance between forest dwellers and the animals is upturned yet again when two royal soldiers enter the scene and demand to know the whereabouts of the *hangul*, Kashmir's celebrated deer.[9] *Shikargah* lampoons the unthinking avarice and cruelty of the foreign military. Here, two royal soldiers speak in a foreign language to a poor Kashmiri peasant and are enraged when he does not understand them. More miscommunication ensues. When the peasant is unable to understand the soldiers, they thrash him with a whip. The play usually ends with the animals prevailing over the hunters and the soldiers, and culminates in a riotous animal dance.

The Bhand Pather use props very sparingly, and in light of this, those that we do see immediately take on particular intensity and symbolic significance. The most commonly used prop is the *koddar*, a whip that makes a nasty lashing sound, but if lashed below the waist it hardly ever hurts the actor. It is not incidental that the most significant prop used in Bhand Pather depicts the physical lashing and humiliation that oppressed Kashmiri subjects experience under the heavy-handed rule of their foreign oppressors.[10] The relationship between the ruler and his subject is mediated and sustained by the symbolic, affective, and material power of this whip.

Although the opening scene of a disruption in Shiva's celestial kingdom may give one the impression that the religious framework

Figure 6.1 Bhand performer as Shiva in *Shikargah*. Photographer: Anant Raina.

dehistoricizes their critique into a timeless litany of oppressions against the rulers, it is important to remember that these dramatic iterations intervene into specific and concrete political circumstances. Kashmir is home to a wide array of flora and fauna: the *chir* tree, the

160

Himalayan cypress, the silver fir, the Himalayan hemlock, and even the famed *chinar* trees, all rapidly disappearing due to commercial exploitation of timber and fuel. The denuded forests also negatively impact industries of domestic carpentry, furniture, railway sleepers, and pulp mills. Add to this the disappearance of Kashmiri wildlife: rare species of animals such as the snow leopard and the Kashmir *hangul* are rapidly becoming extinct.

The aggressive deforestation that began in the wake of colonial forestry practices exacerbated the vulnerability of tribal forest dwellers. The Indian Forest Act of 1865 established the government's claims over forests, which precipitated the draconian Forest Act of 1878, which curtailed centuries-old customary use of communities over their forests and consolidated the government's control over all forests. According to this Forest Act, the use of the forests by villagers was abrogated and then provisionally granted through concessions. Just as the fulfillment of imperial needs was the priority of colonial forest policy, the demands of commercial industry became the cornerstone of postcolonial forest policy.[11] India's Independence brought little benefit to the Kashmiris; the nation-state simply perpetuated the imperious practices of colonial rule. *Shikargah* displays the disruption of Kashmir's biodiversity as a consequence of colonial and national policies that aggressively exploit its natural resources. It offers a biting critique of the hierarchical order of political power, in which forest-dwellers and animals are treated as resources for the voracious and exploitative appetite of foreign rulers. *Shikargah* illustrates the reprisals suffered by those tyrants who disorder the harmonious coexistence of humans and animals.

In addition, the wordplay in *Shikargah* produces a disorienting dislocation of subjecthood and the resultant disintegration of guaranteed subject positions. Arriving at the forest where the forest-dweller lives in harmony with the animals, the cruel hunter brusquely asks the forest-dweller, "Who are you?" – a question that presumes that the hunter is the master of the forest and the forest-dweller is the trespasser. The forest is the home of the forest-dweller, however – indeed, he is the master of this forest. "I am you, but who are you?" responds the forest-dweller, befuddling and confounding the hunter.

When caught in a dizzying volley of words, the hunter, increasingly exasperated by the temerity of the forest-dweller, takes recourse to his whip, the *koddar*, and thrashes the forest-dweller.

Shikargah, like many of the Bhand Pather plays, insists on the radical parity of all earthly beings, and privileges hospitality as a mode of negotiating cultural difference in the world. The enigmatic response of the forest-dweller forces us to consider the ways in which the foreign hunter – by all accounts a visitor and an outsider – turns the host, the forest-dweller, into a hostage through his acts of despotic cruelty. The ruler's authoritarian address, "Who are you?" is mimetically reflected by the forest-dweller, who responds,"I am you, but who are you?"and the refrain plays out in various forms until the very ambivalence of the mimicry unsettles the assuredness of one's position as master.[12]

The mimetic encounter suggests that the hunter and the forest-dweller may not be as far apart as one imagines; indeed, the roles between master and servant are substitutable. This theme is taken up in the *Lear* adaptation in which a similar obfuscation ensues between the roles of king and fool, of Badshah and the Mashkara. The Bhand Pather demonstrates the ways in which satire and the subversive force of comedy destabilize the assured subject positions of hierarchical power relations. Here, laughter presages a process of disintegration of the antagonist: Laughing at the royal oppressor, increasingly angered by the antics of the oppressed forest-dweller, punctures the oppressor's self-importance, pokes holes into his imperturbable kingly facade, and destabilizes and makes visible the cracks in his claim to authority.

Darza Pather

A play that illustrates the absurdity of language politics in Kashmir, *Darza Pather* lampoons the pompousness and vanity of the king. Here, four clowns engage in wordplay with the king; each is flanked on either side by a concubine and played by cross-dressed Bhands. Through imagined and real transgressions of usurping the king's position by cavorting with his concubines and dreaming of the royal *wazwan*, or feast, the clowns mock the king and poke holes in his self-importance. Here, too, much of the humor is derived from the wordplay that follows as a consequence of the failure of communication. Through their jokes, the *pather* poke fun at the absurdity of those who have come to believe in the naturalness of their political authority.

A characteristic feature of the Bhand Pather is the use of the *phir kath*, literally twisted talk, style of dialogue; a rhetorical device that utilizes coded and cryptic idioms. The punning, wordplay, and double-talk enable the folk performers to use ostensibly innocuous comedy to deliver pointed indictments of contemporary society. The double-talk that is distinctive to this series of performance uses local metaphors in ways that make it difficult for non-Kashmiris to follow. The *phir kath* enables the Bhand Pather to critique their oppressive rulers, while at the same time disavowing any obvious, immediate reference to political events.

In addition, the plays were performed in Kashmiri, the local language of the valley, which made it challenging for non-Kashmiris to understand them. Kashmiri Hindus and Muslims speak neither Hindi nor Urdu; they speak Kashmiri. However, the marginalization of Kashmiri and the simultaneous promotion of Urdu, Hindi, or English as the languages of the state demonstrate the incongruence between the Kashmiris and the state. Through its critique of language politics in Kashmir, *Darza Pather* demonstrates the incompatibility between the rulers and their alienated subjects. The repeated refrain in these plays suggest that the state and its people do not speak the same language; the incommensurability between the people and the state is dramatized through the absurd demands by the ruling powers for absolute and unambiguous translatability.

By channeling the disquiet and grievances of the local audiences through comedy, the Bhand plays utilize a creative means to vent their anger toward their oppressive rulers. Kashmiri theatre scholar Javaid Bhat argues that the Bhand Pather's satires played a "therapeutic role" and offered a source of release from the tension of living in the politically volatile region. The comedy offered a release mechanism for the audiences/players to mock, ridicule, and dissipate their frustrations. In the words of Bhat, "The history of the Bhand Pather at the height of its popularity underscored through an overarching mocking tradition the triumph of the small and the weak over the big and the powerful."[13]

Although Bhat rightly focuses our attention on the potential of Bhand Pather to offer a salve to the depredations of everyday life in Kashmir, overemphasizing the "therapeutic" function of comedy as a temporary safety valve that releases tensions within a society and then reinforces the norm disregards the multivalent critique within the Bhand plays. Attending to the multiple components of the Bhand Pather, which include satire, Sufi music, and hybrid cultural practices, allows us to see the cultural and affective resources of an ethic of hospitality in the face of political oppression.

It is important to bear in mind that the humor, language, and even the music work to temporarily constitute a sense of community among their viewer-witnesses. The relay of miscommunication occurs in the presence of the audience; the laughter of the audience secures the bond between the joker and the community of listeners and isolates the tyrant on stage in the process of delineating the boundaries of the community. The community of listeners comes together not only through the dramatic address of the Bhand plays but also through the idiomatic exclusivity of the *phir kath*, which fosters an intimate bond and sense of community among those who "get" the joke. The *phir kath* draws a line between the insiders and the outsiders and fosters an active sense of belonging within the audience.

Taken together, both plays suggest that a ruler who relinquishes his sacred duty toward his subjects will no doubt find his moment of reckoning.[14] The imperative for moral rectitude derives from the divinely ordained duty of the ruler to be just to his subjects and to regard them in a spirit of radical parity. Viewing these plays against a spiritual horizon enriches our understanding of the source of their satirical critique: The humor here derives from the conviction that these sacrilegious and exploitative practices would find their retribution in the afterlife as rulers betray the trust which God placed in them.

Bhand Pather draws its aesthetic and philosophical insights from the robust traditions of Kashmir Shaivism and indigenous Sufism in Kashmir.[15] The transformation of Kashmir from an ancient Hindu system to a Persianized form of Muslim society was generally peaceful. Yoginder Sikand argues that the spread of Islam in Kashmir was the result of Sufi influence and can be traced back to early fourteenth-century missionaries of the Kubravi order. According to Shahzad Bashir, "Hamadani's visit to Kashmir eventually led to a permanent Kubravi presence in the city of Srinagar from the late fourteenth century, and Kashmiri Muslims to this day regard him as the patron saint whose efforts led to the area's Islamization."[16]

Whereas the Sufi orders such as the Suhrawardi, Kubravi, Naqshbandi, and Qadri arrived in Kashmir from Persia, Central Asia, and India, the Rishi order was an indigenous Sufi order that arose in the beginning of the fifteenth century. Commonly known in Kashmir as Nand Resh, Shaikh Nurud-Din is often considered responsible for the growth and popularity of the Muslim Rishi order in Kashmir. Nurud-Din was also inspired by the Bhakti movement in Kashmir that Lal Ded, his senior contemporary, had done much to revive. Whereas the orthodox Sufis' activities ranged from building mosques, constructing educational institutions, and patronage for learned divines, the Rishis stayed away from the establishment of madrasas, missionary activities, politics, and the ruling classes. As Rafiqi puts it, "The Rishis were children of the soil, and though converted to Islam were sympathetic to the mystic traditions of the country."[17] Sufism in Kashmir was not an internally undifferentiated tradition but rife with different strains and often competing and irreconcilable practices and worldviews.[18]

The intermingling of Hindu and Muslim practices also followed from the large flow of Muslims to Kashmir from Multan as well as conversions of Hindus to Islam. What ensued was the gradual Islamization of the valley where Islamic practices were slowly but surely adopted, and local beliefs and customs were Islamized.[19] Situating Bhand Pather within the *longue durée* of cultural syncretism in the valley allows us to see the tenacious and shifting ways in which religious coexistence persist within contemporary cultural practices in Kashmir.

Although the Bhand Pather's critique of oppressive and exploitative state practices acquires its force from an immanent worldview that advocates radical parity as a mode of encountering religious and cultural difference, the political turbulence in the valley over the past two decades has increasingly stifled such critiques. The volatile political landscape in the valley since 1989 has impacted the Bhands as well. While some Bhand players were actively persecuted, and even killed by militants who objected to dance, music, and drama, many others were mistreated at the hands of the military, causing Bhands to migrate from the region and take up other professions.[20] Over the past two decades, the number of Bhand groups in the valley has radically dwindled. In order to understand the marginalization of Bhand Pather, however, it is essential to situate it within the political context of Kashmir, to which we will now turn.

The "problem" of Kashmir

Dominant representations of Kashmir on the subcontinent oscillate between the idyllic "paradise on earth" to its dystopic obverse: "the most dangerous place on earth." The predominant studies on the Kashmir question emerge from social-scientific paradigms and positivist analyses of the conflict in the region. In dominant political and social-science discourse, Kashmir emerges as a "problem" to be rectified by one of three possible solutions: accession to India, accession to Pakistan, and self-determination and possible independence for Kashmir.

The prevailing political science accounts of the conflict overlook the profound sense of loss that pervades the valley. The repression of democratic rights, the loss of lives, and the pervasive fear and suspicion that lurk in the valley are not adequately captured in empiricist and teleological narratives of Kashmir's history. The costs of the conflict have been tremendous: More than 40,000 soldiers, militants, and civilians have lost their lives to the violence in Kashmir during the last twenty years.[21] More than 100,000 Hindu Kashmiri Pandits were displaced.[22] The Association of Parents of Disappeared Persons (APDP) has registered 8,000 enforced disappearances of children – some who have been missing for nearly twenty years.[23] The exploding sounds of shells, grenades, bombs, and mines have intermittently provided the soundtrack to everyday life in the Kashmir valley. The political violence has inscribed death in the heart of the everyday in Kashmir. The unruly history of this region resists empiricist and teleological accounts, which elude the constitutive force of loss in shaping Kashmiri subjectivities.

Any analysis of the conflict in Kashmir must contend with the specter of the violent Partition of British India. Kashmir, often referred to as the "unfinished business" of Partition, has remained the biggest impediment in peaceful Indo-Pakistan relations. Two of the three major wars (1948, 1965) that India has fought against Pakistan were over Kashmir. In 1998, the two nations added nuclear weapons to their existent dangerous and expensive military arsenal. In May 1999, the Kargil War destroyed a promising diplomatic process between then prime ministers Nawaz Sharief and Atal Bihari Vajpayee.

In 1947, at the time of partitioning the two nations, the Instrument of Accession drawn up between the princes and the government of India gave the princely states the formal choice to either accede to India or Pakistan or choose to stay independent. Kashmir was one such princely state. When besieged by ethnic violence, the Hindu king Hari Singh of Muslim-dominated Kashmir, acceded to India, thus precipitating a de facto partitioning of the region between Indian Kashmir, consisting of Jammu, Kashmir, and Ladakh, and Pakistan Kashmir, consisting of Azad Kashmir, Gilgit, and Baltistan.

Pakistan challenged the Accession on the grounds that Kashmir had a Muslim majority. Liaquat Ali Khan, the first prime minister of Pakistan, employed a primordialist argument and reiterated the primacy of religious nationalism as the rationale for Kashmir's incorporation into Pakistan. He argued:

> Geographically, economically, culturally and religiously,
> Kashmir is a part of Pakistan. The overwhelming Muslim
> character of its population, its strategic position in relation to
> Pakistan, the flow of its rivers, the direction of its roads, the
> channels of its trade, the continual intimate association which
> binds it to the people of Pakistan from time immemorial, link
> Kashmir indissolubly with Pakistan.[24]

A different secular conception of nationalism underpins India's claim to Kashmir. India's official rhetoric has bandied secularism and territorial unity as the two key claims for holding on to Kashmir. As the only Indian state with a Muslim majority (95 percent Muslim in Kashmir; 11 percent minority nationwide), Jammu and Kashmir

constitute the crucial grounds for India's claims to secular nationalism. Rejecting the two-nation theory, India claims Kashmir, the only
Muslim-majority state in India to demonstrate that it is indeed a secular nation. Jawaharlal Nehru, India's first prime minister, explains the
importance of Kashmir thus:

> We have always regarded the Kashmir problem as symbolic
> for us, as it has far-reaching consequences in India. Kashmir
> is symbolic as it illustrates that we are a secular state. . . .
> Kashmir has consequences both in India and Pakistan because
> if we disposed of Kashmir on the basis of the two-nation
> theory, obviously millions of people in India and millions of
> people in East Pakistan will be powerfully affected. Many of
> the wounds that had healed might open out again.[25]

In addition to the competing claims to Kashmir made on grounds of
religious nationalism (as in the case of Pakistan) or secular nationalism (as in the case of India), the history of Kashmir's accession is
further undermined by "an unhappy performative." In 1947, following Prince Hari Singh's accession to India, Nehru promised that the
accession should be confirmed by Kashmiri plebiscite once a situation
of normalcy returned to the state. Thus, the Instrument of Accession
was contingent on the condition that the people of Jammu and
Kashmir accept this mandate. On November 2, 1947, Nehru solemnly
"pledged" that "when peace and law and order have been established
... the referendum [shall be]held under international auspices like the
United Nations. We want it to be a fair and just reference to the people, and we shall accept their verdict. I can imagine no fairer and juster
[sic]offer."[26]

   This pledge – that a plebiscite should be held in order to enable
the people of Kashmir to determine their own political future – has
not yet been honored. India defends its position by claiming that it
will indeed conduct a plebiscite but only after Pakistan withdraws
from Pakistan Occupied Kashmir, enabling all the subjects of the
Dogra kingdom to exercise their vote. Meanwhile, Kashmiri agitation
for democratic rights to determine their own political future has been
ongoing for more than sixty years.

But even the unfulfilled pledge did not immediately produce a popular uprising in Kashmir. General discontent with rising unemployment, full press censorship, and unfair elections simmered throughout the 1980s. Ultimately, the disregard for fair elections in 1987 provided the final straw. The late political leader of People's Conference, Abdul Ghani Lone, recalls the sentiment of the younger generation: "'To hell with the democratic process and all that this is about ... let's go for the armed struggle.' It was the flashpoint. The thought was there, the motivation was there, the urge was there, the demand was there, and the opposition was there. The situation became ripe, and then a flashpoint."[27] The frustration with the disregard for Kashmiri democratic aspirations eventually exploded into insurgency.

Lest it be assumed that Pakistan acts as the champion of the oppressed, it is important to note that Pakistan's own record is highly suspect in Azad Kashmir. For example, the Azad Jammu and Kashmir Constitution stipulates that "no person or political party in Azad Jammu and Kashmir shall be permitted to propagate against or take part in activities prejudicial or detrimental to the ideology of the State's accession to Pakistan."[28] Heavy surveillance on bureaucrats and other government employees often results in dismissals. Like India, Pakistan also retains a heavy military presence in Azad Kashmir. While Pakistan agitates for a plebiscite, they maintain that the third option of independence is not feasible.[29]

Although initially militants perpetrated violent acts to gain international support for Kashmiri self-determination and coerce the Indian state to relinquish control of the valley, subsequently the Kashmir cause was hijacked by extremists with little concern for the Kashmiri people. The Islamic militant infiltration from Pakistan and Central Asia into the Kashmiri freedom struggle splintered the movement, alienated religious minorities in the region, and disordered the lives of persecuted Hindu Pandits in the region. Thus, Indian disregard for the basic democratic rights of the Kashmiris and Pakistani sponsorship of militancy laid the foundations for the unrest in Kashmir.

As a result, India's and Pakistan's opposing visions of the greater good for the Kashmiri people quash Kashmir's democratic aspirations. Whereas Pakistan offers an intractably irredentist position by arguing that the freedom of Kashmiri Muslims lies in their accession to a Muslim nation, India, on the other hand, denounces religious nationalism and champions itself as a secular haven for freedom for all minorities. Both Pakistan and India pursue violent means to enact their competing notions of "freedom" for Kashmiris. These instrumentalist arguments, however, obscure a more fundamental drive toward possessing Kashmir: The compulsive attachment to Kashmir derives in no small part from the intense mimetic rivalry between India and Pakistan.[30] The mimetic desire for Kashmir, displayed by both India and Pakistan, causes the antagonists to lose sight of the desired object in their obsessive focus on each other, thus triggering a mimetic rivalry that tends toward interminable revenge.

What emerges from these competing rhetorics of freedom is the persistence of the nation-form as the consummate political vehicle for freedom in modernity. The militant's armed rebellion for an independent Kashmiri nation, the Indian military's repressive strategies to retain Kashmir, and Pakistan's covert sponsorship of terrorist militant activity to bring Muslim Kashmir within its territorial fold are all predicated on a particular notion of the nation as the exemplary conduit to achieve freedom in the modern world. The love for nation, and the readiness to die for it, must be understood within the context of freedom: Dying for the nation guarantees "a life beyond death, a life beyond the finite, merely biological life."[31] The nation offers the modality through which individuals can transcend their own finitude by perpetuating the life of the nation.[32]

Today, even though the militant insurgency appears under control, there is an oppressive tension in the air. The armed forces (500,000 troops, after pulling out 30,000 in 2009) are charged with human rights abuses. Many Kashmiris challenge the presence of the military, most recently demonstrated by the stone-pelting protestors in the summer of 2010.[33]

How does cultural production survive in a context where political violence becomes a routine and banal fact of everyday life? How has the violence impacted the Bhands both in terms of the direct persecution of the performers, as well as in terms of the form itself? How does a comedic form like Bhand Pather accommodate the pervasiveness

170

of grief in the valley? A closer analysis of *Badshah Pather* will allow us to approach some of these questions.

Kashmiri intellectuals and artists have attempted to revive the Bhand Pather tradition in Kashmir, while simultaneously addressing some pressing political issues of contemporary Kashmir through the form. For example, Bhagat Theatre in Akingam, Anantnag was established in 1961 by Mohammad Subhan Bhagat and later patronized by M.L. Kemmu, an award-winning Kashmiri playwright.[34] Kemmu's play *Dakh Yeli Tsalan* written in 1994 depicts the competing worldviews held by Kashmiri militants and Bhand performers. Kemmu critically portrays Kashmiri militants as intolerant of the perpetuation of falsehoods within theatre, and as single-minded in their violent pursuit of political freedom. The altercation between the militants and the Bhand performers plays out on the terrain of mimesis: Is theatre a repository of falsehood, or is nationalism a greater artifice, affectively overwhelming its supporters and soliciting loyalties that privilege attachments to abstractions over attachments to people in one's everyday life? Shashi Shekhar Toshkhani translated the play into Hindi and M.K. Raina directed the translated Hindi version, which was called *Bhand Duhai*.

Distinguished theatre director M.K. Raina is the recipient of several national awards, including the B.V. Karanth Award for Lifetime Achievement in Theatre, the Sangeet Natak Akademi Award (1995), and the Sahitya Kala Parishad Award (1981), among others. His theatre productions include plays written by prominent modern playwrights, including Vijay Tendulkar, Dharam Vir Bharati, Badal Sircar, Mohan Rakesh, and Girish Karnad. Raina's artistic accomplishments reveal compelling intersections between indigenous folk forms and classical high art, between European dramatic literature and avant-garde experimentation, between poesis and politics.

Raina's political commitment gives his artistic work its intellectual precision and imaginative power.[35] Raina's attempt to politicize theatre has often taken him outside the precincts of the bourgeois proscenium auditorium to work with groups that range from the Jan Natya Manch, the pre-eminent street theatre group in India, to the traveling performers of Kashmiri folk theatre, the Bhand Pather. Not only does Raina attempt to revive the dwindling folk theatre form of Bhand Pather, he also offers theatre as a resource to terror-stricken children in the valley, through which to initiate expression, conversation, and healing.

M.K. Raina has worked with the Bhands of Akingam for nearly thirty years. His family, like many other Kashmiri Pandits, migrated out of the valley in 1990s. According to Raina, his many journeys back to the valley were not to recover the home he had lost; rather, Kashmir is formative to his very sense of self. Through his relentless political and artistic work, Raina channels his grief itself into a resource for poesis, for a new kind of world-making, and it is to his Bhand adaptation of *King Lear* that we will now turn.

Badshah Pather

Often described as Shakespeare's most desolate tragedy, *King Lear* meditates on questions of kingship and kinship, property and propriety, justice and the failure of legalism – questions that resonate with everyday life in Kashmir today. When I heard that M.K. Raina was directing a Bhand Pather adaptation of *King Lear*, my first thoughts were: How will Raina accommodate the tragic story of Lear within the satirical style of Bhand Pather? Will the narration resolve this generic tension or hold together the seemingly incommensurable impulses of high tragedy on the one hand and comedic folk critique on the other? Can catharsis and comedy coexist?[36] What will this dramatization reveal to us about contemporary political concerns in Kashmir?

In *Badshah Pather*, M.K. Raina retains the parallel plots of the two fathers, Lear (Badshah), and his three sons: Shamim (Goneril), Karim (Regan), and Rafiq (Cordelia) and the plot of Gloucester, Lear's courtier (Bedar) and his two sons: the illegitimate Kehram (Edmund) and lawful Sikander (Edgar). In his adaptation, Raina transforms the motherless landscape of Lear's play into a world entirely without women.[37] Raina recast the three daughters of Shakespeare's play as three sons, a decision driven by questions of cultural exigency: The repertory consists entirely of male actors, and the members of the Akingam community were reluctant to allow women to act in their bawdy plays. Cross-dressing, while prevalent in plays such as *Darza*

Pather, was not an option for *Badshah Pather* because it verged on caricature and as such would have been inappropriate for the high tragedy of this play.

The performance of *Badshah Pather* took place a few days after I arrived and settled into Akingam.[38] On a bright, warm afternoon the Bhands prepared to put on a show of *Badshah Pather* on a large, open field where they usually perform their plays. I chose a cool spot in the shade of a tree, adjacent to a group of young women. A small group of children, all less than ten years old, surrounded me. Some played in the sun, others wanted to see my camera. As soon as the loud notes of the *swarnai* of the *muqam* (*raag* or musical score) wafted through the afternoon air, the villagers of Akingam began trickling in. The musicians were seated at the bottom of the foothills, with the actors playing in front of them. The audience gathered quickly and settled on the grass in a gender-segregated fashion. There were fewer women, and they, along with the children, sat or stood to the side of the field. The cool afternoon breeze eased somewhat the intensity of the sun beating down on our backs. The music, which consisted of *swarnai* (oboe), *dhol* (drum), *nagara* (percussion), and *thalij* (cymbal), played on for some fifteen minutes, while the audience grew to more than a hundred. Most were Akingam villagers, tired after a day of working hard in the fields. Having finished their afternoon prayers, the Bhand performers got into their costumes and were ready to begin. The sun-induced languor soon gave way to excitement and anticipation.

When the actors were ready to begin, the *swarnai* played its *Badshah Pather muqam* followed by the *dhol*, as a line of brisk and energetic dancers swiftly took on the playing area. After a robust dance, the players moved deftly into Shakespeare's tragedy. The play begins with the display of an enormous map that the actors bring onstage. One of the few props, the map offers a graphic illustration of Badshah's territory and its looming partition into separate states between brothers. The map offers an uncanny reminder of the cartographic power politics at the heart of the Kashmir dispute between India and Pakistan.[39] The map, a fetish of territorial politics, abstracts place and offers a representation of territory that is uncannily bereft of its people. Spatializing Badshah's power, the map consolidates his entitlement to allocate territory according to his desire. The possession of territory organized by the spatial abstraction of the map initiates a fratricidal conflict that culminates in death and dispossession.

The Badshah plot revolves around the haughtiness and subsequent downfall of a king who divides up his kingdom on the basis of a love-test. The parallel plot portrays Bedar (Gloucester, Lear's courtier) and his illegitimate son, Kehram (Edmund) plotting to murder his father by turning him against his legitimate son, Sikander (Edgar). The theme of legitimacy haunts the action on stage: The idea of illegitimacy is embodied in the figure of Kehram (the outlaw son, born out of wedlock). Indeed, the play suggests that loyalty has little to do with legitimacy: Shamim and Karim betray their father as brutally as Kehram deceives his father.

The court in *Badshah Pather* emerges as an arena for theatre that rewards performance rather than sincerity. Refusing to bargain for territory with public declaration of his love, Rafiq withholds flattery and rejects Badshah's economy of filial exchange. As Rafiq leaves the stage after being banished from the kingdom, he turns to his brothers and warns: "Keep your promise. You publicly proclaimed your devotion to our father." He repeats again, "Keep your promise." His words echo as he leaves the stage and raise the specter of broken promises in the kingdom partitioned between two brothers. The fratricidal nature of the conflict reinforces the familial trope of twins, India and Pakistan, warring against each other. Wafadar (Kent), who speaks on behalf of Rafiq, is also virulently banished from court in a scene that forebodes the discontent of the working class and raises the specter of insubordination.

If justice is revealed as performance, then *Badshah Pather* concurrently also turns the theatre into a court. *Badshah Pather* converts the playing field into a theatron, a place for seeing, where the citizen-audience is turned into a witness. The playing space offered a public venue where citizens could dwell on the events of their recent history in a dramatic framework that simultaneously implicated them as witness and also offered some aesthetic distance to reflect on their current imbroglio. Thus a public is temporarily constituted through a poetic address; this discursively constituted public is fostered through an active sense of belonging to an immediate polis.[40] Through the humor and pathos of their stories, the Bhand Pather make shared suffering the generative condition for consolidating a community of witnesses.

Hospitality at the limit of tolerance

At the heart of *Badshah Pather* is the provocative depiction of the claims and failures of hospitality: The pointed depiction of Shamim and Karim turning their father away from his own home brings the idea of hospitality into crisis. Badshah's specious logic at the court – I turn my possessions (my territory) over to my possessions (my sons), and continue to retain my symbolic power – is turned against him. The durability of political power is premised on a promise, which both sons break.

The collapse of received cultural frameworks of hospitality is made vivid when Badshah enters his first son's house, exclaiming: "Where's my *wazwan* [multi-course meal]?" Shamim, the eldest son, immediately undercuts this expansive mood by complaining about Badshah's large retinue. For Badshah, the reduction of his servants is tantamount to a diminution of his royal self: Cutting down his retinue is analogous to cutting him down to size.

Increasingly offended by Shamim's efforts to haggle and reduce his retainers, and rebuffed by the inhospitality of his eldest son, Badshah prepares to visit his second son. Karim, already apprised of the situation by his brother, reprimands his father for his obstinacy and enjoins him to return to Shamim. Karim brusquely informs him that Badshah is not welcome in his kingdom, and he is better off seeking forgiveness from his elder brother. Denied any measure of hospitality from his sons, and repudiated from his own kingdom, Badshah wanders off, disoriented and distraught, into the stormy night. Badshah presumes the claim that he has on his sons but realizes that his claim on kinship is inextricably bound up with his claim on kingship, that the rules of propriety are contingent on the ownership of property.

The shift in political authority from Badshah to his sons is exemplified through the conditions and contingencies that are placed on the performance of hospitality. The word "host" derives from *hospes*, the Latin word for master, often male, and it is this sense of the idea of "host" as master that informs this scene. Hence, relinquishing hospitality demonstrates the shift in political authority and indexes the arrival of a new master.

The two brothers collude to drive their father and his troops out into the howling storm. In their calculated acts of cruelty toward their own father, Shamim and Karim plumb the multivalent etymologies of the idea of host. The word "host" also derives from its affinity to the Latin word *hostis*, meaning enemy/stranger, exemplified in the actions of Shamim and Karim. Kinship here is destabilized and reconfigured as the terrain for politics. The fraternal relations between kin, between Shamim and Karim against their father, and Kehram against Sikander become the ground for the most virulent enactment of hostility. The stakes for betrayal are raised when the narrative reconfigures the filial relationship between father and son into the terrain of the political exemplified in the antagonism between friend and enemy.

We see here that hospitable propriety is contingent on the allocation of property; thus, hospitality transforms into hostility when the circuit of filial exchange – love for property – enacted in the love-test scene, is completed. The promise of filial love, dependent on an instrumental economy of exchange that we first witness in the scene of the lovetest, here comes to its fruition.

If the Badshah plot reveals hosts turning hostile, then in the parallel plot we witness the opposite move: Here the host is taken hostage.[41] If Shamim and Karim turn Badshah out from his own home to the inhospitable stormy heath, then the parallel plot charts Bedar's transformation from host to hostage within his own home. Taking Bedar hostage reinforces the trope of a preposterous world. He pleads with Shamim and Karim: "I am your host. You are robbing me and upsetting the order of things." Shamim and Karim turn a deaf ear to his pleas as they cruelly prepare to gouge his eyes out.

How does one's home become the site of incarceration? How does this resonate with the audience? When I watched the scene of torture, it brought to mind the many stories I had heard about the euphemistically called "interrogation centers," where security forces allegedly tortured those suspected of militant activity.[42] Indeed, Kashmiri nationalists argue that like hostages, they live under the shadow of the military presence – acerbically referred to as "occupa-tion." Or perhaps the audience was reminded of militant activities in the valley: For example, Subhan Bhagat, the founder of the Akingam Bhagat theatre, was taken hostage in his home by five militants in the early 1990s. The militants used his house as a base for four weeks and returned to it several times over the period of that month. Bhagat did not speak about the events that occurred within his home, but this incident dramatically changed him. He lost his desire – indeed his ability – to work with the Bhands. So traumatized was he by this event that he even lost his ability to speak, before succumbing to death. The Bhand performers' fraught encounters with both the militants and the military in the valley made it difficult for me to make any secure interpretive claims regarding the aesthetic representation of *Badshah Pather*.

If the tragic plot of the ill-treatment meted out to Badshah and Bedar turns on the collapse of moral frameworks of hospitality, then what does the satirical Bhand critique make visible? Raina's adapta-tion reinforces the idea that a king, no matter how grand and mighty he has been, is a fool anyway, and inescapably mortal.

The failure of hospitality is indicted in an imaginary court upon the heath through the mock trial of Shamim and Karim. Here, the dispossessed, powerless, crazed Badshah rants, "I am the king! I rule by reckless authority – there is no justice in my kingdom – only my whim – I let all the criminals free – the rapists, the murderers, the thieves. Power is abused by those who go between the state and the people." Badshah continues, in a hoarse, menacing whisper: "You only see the world after you have lost your eyes. Your eyes will deceive you. Look through your ears. Listen to how justice has colluded with the powerful and rails against the poor."[43] Badshah issues a warning not to be fooled by the scopic politics of the region and to attend to the partitions between sight and sound. It is the failure of hospitality that precipitates Badshah's understanding of the social inequities in his own kingdom.

On the heath, the abstraction of territory on the map gives way to the material force of the storm. The ordered and domesticated ter-ritory depicted on the map with its pristine rivers and valleys grows ominous, unleashing its rage and fury. In the disorienting wildness and smoke of the storm, we discern spectral figures; several *dern*, witch-like hags from the Bhand repertoire appear. The *dern* wear black hoods on their faces and are dressed in black costumes covered with straw. They surround and frighten the men on the heath, smothering them with the straw on their costumes. Mashkara and Badshah are terrified and run hither and thither for help, but are besieged by the haunting specters of these *dern* figures, rising up in the smoke.

Illustrating the proximity between the fool and the king, the scene on the heath is played out between Mashkara and Badshah.[44] The Mashkara, in the true spirit of the Bhand style, plays the plain-speaking fool. His coarse speech provides a foil to the smooth hypocrisy of the court and its manners. According to Raina, "The maskharas or jesters are one of the most important characters in the Bhand Pathers and are in fact, its soul.... They lampoon the king and the upper classes by exposing their corruption and greed. The mashkara is the rebel, the one who defies the oppressor."[45] The form of the Bhand Pather with its mocking, satirical humor demystifies political authority and reveals the king as pathetic, fearful, and inexorably mortal.

As with all Bhand plays, our understanding of *Badshah Pather* is limited if we reflect on it only through the interpretive frameworks of western drama. In order to arrive at a fuller understanding of this play, we must take into account not only the eloquence of *King Lear* within the context of a Kashmir partitioned between two brothers, but also consider the framing of the performance through Sufi music. The figure of the dispossessed king, pathetic and forlorn, oscillates between catharsis and comedy, as the incommensurate modes of high tragedy and folk humor are deployed within this scene. Yet a fuller understanding of the scene must locate the king's absolute dispossession within the frame of Sufi music, which crucially informs Bhand Pather more generally and *Badshah Pather* in particular.

Sufi devotional music is generally associated with Qawwali, a predominantly male genre, in which two teams of musicians take turns to sing a mystical poetic text, based on the Perso-Arabic traditions established by Hazrat Amir Khusrau[46]; it is characterized by rhythmic percussive beats, drums, and handclaps that induce

Figure 6.2 Interchangeable roles of Mashkara and Badshah, the jester and the king. *Badshah Pather* by M.K. Raina. Photographer: Jisha Menon.

increasingly ecstatic states in the listeners. The devotional Sufiana Kalam is a spare and less structured mystical genre of poetry typically sung by a solo musician to minimal instrumentation. Qawwali and Sufiana Kalam are both performed at shrines of Sufi saints and at public concerts. Unlike Qawwali, Sufiana Kalam is sung in a monologue and requires less rigid training. Deriving from folk oral melodies, the Sufiana Kalam performers sing in vernacular languages (Gujrati, Punjabi, Kashmiri, Sindhi) to simple stringed instruments such as the *tambur* or *ektara*. Sufiana Kalam aspires toward a spiritual experience not only through the semantic content of texts but also by generating rhythmic cadences within the body.

An integral component of Bhand Pather, the Sufiana Kalam that punctuates the performances is a spare devotional form of Sufi music, often accompanied by Kashmiri folk songs. Each Bhand play has its own specific *muqam* (musical prelude) so the villagers, who are quite familiar with the Bhand Pather, can tell from just listening to the notes which *pather*, or play, to anticipate.

According to ethnomusicologist Regula Qureishi, Sufi music strives to bridge the distance between the Creator and devotee through expressive embodied practices, such as music and dance. Qureshi observes, "The music serves to kindle the flame of his mystical love, to intensify his longing for mystical union, and even to transport him to a state of ecstasy and to sustain him there to the limit of spiritual capacity."[47] Setting to music the quranic texts, the *hadith* enables Sufis to teach the core of religion without the intervention of the clergy.[48] The concept of *sama* is central to Sufi music and is suggestive of the audition or environment created by the music that induces the listener to approach the divine through a sense of ecstatic unity with God.[49] Here, mystical poetry is set to music, which stirs the listener's heart to seek God.

Shemeem Burney Abbas suggests that the recitation through *zikr*, which is based on deep, disciplined breathing exercises and repetitive movements in which the devotee incessantly repeats the god's name, allows the words to move from their overt meaning, *zahir*, to their more buried meaning *batin*.[50] In Sufi discourse the interior world (*batin*) is privileged over the exterior (*zahir*), and the Sufi subjects aspire to interior illumination through the rhythmic practices of the body. As Shahzad Bashir puts it, "Zikr means 'remembrance' and involves repeating one of God's names or a religious formula in conjunction with maintaining or moving the body in particular ways.... When performed with religious sanction, Sufi dance marked moving bodies as conduits between the interior world and the exterior cosmos filled with movement."[51]

Badshah Pather mocks the aspiration for justice through the mediation of constitutional law and suggests a different approach to understanding justice through the Bhand Pather's frameworks of hospitality. It is through the practice of a radical openness to the other, to cultural and religious difference, that we can begin to practice everyday acts of unconditional hospitality, which provide the foundation for a radical parity of all people.[52] The play ends with the scene in which the body of Badshah's beloved son Rafiq is brought in. Rafiq has been killed in conflict. It is a silent scene. Badshah sees the body of his dead son and slowly walks toward it. As he approaches Rafiq,

Figure 6.3 Mad Badshah on the heath. Photographer: Jisha Menon.

Badshah sits down beside him, drops his head on his son's chest, and whispers, "Rafiq!"

The memory of another Rafiq, the most recent victim of police brutality, courses through my body. The time and the space that is breathed into the scene allow my thoughts to drift between Rafiq, the grievously injured boy struggling for his life on a hospital bed, and the Rafiq on stage, his mimetic double. Badshah collapses at the corpse of his son and begins to wail. A parent mourns the untimely death of his young son – how familiar was this scenario to a Kashmiri audience? Raina had instructed his actors to tap into their emotional memory of grieving for their children as resource for fully grasping the horror of this scene.[53]

The loud wailing of Badshah suddenly breaks the grave silence that resounds in the playing field. The force of his embodied expressivity appears almost a reaction to the constant repression of Kashmiri speech, as the body's response to consistent indifference to vocal appeals. Here, Badshah's violent sobs signal the failure of listeners to acknowledge his suffering: When the grief-stricken father's speech falls on deaf ears, his body's expressivity communicates his misery. The play, however, does not conclude on the solemn note of Shakespeare's *Lear*. The musicians in the background take up the wailing of Badshah, lying over the corpse of Rafiq, and the lamentation transforms to a full-throated Sufi song, composed by famous Kashmiri Sufi poet Mahmud Gami.[54] In the song, the grief-stricken parent promises to obliterate the self and the world, transform into a bird, and sing a tender lullaby to the child, while awaiting him at the gates of paradise. All the actors join in a brisk dance as the rhythms of Sufiana Kalam resound in the playing field.

Tragedy regards life as an absolute value, and hence the loss of life initiates the drama of devastation and bereavement. Via the ontological otherness of tragedy, the audiences may safely approach and reflect on the grief in their own lives. This constitutes the pleasure of tragedy: the opportunity to purge oneself of powerful emotions through the witnessing of events, so familiar, yet at a safe distance, occurring on stage.[55] Nevertheless, the tragedy of *Badshah Pather* is not that characters in the play die, but that Rafiq dies: one so pure (*safa*) and so generous (*sakhi*) dies an untimely, indeed a senseless, death. We recall Rafiq as the one who speaks truth to power, whose bold speech triggers his banishment from the kingdom. We mourn the death of this fearless youth who confronts power in a spirit of radical openness that makes him vulnerable to violence. The tragedy of *Badshah Pather* allows us to witness the frailty of human agency.

Tragedies offer ways of making meaning of the turbulent chaos of lives, of shaping messy histories into coherent – even cathartic – experiences. But layering it over with Sufi music suggests that we may need to give up some of our efforts to make sense of the world in which we live. The Sufi songs suggest that we try in vain to master a world that will always elude our grasp. The Sufi music does not contain or bring to closure the critique of geopathologies of state-making; it aims not to incite passions but to offer some modicum of comfort to grief-stricken Kashmiris. In a spirit of hospitality, the Sufi music suggests that approaching adversity with a radical openness precipitates a greater proximity to God.

Although witnessing this particular production may enable the audience to shape the chaos of suffering in Kashmir into a tragic narrative, M.K. Raina's production deliberately chooses not to end on a note of despair. The affirmative Sufi music of Bhand Pather takes its note from Badshah's loud wailing and sutures it to a Sufi song. The music begins slowly, then the percussion picks up in both beat and tempo. All the actors return onstage and begin to dance and sing, and the music resounds in the playing field. From the finality of the death-scene, the Sufi music reopens the cathartic closure of tragedy to an affirmative celebration of the possibility of an imminent union with God. Concluding on this note attempts to comfort and carry the audience from the spectatorial position of mourning witness to a place of spiritual solace that situates its listeners in greater proximity to God. The resounding rhythms of the Sufi music moves *Badshah Pather* from the finality and closure of death to the radical dispossession of the Rishi Sufic philosophy, where after the lamentation for the dead, there may still be music.

In doing so, does Raina pacify his audience and contain the critique of state violence that his production mounts? Raina himself is skeptical about Kashmiri nationalism and firmly believes in the secular credentials of the Indian state. If he had mounted *Badshah Pather* as a cautionary tale that raises the specter of future partitions, the performance itself exceeds and eludes the political intentionality of its director, and moves its audiences in unpredictable ways. The most powerful scene in the play, a father mourning the untimely death of his son, Rafiq, inadvertently connected the play to the ongoing political conflicts in the valley. We were witnessing not what might happen in the wake of a future partition, but what was currently happening in the effort to avert Partition. The viewers of *Badshah Pather* were unwittingly constituted not only as audience to a tragic Bhand but also as witness to the trials experienced by the Kashmiris. The public avowal of grief in the wake of persistent political oppression in the valley became the generative ground on which to bring together a community of witnesses.

On June 20, 2010, Rafiq Bangroo succumbed to his injuries and died in the hospital. This triggered a series of clashes between the security forces and stone-slinging protestors. Kashmir was under cur-few again. By October 15, at least 115 protestors, mostly male youth, lost their lives in the skirmishes triggered in the third consecutive summer of protest in Kashmir.[56] The sense of restiveness continues to simmer in the valley.

7   Afterword

I began this book with a discussion of the ways in which the demolition of the Babri mosque became the occasion for my return to the Partition, a repository of memories that continues to shape public life in India. The generative intellectual discussions that debated the crisis of secularism on the subcontinent, in the wake of the Babri demolition, were frequently polarized between "communitarians," who insisted on a pluralized and decentralized polity that recognized the significance of religion in the lives of those the state purportedly represents, and the "secular liberals," who staunchly advocated uniformity of law and state neutrality in matters of religion. Although both groups differed in their position toward the role of secularism in Indian public culture, they were both vigilant critics of Hindutva agendas of manipulating political theology to persecute India's religious minorities.

On September 30, 2010, the Allahabad High Court ruled that the disputed territory on which the Babri mosque had stood be partitioned among three parties, thus reigniting debates about the politics of majority appeasement, failure of justice, and the accommodation of faith in matters of legal dispute. The question of secularism reemerged here as the active rearticulation of religion in public life that recognized the importance of faith in settling matters of legal dispute, while simultaneously appeasing majority sentiment at the cost of entrenching a sense of minority alienation from the Indian state. Although I am critical of a secularism that haughtily turns away from the very cultural, religious, and spiritual practices that sustain the demographic masses that the state claims to represent, I am wary of attempts that introduce religion into public life without an acute awareness of the ways in which particular religions circulate unmarked in everyday practices of the state. The sense of urgency with which I engage these debates derives from my own self-conscious awareness of my privilege of belonging to the majority Hindu community, and my resistance to the ways in which political Hinduism serves the instrumental needs of the Hindu right in India.

However, another crucial event shaped my engagement with questions of religious difference, minority politics, and the crisis of secularism. The attack on the World Trade Center on September 11, 2001, and the subsequent acts of state and nonstate violence that it produced in its wake returned me to the question: How does one negotiate religious difference in our world today? If the demolition of the Babri mosque in 1992 compelled me to acknowledge my own privileged position as a Hindu, the events of September 11, 2001, positioned me as a racialized minority living in the United States. Such a positionality was crucial in my effort to read the archive of the Partition through the practice of what Edward Said terms "secular criticism."[1]

For Said, secular criticism entails the critical practice of re-creating the affiliative bonds between texts and the world, returning aesthetic products to their materiality and placing them in dialogic, contrapuntal relationship with other texts, classes, and institutions. The mimetic affinities between texts and the worlds that they circulate in circumvent reductive teleological accounts of the relationship between reality and its aesthetic representation. Moving away from such a linear and progressivist account, Said forwards secular criticism as a critical practice that situates cultural production within the currents of history, politics, and power.

Using Auerbach, the Jewish German author of *Mimesis*, writing on canonical European literature in wartime Istanbul as his exemplar, Said uncovers the ways in which Auerbach's position as one who is simultaneously insider and outsider becomes the generative condition for critical practice. By writing *Mimesis*, Auerbach was not merely practicing his profession but was rather performing an act of cultural –even civilizational –survival of the highest order. According to Said, "By not writing he would have fallen to the dangers of exile:

loss of texts, traditions, continuities that make up the very web of a culture."² Secular criticism, as Edward Said formulated it, cultivates the practice of criticism from the point of view of the dispossessed, the exiled, the minority – in short, someone who stands in a vexed relationship to hegemonic culture.

The secular critic, then, attends to the noncoincidence of the self with the self, the trace of otherness that is constitutive of the self. Emphasizing the mimetic double-ness that constitutes the subjects of Partition, I have argued, begins the process of recognizing the manifold affinities that exist among people, artificially classified into the reified categories of community and nation. The dialectical constitution of the nonidentical puts the very idea of unified, sovereign subjects of autonomous nation-states of India and Pakistan into crisis. *The Performance of Nationalism: India, Pakistan, and the Memory of Partition* inquires into the nonidentity at the heart of the national political subject by turning to mimetic double-ness that fractures the bounded and coherent subjects of the Partition.

And where better to recognize the otherness that perdures at the heart of the self than within tropes of acting? Bertolt Brecht reminds us that in life, as on stage, "the smallest social unit is not the single person but two people. In life too we develop one another."³ Turning to the trope of acting and performance enables me to account for the particular embodied dimensions of nation-making, thus exposing the ways in which the complex and messy concreteness of lived experience is subsumed under grand narratives of religion, community, and nation.

The Performance of Nationalism: India, Pakistan, and the Memory of Partition recuperates mimesis to think through the relationship between history and aesthetics as mimetic discourses of the Partition. If the Partition's residual memory is reinvented in India's antagonistic relationship with Pakistan, then the Sikh pogroms of 1984 were an explicit reminder of the ways in which the violence can turn inward on the nation. The post-1984 representations of the Partition in the public sphere raised questions of national belonging, minority identity, and religious affiliation. The Partition's reemergence into public discourse at this historical moment signals its resilience in social memory and its analytical usefulness for thinking about religious conflicts and the crisis of secularism on the subcontinent. Likewise, contemporary political scenarios intervene into cultural memories and reshape narrations of the Partition. Memories of the Partition inhabit a diachronic doubleness of time that mediates present ethnic and national identities.

The various performances I consider here, from Wagah border ceremonies to films and theatre, also allow us to think about the ways in which the traumatic performance of the Partition offers the occasion for the constitution of publics. The audience, or the community of listeners, in turn becomes the witness and bearer of these stories of displacement, violence, betrayal, and courage. Through their active listening, the audience constitutes a polis, an embodied archive, a community of memory. If tragedies on stage, as in life, remind us of the frailty of human action, then the performative public space it creates offers the promise of the persistence of memory. Performance works here not as an ephemeral event that vanishes and leaves no trace behind but rather situates the audience as the bearer of stories. The narration of the Partition constitutes a community of witnesses and facilitates the formation of a public that attends and bears witness to the particular and incommensurable accounts of the Partition.

The specter of the Partition continues to haunt and even structure contemporary ethnic relations within the Indian subcontinent. Its reemergence in public discourse at a historical moment when the nation is witnessing an alarming increase in hate crimes directed against minorities reveals the lingering ways in which the Partition shapes community and public life in India and Pakistan. This book aspires to configure an urgent responsibility and an ethical relationship to the traumatic past. To reiterate the performative constitution of religious and national identity is especially crucial at a time when theories about the "clash of civilizations" proliferate all over the world. Foregrounding the mimetic formation of the nonidentical "other" complicates discrete, static, and exclusive notions of culture and identity, thus offering the opportunity to imagine new kinds of political communities.

188

Notes

1 Introduction

1 On December 6, 1992, Babri Masjid, the sixteenth-century Muslim mosque, collapsed under the collective effort and will of Hindutva activists. The mosque was built by Babar, the first Muslim emperor in India, and stood in Ayodhya, a Hindu pilgrimage town. Ire against the Babri mosque was founded on the belief that the mosque stood on the grounds of Ayodhya, which was the mythical birthplace of the Hindu god Ram. It paved the way for vociferous demands to reclaim Ayodhya, culminating in the destruction of the mosque and the construction of a Hindu temple in its place. The uproar of communal riots over the issue in 1992 claimed about 2,000 lives. On September 30, 2010, the Allahabad High Court gave its verdict of a proposed three-way division of the disputed Ram Janmabhoomi-Babri Masjid site among the Sunni Wakf Board, Akhil Bharat Hindu Mahasabha, and the Nirmohi Akhara. The verdict generated heated debates on the role of history and archaeology, secularism, and democracy in contemporary India. See, for instance, Thapar, "The Verdict on Ayodhya."

2 Chakrabarty, *Habitations of Modernity*, 140.

3 The Sangh Parivar refers to the family of organizations of Hindu nationalists, which include the Rashtriya Swayamsevak Sangh (RSS), Bharatiya Janata Party (BJP), and the Vishva Hindu Parishad (VHP), among others.

4 Taran, as quoted in Menon and Bhasin, *Borders and Boundaries*, 246.

5 Ibid., 5.

189

6 Butalia, *The Other Side of Silence*, 4.

7 Ibid., 4.

8 See Zamindar, *The Long Partition* on the enduring effects of the Partition. See also Ansari, *Life after Partition*.

9 Futehally, as quoted in Hasan, "Prologue," 12.

10 Kaul, "Introduction," *The Partitions of Memory*, 1.

11 Nandy, "The Days of the Hyaena," 2.

12 For an excellent account of the causes, consequences, and legacies of the Partition, see Talbot and Singh, *The Partition of India*.

13 See India Ministry of Information and Broadcasting, *Millions on the Move*.

14 Menon and Bhasin, *Borders and Boundaries*, 70.

15 See Talbot and Singh, *The Partition of India*.

16 Ibid.

17 Ibid., 61.

18 Said, *Orientalism*, 72.

19 See Ludden, "Orientalist Empiricism."

20 Pandey, *The Construction of Communalism in Colonial North India*.

21 Kaviraj, "The Imaginary Institution of India," 26. As Kaviraj puts it, because members of fuzzy communities did not consider their power in terms of numbers, "they could not consider what they could wreak upon the world for their collective benefit, through collective action."

22 Chakrabarty points out that accounting practices reconstituted the meaning of "community" in three important ways. First, the centrality of numbers for gaining political clout was crucial for the authority of the political groups. Next, socioeconomic progress could be measured by examining the share of each community in public life. Finally, quantitative governance enabled governments/communities to devise objective tests for relative "backwardness" of a given community. As a result, Chakrabarty argues that professing simplistic, homogenous religious identities in public life (disregarding the heterogeneity and diversity of Indian social practices) became a crucial means for taking advantage of equal opportunity legislation. See Chakrabarty, "Modernity and Ethnicity in India."

23 Appadurai, *Fear of Small Numbers*, 53.

24 See Chris Bayly for a historical survey of religious conflict in precolonial India. Bayly, "The Pre-History of Communalism."

25 Metcalf, *Ideologies of the Raj*, 224.

26 For significant scholarship in this field see the classic study by Geertz, *The Negara State*. See also recent scholarship of Aggarwal, *Beyond Lines of Control*; Askew, *Performing the Nation*; Ebron, *Performing Africa*; Kaur, *Performative Politics and the Cultures of Hinduism*; Kruger, *The National Stage*.

27 See the excellent scholarship of Ludden, *Making India Hindu*; Hansen, *Wages of Violence*; Mankekar, *Screening Culture, Viewing Politics*; and Rajagopal, *Politics after Television* on the performative politics of the Hindu right.

28 Kelley Askew, in her study of performance, Swahili music and Tanzanian nationalism, has generatively suggested that we shift our categories of analysis from the constative fiat of the "imagined nation" to consider the performative production of "national imaginaries" and pay attention to its "multivalent, multivocal, polyphonic – perhaps even cacophonous" iterations of national imaginaries. See Askew, *Performing the Nation*, 273.

29 Anderson, *Imagined Communities*. Richard Davis points out that the same technologies that produced and disseminated mass-reading publics also widely disseminated visual imagery through posters, photographs, postcards, illustrations, etc. See Davis, *Picturing the Nation*, 5.

30 See Anderson, *Imagined Communities*; Bhabha, *Nation and Narration*; Timothy Brennan, "The National Longing for Form" in *Nation and Narration*. In the context of Partition, Jill Didur explores the rhetorical dimensions of Partition literature. See Didur, *Unsettling Partition*.

31 Freitag, "Visions of the Nation," in Dwyer and Pinny, eds., *Pleasure and the Nation*, p. 39.

32 See the edited volumes of Davis, *Picturing the Nation* and Ramaswamy, *Beyond Appearances* for a range of scholarly essays that take up and complicate the question of visuality in relation to the nation. See especially Ajay Sinha and Kajri Jain.

33 *The Republic* depicts an imaginary conversation between Socrates, Thrasymachus, Glaucon, and Adeimantus, set some fifty years earlier, at the height of the Peloponnesian War – sometime between 431–411 BC. In his treatise, Plato imagines an ideal republic, governed by power-averse philosophers, with resolute knowledge of what constitutes the greater good, thus bringing unity, harmony, and order to the city and those within it.

34 In *The Republic* Socrates warns, "If we let our pity for the misfortunes of others grow too strong it will be difficult to restrain our feelings in our own" (Plato, 606, b, 350). See also Halliwell, *Aesthetics of Mimesis*, 93–97.

35 See Nuttall, *Why Does Tragedy Give Pleasure?*

36 See Halliwell on Aristotelian mimesis as parallel world-making, *Aesthetics of Mimesis*, 166. Aristotle takes emotion and recognition, pleasure and pain as fused in the aesthetic experience (186). I argue that aesthetic pleasure derives not only from mimetic action on stage but from a sense of shared witnessing and public recognition of the sufferings one has endured. Rather than privatizing, grief when collectively witnessed offers the ground to generate a powerful sense of solidarity.

37 According to Aristotle, tragedy in particular offers us an opportunity to witness the precariousness of human action. Tragedy exposes the frailty of all action, good and bad, and the inability of agents to guard against the vicissitudes of chance. Aristotle stresses the transformational power of tragic pity: a responsiveness to the suffering of another that has the capacity to remake one's own sense of moral self. Drawing the audience into an intimate proximity with the suffering of another, tragic pity enables a profound witnessing without dissolving into a complete spectatorial identification with the character. I explore the relationship between tragedy and civic culture in Chapter 6 on Kashmir.

38 See Gebauer and Wulf, *Mimesis: Culture – Art – Society*, especially Part II, "Mimesis as Imitatio" 61–104.

39 See, for instance, Horace, Seneca, and Longinus.

40 See Gebauer and Wulf, *Mimesis*, 146–147.

41 Within Sanskrit aesthetic theory, the concept of anukarana (derived from "anu" for after and "karana" for creation) reinforces the centrality of aesthetic creation as re-creation. Bharata suggests in his treatise on dramaturgy, Natyashatra, (c. 2nd century BC) that imitation is the heart of drama, "Drama is the reproduction of the mental states, actions and conducts of people" (Natyashatra, I, 106–112.) Abhinavagupta, (tenth century) argues that drama cannot be reduced to a narrow understanding of reproduction; its power derives from its capacity to trigger a particular constellation of essential emotions. Abhinavagupta foregrounds the sympathetic proximity of actor and spectator: The actor does not "reproduce" but rather draws from similar experience to enact a role – similarity rather than identity generates aesthetic re-creation. It is the "sympathetic vibration of the heart" (hrdayaspandana) that brings character, actor and spectator together to produce rasa or aesthetic pleasure. For a detailed discussion on imitation in Indian aesthetic theory, see V. K. Chari, "The Nature of Poetic Truth: Some Indian Views," *British Journal of Aesthetics*, 1979, 19 (3): 213–223.

42 For example, in "Education, The First Stage," Socrates explains the relationship between mimesis as aesthetic practice and mimesis as subject constitution: "For have you not noticed how dramatic and similar representations, if indulgence in them is prolonged into adult life, establish habits of physical poise, intonation and thought which become second nature?" (Plato, 395, d, 89).

43 On colonial mimesis, see Eaton, "Between Mimesis and Alterity." See also Shimakawa, *National Abjection* on "critical mimesis," which draws on Irigaray to discuss Asian American abjection within the American national imaginary.

44 Diamond, *Performance and Cultural Politics*, 107.

45 Recent scholarship on the depiction of Partition in fiction includes work by Jill Didur, Kavita Daiya, Priyamvada Gopal, and Priya Kumar, among others.

46 See Ramaswamy's idea of bodyscapes to consider the work of cartography in producing the nation as gendered space. Ramaswamy, *Goddess of the Nation*.

47 Moving away from an understanding of discourse as Habermasian
   communicative rationality, Michael Warner explores the multige-
   neric, cross-citational heterogeneous social field of discourse, which
   projects for the public a concrete livable world and attempts to realize that world through its address. The circularity is a key feature of
   Warner's conception of the public: An addressable object is conjured
   into being in order to enable the very discourse that gives it existence.
   He differs from Hannah Arendt in that he posits work or poesis rather
   than action as the ground for political publicity. For Hannah Arendt,
   action has been devalued and subordinated to a life of contemplation.
   By putting forward action as the key mode of human togetherness,
   Arendt revives a conception of the Athenian polis, where individuals
   encounter one another as members of a community through nonin-
   strumental action. Arendt writes, "Theatre is the political art par
   excellence; only there is the political sphere of human life transposed
   into art. By the same token, it is the only art whose sole subject is man
   in his relationship to others." See Arendt, *The Human Condition*,
   188, for an elaboration of the importance of action in public life.
48 I draw from the scholarship of Judith Butler. See especially *Precarious
   Life*.
49 Said, *The World, the Text, and the Critic*, 50. Said suggests that
   once we overcome the Platonic linearity that posits art as copy to
   primary experience, and begin to recognize its theological under-
   pinnings, we can begin the process of "secular criticism," which
   avows the manifold mimetic associations within the social
   world.
50 Pointing to the role of colonialism in shaping what constitutes legitimate, "reliable" evidence of the past, Antoinette Burton notes that
   the emergence of the gendered precincts of history and literature
   itself can be traced back to the eighteenth century. The segregation
   of history from literature coincides not incidentally with the emergence of "archival rationalization" – a process by which archives
   become part of the quest for a "truth apparatus" that, she argues,
   underpinned diverse social science practices. See Antoinette Burton,
   Dwelling in the Archive. For an analysis of the intersection of
   Holocaust history and performance, see the significant contribution

of Rokem, *Performing History* and Patraka, *Spectacular Suffering*. See also the influential scholarship of Taylor, *The Archive and the Repertoire*.

2 Bordering on drama: the performance of politics and the politics of performance

1 For a critique of the dominant approaches to the study of politics through the interpretive frameworks of Weberian and rational choice theory, see Strauss and O'Brien, eds., *Staging Politics*.
2 Unlike recent subaltern historiographies that attempt to recover histories of the marginalized and dispossessed, the term "high politics" connotes the political arrangements of the colonial and nationalist elite in the 1940s.
3 I refer here to Diana Taylor's influential book, *The Archive and the Repertoire*. In her compelling analysis, Yasmin Khan takes the binaristic model of Partition studies – one that bifurcates "high politics" and "human dimensions" and weaves it into a dialectical narrative that examines the way in which the Partition juggernaut drew from the co-implicated politics of elite policies and mass mobilizations. See Khan, *The Great Partition*.
4 Kaviraj is specifically interested in the ways in which people in colonial India begin to imagine themselves as a single political entity. He argues that "narrative" provided one particular figuration of discourse to encrust and crystallize this imagined Indian-ness. Drawing upon Austin's notion of "the performative," Kaviraj argues that the narrative of Indian-ness sedimented through a process of citing the imagined India. According to Kaviraj then, the repeated inculcation of "India" works through the reiterative power of discourse to produce phenomena that it regulates. See Kaviraj, "The Imaginary Institution of India."
5 Stanley Cavell turns to the neglected dimension of passionate speech in Austin's analysis of performative speech acts and reminds us that while illocutionary performative speech enacts what it names, perlocutionary speech acts (often disregarded by the analytical philosophers) expresses desire. According to Cavell, passionate expression makes demands upon the singular body in a way that illocutionary

force forgoes. A passionate utterance, as Cavell puts it, "character-istically puts the future of our relationship, as part of my sense of my identity, or of my existence, more radically at stake." See Cavell, *Philosophy the Day after Tomorrow.*

6 Farzana Shaikh argues that the League's claim to exclusive represen-tation owed its ideological authenticity to the Islamic conviction that Muslims were "bound by a substantive consensus and that such a consensus demanded a single Muslim medium." See Shaikh, "Muslims and Political Representation in Colonial India."

7 Jinnah, "An Extract from the Presidential Address of M.A. Jinnah – Lahore, 1940," 56.

8 Jinnah, as quoted in Asim Roy, "The High Politics of India's Partition," 108.

9 The word "personality" and even the more sober "personhood" derive from *persona*, for mask or dramatic character, thus forcing us to take seriously the possibility that "persons" may be iteratively produced through performance. See Goffman, *The Presentation of Self in Everyday Life.*

10 Asim Roy, 112.

11 Ibid., 110. The words in quotes are his own from an earlier review of Jalal's *The Sole Spokesman.*

12 See Nair, *Changing Homelands,* which considers the politics of Punjabi Hindus in the first half of the twentieth century. Nair traces the shifting allegiances of the Punjabi Hindus, a religious minority in undivided Punjab, who aligned themselves with Punjabi Muslims and Sikhs during critical moments in the anticolonial struggle. The book considers the transformation of this group from cross-religious alliances to an increasingly "communal" politics.

13 See, for example, Hasan and Asim Roy in *India's Partition.*

14 See Hasan, "Introduction," *India's Partition.*

15 See Asim Roy, "The High Politics of India's Partition," *India's Partition,* 130–132.

16 Ibid., 105.

17 Conquergood, "Performance Studies," 146.

18 Auden, "Partition," 604.

19 Divested of all poetic flourishes, "Partition" stands in stark relief to the political idiom of the time that was embellished in rhetorical excesses. In Auden's words, "The ideal at which I aim is a style which shall combine the drab sober truthfulness of prose with a poetic uniqueness of expression." See Goethals, "Poetry and History."

20 In the words of Joya Chatterji, "Mountbatten's concern to protect his Government's image overrode all other factors ... a man who enjoyed pomp and circumstance ... he was particularly anxious that no unpleasantness should mar the transfer of power celebrations in which he would play viceroy for the last time. See Chatterji, "The Fashioning of a Frontier," 195. Talbot, on the other hand, cautions against overreading Partition as Britain's "parting gift" to India. He points out that Mountbatten attempts to revive conversations about the Cabinet Mission proposal but gave up when it became increasingly apparent that Partition was now a more realistic option. Partition was "self-consciously willed by the All-India Congress and Muslim League leaders and, above all, reflected their fears and mistrusts, as well as hopes, that a 'right-sized' state would deliver to them the power to construct a new political, economic and social order in a free subcontinent." See Talbot and Singh, *The Partition of India*, 41.

21 See Nair, *Changing Homelands*, 9, 180.

22 As Chester skillfully argues, Radcliffe chose not to leave this thankless job but persisted, owing to a sense of duty and perseverance. In her words, "Radcliffe regarded his work on the Boundary Commission as a burden to be carried to whatever end resulted, no matter the personal cost. Unfortunately, the millions of people who lost their lives or their property in the 1947 partition did not have that choice – and they risked far more than Radcliffe did." Chester, *Borders and Conflict*, 181.

23 Auden, "Partition."

24 Ibid.

25 See Chester, "The 1947 Partition."

26 The four parties that presented the Hindu case included Congress, Hindu Mahasabha, Indian Association, and New Bengal Association.

Muslim interests were represented by the Muslim League. See Chatterji, "The Fashioning of a Frontier," 188–189. Chatterji highlights, "The partition vote was necessarily an imperfect one because members of the West Bengal Assembly voted for partition without knowing for certain whether their constituencies would continue to be in West Bengal when the Award was finally made. Whether or not such foreknowledge would have made a difference to the final outcome – the majority in the West Bengal Assembly deciding in favor of Partition – must remain a matter of conjecture. But it is significant that the procedure for establishing the will on a question of such momentous import was dealt with so summarily."

27 Ibid.

28 He visited Calcutta, Lahore, Simla, and Delhi, the locations where the commissions held their public meetings. See Chester, *Borders and Conflict*, 55.

29 As Chester puts it, "The census data and gazetteers that Radcliffe perused portrayed a land in which people identified themselves in categorical terms, as Hindu, Muslim, Sikh etc. they did not reflect local understandings of an individual or community's various identities or the interplay of religious affiliation, kinship ties, political associations, and economic links. By demonstrating that Hindus, Sikhs, and Muslims lived in intermingled communities, the information Radcliffe saw did make clear that these groups could not be divided easily; unfortunately, the reality on the ground was even more complex than Radcliffe's documents showed." Chester, *Borders and Conflict*, 21.

30 Auden, "Partition."

31 Chester, *Borders and Conflict*, 109.

32 Chatterji, "The Fashioning of a Frontier," 213.

33 Ibid., 21.

34 Radcliffe gave sections of Gurdaspur, in northern Punjab, to India as a vital corridor to Kashmir: The waters feeding the essential irrigation systems of both Indian and Pakistani Punjab originate in the Kashmir mountains. Chester, *Borders and Conflict*, 7, 137.

35 See Chester, *Borders and Conflict*.

36 See Kalra and Purewal, "The Strut of the Peacocks," 54–68.

37 See Talbot and Tatla, eds. *Epicentre of Violence*, 2.

38 See Talbot, *Divided Cities*, xvii–xix.

39 I borrow this phrase from Marya Mannes's poem. See Mannes, *Subverse*, 12.

40 I visited Wagah in December 2002.

41 Chetan Singh is a pseudonym.

42 See Talbot, *Divided Cities*, xxxi.

43 All railway communication between India and Pakistan ceased after December 13, 2001, when the Indian Parliament house was attacked. The services were subsequently restored on January 15, 2004.

44 The Attari Special train takes passengers bound for Lahore from New Delhi to the border station of Attari. After immigration and customs clearance at Attari, passengers board the Samjhauta Express and leave for Wagah, from where they board a Pakistan Railways train to Lahore.

45 See Foucault, *Discipline and Punish*.

46 See Zamindar, *The Long Partition* for the role of bureaucratic productions of the border. I discuss this is in greater detail in Chapter 4, "The Poetics and Politics of Accommodation."

47 Alter, *Amritsar to Lahore*, 58. Alter observes that land borders are instilled with a greater sense of awe through the vivid assertion of state authority. He explains that whereas an airport can be located anywhere in the country, the border post is not only a point of entry and exit but also "a locus of friction and conflict" (59).

48 In 1999, Pakistani Prime Minister Nawaz Sharief and Indian Prime Minister A.B. Vajpayee inaugurated a bus route that took Indians or Pakistanis across Wagah for reunions with kin separated by Partition. In an attempt to ameliorate international opinion after the BJP conducted nuclear tests a few months earlier, Vajpayee initiated a unilateral gesture of "bus diplomacy," a phrase coined by Aijaz Ahmad in "Many Roads to Kargil."

49 Here is how one Pakistani passenger, Mubashir Hasan, describes his journey: "Through crowded towns and highways, the bus to Delhi hurtles like the VIP cavalcade which is late for its appointment. On every road crossing of its 530 km journey, police ensures its passage

without a stop. One for each district administration en route, a relay of police vehicles, two in front, flying red flags and one carrying an armed guard in the rear roar to guarantee the safety and unhindered passage of the bus. With sirens blowing all the way, men in pilot vehicles clear the way for the bus with merciless zeal, waving battens in the air, sometimes hitting drivers of scooters, scooter rickshaws and their vehicles which are slow in yielding the way. All red lights are violated with impunity. It is an ugly sight. The aggressive behaviour of the police in the two Punjabs, Haryana and Delhi is identical in this respect. At Lahore and Delhi and at five stops on the way, there is heavy presence of police and security men and women in plain clothes guard the passengers and the bus." See Hasan, "Bus to Delhi."

50 Kalra and Purewal, "The Strut of the Peacocks," 59.

51 Choran Bazaar (Thieves Market) in Amritsar is famous for its goods, smuggled across the border. Kalra and Purewal observe in "The Strut of the Peacocks" that smugglers have well established ties with the BSF and local police; smuggled goods include tea, videos of Hindi movies, cigarettes, cloth, electrical products, whiskey, dried fruits, and goods that are hard to procure in either country.

52 As quoted in Harkirat Singh, "Wagah, Wagah."

53 See Nair, "Singing a Nation into Being" on the role of national anthems in the affective imagining of the nation.

54 Vasudevan, "A Response to the Discussion on Visual Culture," in online discussion on visual culture in India. See www.cscban.org.

55 Personal communication, interviews with tourists, December 2002.

56 According to Jeffrey Green, "Being-ruled – that is, the spectatorial engagement with politics characterized by *involvement without participation* – is a form of citizenship that is extremely prevalent within twenty-first century conditions, yet nonetheless something that has been neglected by the major discourses constituting the contemporary study of democracy." See Green, *The Eyes of the People*, 34 (italics given). I thank Sebastian Calderon for bringing this book to my attention.

57 See Hansen, "Politics as Permanent Performance," 20.

58 Another incident that illustrates the unpredictability and volatility of live performance: in the wake of the Parliament attacks in December 2001, during the Retreat Ceremony in October 2002, an Indian soldier, allegedly, attacked his Pakistani counterpart. See *The Tribune*, "Heated Exchange at Wagah during Retreat Ceremony," October 21, 2002.

59 See Phelan, *Unmarked*; Auslander, *Liveness*; Blau, "Universals of Performance"; and Schneider, *Performing Remains*. Jill Dolan's contribution to the study of liveness has focused on its potential for creating democratic public spheres. She contends, "Performance of the moment also creates community, images, and energy for protestors to rally around, take pride and pleasure in; it focuses anger, as well as political momentum and desire." See Dolan, "Rehearsing Democracy," 1–17.

60 Hansen reminds us that the Shiv Sena "grew for years in the protective shadow of the Congress party." See Hansen, "Politics as Permanent Performance," 26.

61 See Banerjee, "Civic and Cultural Nationalism in India," 50–82.

62 See Ashis Nandy for an analysis of the distinction between patriotism and nationalism. He writes, "Nationalism is more specific, ideologically tinged, ardent form of 'love of one's own kind' that is essentially ego-defensive and overlies some degree of fearful dislike or positive hostility to 'outsiders'.... Patriotism, on the other hand, presumes the existence of communities other than the country and gives them due recognition, sometimes even priority. It is at least vaguely aware that there can be contradictions between the demands of the nation and of these communities." Nandy, "Nationalism, Genuine and Spurious," 3502.

63 I borrow the term "invented tradition" from Eric Hobsbawm and Terence Ranger's influential book, in which they remind us that "most of the occasions when people become conscious of citizenship as such remain associated with symbol and semi-ritual practices (for instance, elections), most of which are historically novel and largely invented: flags, images, ceremonies and music." See Hobsbawm's "Introduction" in *The Invention of Tradition*, 12.

64 BSF recently announced its plans to have women officers participate in the Retreat ceremony in an effort to soften the machismo and aggression of the ceremonies, which have been increasingly criticized across the media.

65 The British empire in India paid particular attention to the dramatization of imperial power in the public sphere. See Cannadine, "The Context, Performance and Meaning of Ritual: The British Monarchy and the 'Invention of Tradition,' c. 1820–1977" in Hobsbawm and Ranger, eds., *The Invention of Tradition*, 101–164. See also Cohn, "Representing Authority in India" in the same volume, 165–211. On imperial pageantry, see Strong, *Art and Power.*

66 The Watch Setting, described in the "Rules and Ordynaunces for the Warre" dated 1554, may be an early precursor to the contemporary Beating the Retreat ceremony. In 1727, Humphrey Bland's "Treatise of Military Discipline" states, "Half an hour before the gates are to be shut, generally at the setting of the sun, the Drummers of the Port Guard are to go upon the ramparts and beat a Retreat to give notice to those without that the gates are to be shut. See www.army.mod.uk/events/ceremonial/3052.aspx, accessed July 21, 2011. See also Sounding ceremonies www.army.mod.uk/music/corps-band/20042.aspx,accessed July 21, 2011.

67 Peggy Phelan reminds us that "precisely because of representation's supplemental excess and its failure to be totalizing, close readings of the logic of representation can produce psychic resistance and, possibly, political change."Phelan, *Unmarked*, 2.

68 Murphy, "Performing Partition in Lahore," 183–207.

69 See Kamra, *Bearing Witness* on political cartoons and Bhaskar Sarkar, *Mourning the Nation* for his work on Partition and Indian cinema.

70 This widespread notion echoes one of the Indian immigrations officials: "Relations are very cordial between us (officers). It is only the politicians who are bloody idiots." As quoted by Thorold, BBC Radio 4, March 13, 2004.

71 As quoted in Benjamin, *Illuminations*, 153.

72 See Bhabha on the "iterative plebiscite" displacing "the totalizing pedagogy of the will." Bhabha writes, "The deeply repressed past initiates a strategy of repetition that disturbs the sociological totalities

within which we recognize the modernity of national culture."
Bhabha, "DissemiNation," 304.

73 Bajwa, *The Falcon in My Name.* 238–239. In a similar move, Pakistani
playwright Shahid Nadeem's children's play "Border-Border" narrates the story of nearly identical, transposable children of two families who get lost on either side of the Wagah border. The play was
enacted in June 2001 by Indian and Pakistani children. See Nadeem,
"Border-Border."

74 Mehta, "Reflections: A Fatal Love," www.himalmag.com/compo-
nent/content/article/1703-A-Fatal-Love.html

75 Ibid.

76 See Hannah Arendt on "political fact" in her illuminating essay
Men in Dark Times.

3   Ghatak's cinema and the discoherence of the Bengal Partition

1 I borrow the concept of nonsensuous similitude from Walter
Benjamin, whose meditations on translation look at language as an
archive of nonsensuous similarity within which to find constella-
tions of affects, associations, evocations of a field of semantic resonances, and involuntary memories that a particular concept may
generate to find affinity with/across another language. See Benjamin,
"On the Mimetic Faculty."

2 I prefer to use the term "parity" to avoid the freighted connotations of the liberal use of the term "equality." In addition, where
equality derives from enumerative understandings of fairness (and
so introducing an idea of abstractness into such measurements of
opportunity and redistribution), parity derives from the idea of pairs,
thus reinforcing my argument about the mimetic relationality at the
heart of the fraternal encounter between India and Pakistan.

3 Brecht, "Short Organum," in Willet, *Brecht on Theatre*, 204.

4 Satyajit Ray, often considered one of India's finest filmmakers,
acknowledges Ghatak's epic style: "Ritwik was one of the few truly
original talents in the cinema this country has produced.... As a creator of powerful images in an epic style he was virtually unsurpassed
in Indian cinema." See Robinson, *Satyajit Ray*, 334.

5 Ghatak, *Rows and Rows*, 51. [CE: quote not necessary]
6 Tagore functions almost as Ghatak's conscience; on Tagore's influence, Ghatak notes, "I cannot speak without him. That man has culled all my feelings long before my birth. He has understood what I am." See Ghatak, *Rows and Rows*, 94.
7 Ghatak, *Rows and Rows*, 49.
8 After the India-Pakistan War in 1965, all Indian films were taken off the screen from cinemas in Pakistan, and a complete ban was imposed on Indian films. The ban had existed since 1952 in West Pakistan and since 1962 in East Pakistan (now Bangladesh), but was exercised rigorously after the conflict. Former Pakistani president Pervez Musharraf finally lifted the forty-year-old ban on Indian films in February 2008. Because of the active – and largely undisturbed – smuggling trade, however, the ban was never particularly effective. In Bangladesh, the ban on import and display of Indian films in the country's cinema halls was imposed in 1972, soon after Bangladeshi independence, and despite recent state attempts to lift the ban to revive Bangladesh's film industry, the ban was reimposed due to popular support.
9 Bagchi describes the conflation of Bengal and the mother-goddess thus: "Sonar Bangla, the youthful golden Bengal, the honey-tongued mother whose sons weep if there is a flicker of sadness on her face. Partition was an ever-unfolding story of the abduction of this young mother from which there was no recovery, state planned or otherwise." See Bagchi, "Freedom in an Idiom of Loss," 17.
10 In her discussion of the *bhadralok*, Joya Chatterji describes the ways in which the landed elite in Bengal lived off of rental income. Not accustomed to manual labor, the *bhadralok* gentleman shunned physical exertion and was in many ways the antithesis of the horny-handed son of the soil. Shunning manual labor, the *babu* saw this as the essence of the social distance between himself and his social inferiors, including Muslims and *dalits*. See Chatterji, *Spoils of Partition*, 12. See also Sinha, *Colonial Masculinity*.
11 "The act of production," Marx reminds us in the *Grundrisse*, is "in all its moments also an act of consumption" (90). See also Stephens and Weston, "Free Time: Overwork as an Ontological Condition."

12 I am drawing on the etymological root of "preposterous," literally "before-behind," that suggests a topsy-turvy disordered world.

13 Bagchi and Dasgupta, "Introduction," 5–6. She observes, "What gets elided is the agency of women who start up the family routine in changed circumstances, re-build the rhythms of daily subsistence ... the caring, nurturing role of women hounds them in these moments of public rupture."

14 Butalia, *The Other Side of Silence*, 6.

15 Tanika Sarkar, "Foreword," ix.

16 Chakravartty, *Coming Out of Partition*, xi.

17 Ibid., 87.

18 Ibid., 91 (italics added).

19 Ibid., 92.

20 Rajadhyaksha, *Ritwik Ghatak*, 53. Ashish Rajadhyaksha further notes, "Ghatak's splitting of individual from the archetypal exposes the exploitative aspect of the latter; the creative and destructive principles, at one level manifested in the Jagaddhatri and the Kali, at another also get linked to the tendency of the archetype to free and to bind." Rajadhyaksha, *Ritwik Ghatak*, 65. See also Bhaskar Sarkar, who makes a similar point: "In *Meghe Dhaka Tara*, the three female characters are turned into archetypal symbols, embodying three traditional aspects of feminine power: the mother represents cruelty; the heroine Neeta embodies the nurturing aspect of femininity; Geeta, her sister, is the sensual woman." See Bhaskar Sarkar, *Mourning the Nation*, 213. Likewise, Kumar Shahani, avant-garde film director and student of Ghatak, notes, "The feminine principle, borrowed from our earlier lower level of materialist culture, also suffers the split into the three principal women characters – the cruel mother, the sensual daughter and the preserving and nurturing heroine. The triangular compositions and the multiple allusions to Durga on the rich sound-track reinforce the pattern." Shahani, "Violence and Responsibility," 79. Writing of the mother in *Meghe Dhaka Tara*, film theorist Ira Bhaskar writes, "The realization of the destructive, militant Kali image is complete. Nita is sacrificed so that the rest of her family may survive. The deconsecration of Nita has begun." Bhaskar, "Myth and Ritual," 48. The prominent film

critic, Chidananda Dasgupta, however, rejects the aforementioned film scholars' archetypal reading of the mother as Kali by pointing out, "In mythology, Kali's destruction is a motiveless cycle, not born of the earthly want to which the poor mother is subject. Ghatak's film-making is so sharp and his feelings so acute that he elevates these stereotypes to real people whose lives are distorted by want. If there are shades of mythological archetypes they are, at best, his own theoretical overlays, at worst, mere conjecture on the part of his disciples." See Dasgupta, "Cinema, Marxism, and the Mother Goddess," 130.

21 Anindya Sengupta observes, "The editing does not allow the image to be conventionally narrativized – ie. continuity editing does not precede or follow the shots. Sengupta, "The Face of the Mother," 171.

22 Rabindrasangeet conjoins the divine with nature and person. Appropriately, the collection of Tagore's 2,200 odd songs is known as *Gitabitan*, or "garden of songs."

23 The word "Baul" derived from the Sanskrit word *vatula*, which means "divinely inspired," or from *vyakula*, which means "impatiently eager," connotes its modern meaning of an inspired people with an ecstatic eagerness for spiritual life. The Baul religious practices draw from Tantric Buddhism, Tantric Hinduism, Vaishnavism, and Sufi Islam. According to Pravina Cooper, the Bauls exemplified the Bhakti movement, a reformist movement that targeted Brahminical feudal powers. The Bauls' assertion of the individual's personal relationship to the divine had the political effect of disturbing the feudalistic order of the Brahman (upper caste.) See also Sudipto Chatterjee's creative work on Lalon Fakir, "Man of the Heart."

24 According to Reba Som, "It amazed Tagore that this band of wandering minstrels who were amongst the lowest in the caste hierarchy, denied access into temples, unschooled and poor, should have such an evolved philosophy of life with which they could defy social pressures and taboos, declare with aplomb that they did not need admission into temples since their body was God's temple and claim with pride an equal dependence between the divine

and man." See Som, *Rabindranath Tagore*, 73. See also Vasudha Dalmia, "Tagore's work, particularly his poetry, but also his drama, is shot through with the lyrical impetus received from the rural countryside, with the songs of the itinerant singers, particularly the Bauls he had heard in his East Bengal estates." Dalmia, *Poetics, Plays, and Performances*, 156.

25 Ghatak, *Rows and Rows*, 2000, p. 50.

26 The *"Raag Malhar"* celebrates the rain and is one of the oldest and most melodious ragas of Hindustani classical music, with many versions.

27 See Rajadhyaksha, *Ritwik Ghatak* for an excellent analysis of the role of music in Ghatak's cinema.

28 Bagchi and Dasgupta, "Introduction," 8.

29 Chakravartty, *Coming Out of Partition*, 97.

30 Ibid.

31 Bhatia, *Acts of Authority*, 77. See also Vivek Bhandari's discussion of IPTA as a counterpublic. Bhandari, "Civil Society and the Predicament of Multiple Publics."

32 Benegal, "A Panorama of Theatre in India," 13.

33 See Khan, Bose, and Chakrabarti, "Left Cultural Movement in West Bengal."

34 In the Sanskrit play, Kalidasa reworks the mythological story in the *Mahabharata*. Significantly, he adds the curse of Durvasa, the visiting hermit who is rebuffed by Sakuntala's absorption in Dusyanta. Durvasa's curse works in the narrative to justify Dusyanta's callous failure to remember Sakuntala. The curse is also indicative of the dangers of absorption, of immersing the other into the self to such an extent as to preclude sociality and, indeed, hospitality. In *The Modernity of Sanskrit*, Simona Sawhney argues that the figuration and articulation of the lost immediacy in the representation of love in the Sanskrit drama of Kalidasa offers a reprieve for Tagore from the sense of exilic banishment and alienation constitutive of modern life. In her words, "the trope of a universal and a historical longing offers the modern reader nostalgic for a plenitude now lost the connection he wishes to have with the past" (47).

35 See Brecht on gestus, *Short Organum*.

36 "Emotional memory" is a term coined by the Russian director Konstantin Stanislavski, who attempted to expunge the mechanical acting that was increasingly pervasive in Russia at the turn of the century in an attempt to restore some "truth" to acting. Elsewhere, Ghatak remarks on Stanislavski's influence on his career: "I have learnt the most through rummaging through the works of Konstantin Stanislavski." See Ghatak, *Rows and Rows*, 73.

37 Anasuya also invokes Shakespeare's *The Tempest* and draws parallels between her story and that of Ferdinand and Miranda.

38 Bhaskar Roy captures this displacement when he writes, "Uprooted from the riverine East Bengal, the people born of the wombs of the mighty Padma, Meghna, Buriganga – massive turgid water courses – now lived by the side of putrid canals, clogged streams, or scum layered swamps." See Bhaskar Roy, *An Escape into Silence*, 77–78.

39 See, for instance, Moinak Biswas, "Her Mother's Son: Kinship and History in Ritwik Ghatak," in *Rouge Electronic Journal*: www.rouge.com.au/3/ghatak.html (2004), accessed December 5, 2011.

40 Ghatak, *Rows and Rows*, 50.

41 In dismissing his work as melodramatic, Ghatak's detractors attempt to discredit the seriousness and experimentalism of his work. When Ghatak does employ melodramatic tropes such as frontality, he does so with a sense of irony, with a critical distance, with self-reflexivity that produces difference out of sameness.

42 Chatterjee, Review of *Rows and Rows of Fences*.

43 As quoted in Bhaskar Sarkar, *Mourning the Nation*, 218.

44 Ghatak, *Rows and Rows*, 51.

45 *Bahurupi*, derives from the Sanskrit word for many (*bahu*) forms (*rupa.*) The *bahurupis* are nomadic solo folk performers who travel in and around the regions of Birbhum, Burdwan, Murshidabad, Hooghly, Medinipur, and Nadia in West Bengal. Skilled at the art of costuming and makeup, these performers don multiple roles, from mythological gods and goddesses to village saints/*fakirs*. Using acrobatics, music, and dance, they portray several hundred characters, from gods to lepers to animals and demons, doctors and engineers, children and birds, holy men, professional men and tribals, tradesmen and rogues, beggars and fools.

46 Ghatak, *Rows and Rows*, 50.

47 According to O'Donnell, "Ghatak frames Sita as part of the surrounding expanse of landscape and nature while she sings this song
of longing so as to identify Sita, as Sita her namesake, with her
mother, Earth, and to depict Sita, as Radha, singing her song of love
in separation to Abhiram, as Krishna. Ghatak's use of a wide-angle
lens serves to fuse together the vast, open vista and the image of Sita
as iconic motherland." O'Donnell, "'Woman' and 'Homeland.'"

48 See Cooper, "Between the Messianic and the Material," 104–105.
Bhaskar Sarkar in *Mourning the Nation* also considers Ghatak's oeuvre in a Benjaminian vein.

49 See Ghatak's film *Subarnarekha*.

50 As quoted in Banerjee, ed., *Ritwik Ghatak*, 70.

51 Ghatak draws from T.S. Eliot's *Wasteland* to depict the depredations
of modern life in Calcutta.

52 See O' Donnell, "'Woman' and 'Homeland.'"

53 Ganesh, "Mother Who Is Not a Mother," 60.

54 Dasgupta, "Cinema, Marxism, and the Mother Goddess," 123.
Dasgupta also notes the sexual restraint in Ghatak's cinema as bearing a distinctly Tagorean stamp. He also points out that whereas
Tagore as a Brahmo-Samajist inspired by the Upanishadic tradition
believed in God as father, Ghatak's own cinema invokes Tagorean
sonic nature in juxtaposition to the cult of mother goddesses that
were explicitly invoked in the Bengal resistance movement, which
culminated in the Partition of the country.

4 The poetics and politics of accommodation

1 Rakesh, "The Owner of Rubble," 67–77.

2 Ibid., 67.

3 Ibid., 69.

4 See Butalia, *The Other Side of Silence*; Das, *Critical Events*; and
Menon and Bhasin, *Borders and Boundaries: Women in India's
Partition* for their work on Partition and gendered violence. I explore
this question in detail in Chapter 5.

5 I am drawing here from Homi Bhabha's idea of unhomeliness: The
image of the charred door frame represents, in its desolate aura, what

Bhabha has described as "the shock of recognition of the world-in-the-home, the home-in-the-world." Bhabha here develops his idea of the "unhomely" from Freud's notion of the *unheimlich*, as the name for everything "that ought to have remained secret and hidden but has come to light." For Freud, the *unheimlich* represents the return of old, familiar, and hitherto repressed experiences as present anxieties. Bhabha displaces Freud's psychosexual economy by inserting the *unheimlich* within larger frames of political history. See Bhabha, "The World and the Home," 445. See also Freud, "The Uncanny," 225.

6 See Sidhwa, *Ice-Candy Man*.

7 Manto, "Mozel," 455–478.

8 *Lahore* and Govind Nihalani's television serial *Tamas* (based on the novel by Bhisham Sahni) were presented the same year. While *Tamas* made visible the violence of the Partition, *Lahore* explored the ambivalent negotiations of minority identity and national belonging.

9 Consider, for example, responses by Muslim migrants in Lahore, interviewed in Satti Khanna and Peter Chappell's film *A Division of Hearts* says, "Do whatever you want to do but be faithful to the soil you live on. If you are not faithful to your soil, you are not faithful to yourself. Another interviewee declares, "Misfortune, murder, no matter what – don't leave the land of your birth. This is what I tell all future generations, because that has been my experience, after leaving my homeland. Even if you are going to be wiped out, then die by another's hand but never leave the land where you were born, that's what I say." Yet another interviewee declares, "I don't have the heart to return to visit my former homeland. I myself can't comprehend why I don't want to visit. I can't understand it. I just don't want to go. That's just how it is." Khanna and Chapell, *A Division of Hearts*. All translations of *A Division of Hearts*, *Garm Hawa*, and *Lahore* are mine.

10 Malkki, "National Geographic," 61.

11 As quoted in Gopal, *Anatomy of a Confrontation*, 15. Emphasis mine.

12 Gandhi, The Collected Works of Mahatma Gandhi, 76, 238.

13 As quoted in Pawar, "The Lion Still Roars."

14 Mukul Kesavan has argued that because of the affective richness of Urdu, it is the language par excellence of Hindi cinema. Thus according to Kesavan, Hindi cinema is the last bastion for the Urdu language, and Islamicate culture has been crucial in the development of Hindi cinema. See Kesavan, "Urdu, Awadh, and the Tawaif," 244–257.

15 The *chamars*, the so-called "low-caste" Hindus, engage in the tanning industry.

16 Both *Lahore* and *Garm Hawa* ratify the prevailing nationalist discourse in India that the Muslim League demanded Partition and underestimate the complicity of the Congress in seeking it. Jalal makes an intervention into the widespread idea that the Muslim League stood for Partition and the Congress stood for unity. Jalal, *The Sole Spokesman*. See also Nair, *Changing Homelands*.

17 As Chapter 2 illustrated, the governments of India and Pakistan closely guard the borders; Indians and Pakistanis require visas to enter either nation. Further, they need to report at the police station in the city they are visiting as soon as they arrive and before they depart and are not permitted to visit more than five places during any one trip. The recently signed liberalized visa agreement between India and Pakistan has relaxed some of the earlier restrictions. According to Zamindar, *The Long Partition*, 82: "The partition council which oversaw the administrative division of British India, had left the question of nationality laws to the two emerging states but had gone far to amend British passport rules, which declared that 'there should be no restrictions on the movement of persons from one Dominion to another.' Then the government of India unilaterally announced on July 14, 1948, the introduction of a permit system across its western frontier with Pakistan and then promulgated a parallel Pakistan (Control of Enemy) Ordinance 1948. Together these measures formed the first set of restrictions on movement of people between the two postcolonial states, and even though they affected movement across the western border only, it was, for many, the 'real' Partition."

18 As quoted in Pandey, *Remembering Partition*, 161.

19 Ibid., 162.

20 Gandhi, The Collected Works of Mahatma Gandhi, 415.

21 The scene evokes the popular image of Shah Jahan, under house arrest, gazing upon the Taj Mahal where his beloved wife, Mumtaz was interred. There are several shots of the Taj Mahal throughout this film that evoke the idea of intimate betrayals and put the stability of kinship itself into crisis. The multiple perfidies between kin experienced during the Partition complicate the grand narratives of ethnic antagonisms. The film shows several images of these monuments and captures the deep Muslim ethos in cities such as Agra.

22 Singh's *Train to Pakistan* features a scene in which Nooran, a Muslim girl, goes to bid farewell to her Sikh lover, Jugga, before leaving for Pakistan but finds only his mother there. The moment captures some of the gendered ambiguities that interrupt national belonging for women, as Jugga's mother comforts Nooran, saying that her son will bring her back as his wife. Singh writes, "A vague hope filled Nooran's being. She felt as if she belonged to the house and the house to her; the charpoy she sat on, the buffalo, Jugga's mother, all were hers. She could come back even if Jugga failed to turn up. She could tell them she was married" (153). As a woman, Nooran is constituted as an ambivalent national subject, whose national identity is mediated through marriage. See Singh, *Train to Pakistan*.

23 Zamindar, *The Long Partition*, 209. See also Shyam Benegal's film *Mammo* (1994) for a touching portrayal of one Muslim widow's journeys between India and Pakistan as she finds herself homeless after the death of her husband. Benegal captures the ways in which the bureaucratic mechanisms of the state in the forms of permits, visas, and passports interrupt Mammo's ability to live with her sister in India. The film reveals how Mammo must "die" (and indeed she stages her own death through a false death certificate) in order to live with her kin in India.

24 Although dowry is not Islamic practice, it is widely prevalent among Indian Muslims possibly influenced by Hindu practices on the subcontinent.

25 Jinnah, "Presidential Address," as quoted in Burki, *Pakistan: A Nation in the Making*, 26.

26 Talbot, Pakistan, 254.

27 For example, by yielding to the pressure to declare Ahmedis a non-Muslim minority, Zulfikar Bhutto (1974) legally authorized their disenfranchisement and laid the foundation for further Sunni demands to define, ever more narrowly, a sectarian definition for Pakistan.

28 See Fawzia Afzal-Khan for a discussion of the ways in which secular theatre activists in Pakistan intervened into juridical discourses that inculpated women. In her book, *A Critical Stage: The Role of Secular Alternative Theatre in Pakistan*, Afzal-Khan studies the contemporary alternative theatre scene in Pakistan through an interdisciplinary approach that carefully locates the performance interventions of groups such as Ajoka, Tehrik-i-Niswan, and Lok Rehas within the political economy of increasing Islamization of state policies, corporate globalization, nongovernmental organization culture, and questions of women's issues.

29 See Shaikh, Making Sense of Pakistan. See also Talbot, Pakistan and Burki, Pakistan.

30 Khilnani, *The Idea of India*, 56.

31 See the feminist scholarship of Zoya Hasan and Rajeswari Sunder Rajan on this issue. Hasan argues that minority patriarchies and larger structures of politics have worked together to produce legal inequalities. The Hindu right seized this opportunity to articulate their logic of minority appeasement, thus creating a competitive discourse between minority and majority community patriarchies regarding the appropriate policing of their women. See Hasan, "Minority Identity, State Policy, and Political Process" and Sunder Rajan, *The Scandal of the State*.

32 See Basu and Kohli, "Introduction" in *Community Conflicts*, 2.

33 My discussion draws from the dramatic text and three productions that I viewed: the video recordings of the productions directed by Dinesh Thakur (Ank, Mumbai), Sheema Kermani (Tehrik-i-Niswan, Karachi), and a live performance directed by Monica Chitkara (Natak, Palo Alto).

34 Wajahat, personal communication, 2002.

35 Foregrounding the dissent expressed by the ulamas, the Ahrars, the Shias, the Khudai Khidmatgars, and the Momins who staunchly

repudiated the two-nation theory and stuck to their vision of a secular India, Mushirul Hasan writes, "They were insulted, rebuffed and violently attacked, but refused to capitulate to the forces of political reaction and religious fanaticism. Their role must not be written off or relegated to a historian's footnote. In the evolution of a composite, nationalist ideology, which no doubt suffered a jolt during the dark days of 1947–1948, the turbaned men with flowing gowns had as much role to play as their counterparts among the western-educated intelligentsia." See Mushirul Hasan, *India's Partition*, 29.

36 See Zamindar, *The Long Partition*, 72.

37 Legislative Debates in February 1948, *Constituent Assembly Debates*, 1048.

38 Wajahat, *Jis Lahore NaiDekhya O Jamya Nai*, 14, my translation.

39 See Joseph Roach on surrogation. See also Rebecca Schneider's discussion of Joseph Roach: "To be necessarily contingent, in Roach's way of thinking about performance, is not necessarily to disappear, though it is certainly to move, to step, to shift, to jump across bodies, objects, continents, and to be given to irruptive and even 'desperate' repetition and revision." See Roach, *Cities of the Dead* and Schneider, *Performance Remains*.

40 Roach, *Cities of the Dead*.

41 See Malkki, "National Geographic," 62.

42 I am drawing upon Levinas's ideas about substitutability in *Otherwise Than Being*. See also Judith Butler, *Precarious Life*.

43 Basir Kazmi, son of Nasir Kazmi, confirms that while all the poems are taken from Nasir, the majority of these poems were written in the late 1950s and early 1960s. The poems span some twenty-five years, between 1947 and 1972. Moreover, at the time of the Partition, Nasir Kazmi was twenty-two years old. E-mail communication, January 16, 2011.

44 Born in 1925 in Ambala, Punjab, Nasir Kazmi was the son of an army major and a schoolteacher. Nasir Kazmi migrated to Lahore in September 1947 – the family lost their home and land in one stroke. Suddenly poor, Nasir worked hard to survive. His parents died within two years of moving to Lahore, and at twenty-three, he was responsible for his younger brother. He published his first book

of poems, *Burg-e-Nai* (Bamboo Leaf) in 1952, edited several literary
magazines, including *Auraq-e-Nao* (New Pages), *Humayun, Mah-e-
nao*, and *Khayaal*, in addition to taking on a range of government
jobs. Kazmi also wrote a play entitled *Sur ki Chaya* (1957), which,
along with his poems, was published in the magazine *Savera*. He
was a voracious reader of literature from all parts of the world, and
when he died, a copy of Lorca's book was found at his bedside. See
Kazmi, *Generations of Ghazals*.

45 Prominent Persian and Urdu *ghazal* poets include Jalal al-Din
Muhammad Rumi (thirteenth century), Hafez (fourteenth century),
and the Azeri poet Fuzuli (sixteenth century), as well as Mirza
Ghalib (1797–1869) and Muhammad Iqbal (1877–1938.) See Ali and
Suleri, *Ravishing DisUnitites*.

46 See Pritchett, *Nets of Awareness*, 28.

47 Naim, "Consequences of the Indo-Pakistani War," 271.

48 See Ali and Suleri, *Ravishing DisUnities*, 8.

49 Bryant quoted in Patel, *Lyrical Movements*, 205.

50 Translation, Basir Kazmi.

51 I thank Basir Kazmi, son of the late Nasir Kazmi, for his assistance
with the translations.

52 Aamir Mufti, *Enlightenment in the Colony*, 232.

53 See Pandey, *Remembering Partition*, 205.

5 Somatic texts and the gender of partition

1 See Menon and Bhasin, *Borders and Boundaries*, 71.

2 See Das, *Life and Words*, 21–26. According to Veena Das, "The story
of recovery and abduction acts as a foundational story that author-
izes a particular relation between social contract and sexual contract – the former being a contract between men to place women
within the home under the authority of the husband/father figure ...
the origin of the state is located in the rightful reinstating of proper
kinship by recovering women from the other side."

3 The significant contributions of Ritu Menon, Kamla Bhasin, and
Urvashi Butalia have addressed the question of women during
Partition and have been central in my analysis of female bodies as
political artifacts. See Menon and Bhasin, *Borders and Boundaries*

and Butalia, *The Other Side of Silence*. See also Sinha, *Specters of Mother India* for an analysis of the feminist responses to Katherine Mayo's controversial book, *Mother India*.

4 All translations are mine. The analysis of this play is based on the 2001 production at the National School of Drama, New Delhi; the dialogues have been transcribed from a video recording of the same production.

5 Butalia, *The Other Side of Silence*, 19. Veena Das distinguishes speech from voice: "I cannot tie voice to presence and writing to absence as suggested by Jacques Derrida," writes Das (*Life and Words*, 8). It is precisely the horizon of voice as communication of consciousness/presence, however, that Derrida attempts to challenge. Derrida reminds us that speech is also graphematic in structure; that is, it bears the radical trace of absence.

6 O'Hanlon, "Recovering the Subject." See also Menon, *Recovering Subversion* for a consideration of the limits of constitutional amendments, legal redress, and rights discourses within liberal feminist movement in India.

7 Elsewhere Joan Scott comments, "If one grants that meanings are constructed through exclusions, one must acknowledge and take responsibility for the exclusions involved in one's own project. Such a reflexive, self-critical approach makes apparent the particularistic status of any historical knowledge and the historian's active role as a producer of knowledge. It undermines claims for authority based on totalizing explanations, essentialized categories of analysis (be they human nature, race, class, sex, or 'the oppressed,', or synthetic narratives that assume an inherent unity for the past)." Scott, "Experience" in *Feminists Theorize the Political*, 25.

8 Joan Scott, "Experience" in *Feminists Theorize the Political*.

9 On the challenges and pitfalls of anti-foundationalist histories that highlight the fragmentariness of discourses, see the exchange between Rosalind O'Hanlon and Gyan Prakash. O'Hanlon and Washbrook, "After Orientalism" and Prakash, "Writing Post-Orientalist Histories of the Third World," in Vinayak Chaturvedi (ed.), *Mapping Subaltern Studies*.

10 Hashmi, "The Exile," in *Stories about the Partition of India*.

11 For a discussion of the Ramlila, see Anuradha Kapur, *Actors, Pilgrims, Kings, and Gods: The Ramlila at Ramnagar.*

12 The *Ramayana* is an ancient Sanskrit epic ascribed to the sage, Valmiki. It depicts the tribulations of King Rama after he was banished to the woods with his wife, Sita, and younger brother, Lakshman. Ravana, King of Lanka and a well-reputed scholar, is cast as the demon in this tale in which he covets Sita and kidnaps her. Rama fights a prolonged war to rescue Sita. Subsequently, after Sita is restored, Rama banishes her again because of rumors he overhears from a washerman surrounding her chastity after she lived with Ravana. Therefore the concept of Ramarajya (the just rule of Rama where even a washerman will be heard) is very problematic for feminist scholars, as it endorses caste/class equality even as it is predicated upon gender inequities.

13 Constituent Assembly Debates, 1949.

14 *Organiser*, July 10, 1947.

15 Constituent Assembly Debates, 1947–52.

16 Hashmi, "The Exile," 60.

17 See Shoshana Felman on threats as performative speech acts in "The Scandal of the Speaking Body."

18 This scene mimetically parodies the scene from *Mahabharata* where Arjun "wins" Draupadi through a contest set up by her father and brings her home to his mother, Kunti.

19 Here, I am drawing upon Foucault's idea that the discourse of the soul functions as a technology of power over the body. According to Foucault, to say the soul is an illusion is a flawed claim; the soul exists not as an ideological effect but is produced permanently around, on, within, the body. The soul is a surface signification that contests and displaces the inner/outer distinction itself, a figure of interior psychic space inscribed on the body as a social signification that perpetually renounces itself as such. Foucault, *Discipline and Punish*, 39–40.

20 See Devi, *The River Churning* and Das, *Life and Words* for a critique of the idea of the socially dead woman. See also Didur, *Unsettling Partition* for a discussion of women's experience of the Partition in fiction.

21 Foucault's discussion of subjectivation is apropos here: The subject comes into her subjecthood through processes of subjection. See also the excellent scholarship of Saba Mahmood and her critique of liberal feminism in the context of the piety movement among Egyptian women. Mahmood, *Politics of Piety*. See also Talal Asad, *Formations of the Secular*.

22 See Rajan's classic work on postcolonial feminism, *Real and Imagined Women*.

23 In Gurdas Mann's Punjabi film *Shaheed-e-Mohabbat*, Buta Singh is cast as a martyr to love, and a memorial has been erected to honor his commitment to his love. The same film, however, is ambivalent about Zainab and gestures toward her cowardice and moral infirmity in disclaiming her husband.

24 Das, *Critical Events*, 79.

25 For a detailed treatment of this question, see Devi's novel, *The River Churning*.

26 Das, *Critical Events*, 83.

27 Ibid., 67.

28 In her excellent book entitled *Ghosts*, Alice Rayner makes the argument that the unsettling doubleness of the actor/character undoes metaphysical arguments about ontological being. "When I say theatre is an arena for the phantasmic, I refer, then, not primarily to the illusions of theatre but to the strangeness of the fact that what is singularly visible is at the same time a double: something else is manifestly present but not necessarily identical to what is manifest.... Theatre, in this view, undermines ontology, for whatever is on stage becomes itself in some sense by denying itself, generating what Herbert Blau has called the 'dubious spectacle'" (x).

29 Paola Bacchetta points out that the state continues to cast women as property of their communities, as the Shah Bano case makes clear. See Bacchetta, "Re-interrogating Partition Violence," 567–585.

30 In a highly stylized and carefully choreographed scene, Jain stages the ritual killing of a row of women by the patriarch of the family.

31 The television serial *Tamas* dramatizes this scene. Based on Bhisham Sahni's novel, the television serial was adapted and directed by Govind Nihalani. For an excellent ethnographic analysis

of this television series, read Mankekar, *Screening Culture, Viewing Politics*.

32 Butalia, *The Other Side of Silence*, 164.

33 Ibid., 158.

34 I made this argument in an earlier version of this chapter, which appeared in *Feminist Review*, 2006. However, this chapter revises that argument. Psychoanalytic theories of trauma do not adequately capture the particular negotiations between bodies and language in this particular context. See Menon, "Rehearsing the Partition."

35 This analysis is indebted to the brilliant scholarship of Judith Butler who takes up the question of the perlocutionary force of language in *Excitable Speech*.

36 Caruth, "Introduction," in *Trauma: Explorations in Memory*, 151.

37 Das, *Life and Words*, 1.

38 Ibid., 54.

39 Ibid., 8.

40 Butalia, *Other Side of Silence*, 18.

41 For excellent analyses on gendered violence and the crisis of masculinity in Partition literature, see Priyamvada Gopal, *Literary Radicalism in India* and Kavita Daiya, *Violent Belongings*.

42 Manto, "Sorry," 118.

43 See Alok Bhalla, "The Politics of Translation: Manto's Partition Stories and Khalid Hasan's English Version," in *Social Scientist* Vol. 29, No. 7/8 (July–August 2001), pp. 19–38.

44 As quoted in Flemming, *Another Lonely Voice*, 12.

45 Ibid., 32.

46 See my essay on Rukhsana Ahmad's dramatic adaptation of Manto's short story, "Kali Shalwar," entitled "Unimaginable Communities."

47 I am drawing on Adorno's discussion of the shudder in *Aesthetic Theory*.

48 In a perceptive analysis of two stories by Manto and one by Khwaja Ahmed Abbas, Priya Kumar argues, "These fictions of rape scripted by the male writer are essentially male stories of male trauma around female silencing or of masculine agential transformation." She argues that such depictions reify women's victimhood and deny

them "any agency or capacity for effecting change in her life ...
indeed she is often denied the right to life itself." By looking to the
hermeneutic horizon of his fiction, Kumar looks away from the performative force of Manto's stories. Manto's stories literally destabilize his readers; he deterritorializes us with the abrupt inversion that
his stories culminate with. See Kumar, *Limiting Secularism.*

49 Singh, *Train to Pakistan,* 65.

50 Ibid., 162.

51 I borrow this phrase from Joseph Roach, who defines "kinesthetic
imagination" as "a way of thinking through movements – at once
remembered and reinvented." Roach, *Cities of the Dead,* 27.

6 Kashmir: hospitality and the "unfinished business" of partition

1 See Muzamil Jaleel, "Fake Encounter at LOC," in *Indian Express,*
Srinagar, 29 May 2010.

2 See "India 'to Cut Kashmir Troops by a Quarter'" January 14, 2011.
BBC News, South Asia.

3 See Taylor, *Disappearing Acts* on percepticide, acts of self-inflicted
violence that disavow what is patently visible.

4 See Sikand, *The Role of Kashmiri Sufis.*

5 See M.K. Raina: www.koausa.org/BhandPather/index.html.

6 Javaid Iqbal Bhat, "Loss of a Syncretic Theatrical Form," *Folklore
Electronic Journal,* 2006, 34:39–56: www.folklore.ee/folklore/vol34/
bhat.pdf, accessed December 4, 2011.

7 Chitralekha Zutshi, *Languages of Belonging,* p. 2.

8 Vasudha Dalmia has astutely demonstrated the ossification of the
category of folk through its interaction with colonial and national
agendas. A relational category, folk emerges in contradistinction from
elite forms of cultural production. She writes, "There was at least a
two-fold use of 'folk' by urban theatre people. In the first period its
extensive usage (IPTA), the use was entirely and self-proclaimedly
functional. Folk forms were used to address folks, to radicalize politics, and at the same time to reinvigorate urban theatre practice, once
again, for social rather than aesthetic ends. After Independence, the
term 'folk' came to be used increasingly to manipulate and integrate

into the grand national master narrative." See Dalmia, *Poetics, Plays, and Performances*, 211.

9   The *hangul* is Kashmir's state animal, an endangered species, and the only surviving subspecies of the red deer family of Europe. Known for its magnificent antlers, *hanguls* have dwindled in number from roughly 3,000 to 5,000 in the 1940s to 160 in 2008.

10   Bhand Pather repertoire creatively records a long history of oppression where only the identities of the oppressors have changed; the politics, methods, and frameworks of oppression persist from precolonial through colonial and postcolonial forms of government.

11   Whereas communities were excluded from using forests, many industries were granted raw materials at extremely low prices. Large tracts of forest were diverted for agriculture, hydroelectric projects, and other development projects in the years after Independence. See Mitra and Gupta, "Indigenous Peoples' Forest Tenure in India," in Jayantha, ed., *Land and Cultural Survival*.

12   I am drawing here from Homi Bhabha's work on mimicry and ambivalence. See Bhabha, *Location of Culture*.

13   Bhat, "Loss of a Syncretic Theatrical Form," 52.

14   Abdul Qaiyum Rafiqi notes in his study on Sufism in Kashmir that the idea of the just king was central to the Kubravi saint Saiyid Ali Hamadani, who records several warnings in *Zakhiratu'l-Muluk* from prophets to Sultans and high officers of state, cautioning rulers that they will be subjected to torture in the afterlife should they betray the trust that God has placed in them. "When a ruler follows the path of justice and equity and strives to establish the Divine law and executes the decrees of religion he is the chosen deputy of God, and his Shadow and vice-regent upon earth," writes Saiyid Ali. See Rafiqi, *Sufism in Kashmir*, 75.

15   Abdul Qaiyum Rafiqi observes that Mahmud Ghazni's incursions into Kashmir in 1014 and 1016 set the groundwork for the penetration of Muslims into the valley. The absorption of Muslim cultural practices continued through the Lohra dynasty (1003–1320). The Shah Mir dynasty (1339–1561) witnessed increased immigration from Persia and Central Asia into Kashmir. The work of the Sufi saint Saiyid Ali Hamadani accelerated the process of Persianization

of the administration and the development of a new way of life quite different from that of old Kashmir.

16 Bashir, *Messianic Hopes and Mystical Visions*, 199. Bashir traces the fortunes of the Nurbakshiya in Kashmir from its initial success in the fourteenth century to its eventual decline and the consolidation of Sunni Mughal domination in India.

17 See Rafiqi, *Sufism in Kashmir*, 207.

18 I take my cue from Carl Ernst who cautions against orientalist descriptors that fix Sufism as a timeless religious doctrine or sociological category. Sufism is neither monolithic nor homogenizes the religious practices of millions of people. Ernst writes, "While Orientalists were interested in Sufism as a descriptive term for a body of religious beliefs and practices, Muslim mystics traditionally used the term Sufi in a prescriptive way to convey certain ethical and spiritual ideas." See Ernst, *The Shambala Guide to Sufism*, xvi. This chapter looks at particular Sufi practices within their social and political context rather than the abstract mystical philosophy of Sufism.

19 Sikand, *The Role of Kasmiri Sufis*, 7. See also Shahzad Bashir, *Messianic Hopes and Mystical Visions*, especially chapter 6.

20 See Jeelani, "The Insurgent." See also Pankaj Rishi Kumar's documentary film *Pather Chujaeri*, which documents the disappearance of the folk theatre of the Bhands from the region. For a very different mood and treatment of Bhand theatre as cultural fetish of Kashmir, see Siddharth Kak's early film on Bhands, *The Bhands of Kashmir*. My sincere gratitude to Professor John Emigh for sharing his copy of this film with me. Among the most active folk theatre groups include Bhagat Theater in Akingam, Anantnag; National Bhand Theatre in Wathora-Chadora, Badgam; Alamdar Bhagat Theatre, Mohripora-Anantnag; Wuller Folk Theatre, Zaingair-Baramulla; Gulmarg Luka Theatre, Palhalan-Pattan, Baramulla; and Dilkash Folk Theatre, Hatmulla-Kupwara.

21 See *Times of India*, Randeep Singh Nandal, "State Data Refutes Claim of One Lakh Killed in Kashmir," TNN, June 20, 2011:http://articles. timesofindia.indiatimes.com/2011-06-20/india/29679480_1_milita nts-security-forces-sopore,accessed March 27, 2012.

22 According to Sumantra Bose, roughly 100,000 migrated to Jammu and Delhi, among other places. Roughly 20,000 Pandits still live in Kashmir. See Bose, *The Challenge in Kashmir*, 71.

23 The APDP alleges that more than 10,000 people are missing in Jammu and Kashmir. The government has admitted that nearly 4,000 people are missing but claims that some of them may have crossed into Pakistan to join militant groups. See Seema Kazi for a discussion on the gender politics of the violence in the valley. Kazi, *Between Democracy and Nation*.

24 Liaquat Ali Khan, Speech to the Constituent Assembly of Pakistan, 17.

25 Jawaharlal Nehru, Speech to Lok Sabha, 3995.

26 Nehru, Constituent Assembly. "In accepting the accession, however ... we made it clear that as soon as law and order had been restored in Kashmir and her soil cleared of the invaders, the question of the State's accession should be settled by reference to the people."

27 As quoted in Widmalm, *Kashmir in Comparative Perspective*, 80.

28 As quoted in Bose, *The Challenge in Kashmir*, 68.

29 Sumantra Bose describes Pakistan's position on Kashmir in this way: "The official Pakistani stance on Kashmir is the mirror-image of its Indian counterpart. It is born of the same narrow nationalist obsession with sovereignty and territory. Pakistan's obsessive interest in Kashmir is not motivated by any concern for the aspirations of Kashmiris to a dignified existence and a democratic political life. Instead, Pakistan's national project is seen as being incomplete unless and until 'Muslim' Kashmir is brought into the fold. This is not only a dogmatically irredentist position, but it is permeated with a virulently communal content. Lip service to the democratic and human rights of Kashmiris merely provides a handy stick with which to beat the Indians, who are indeed violators of those rights." See Bose, *The Challenge in Kashmir*, 176.

30 According to Rene Girard, the triangulated mimetic rivalry does not arise because of "the fortuitous convergence of two desires on a single object; rather, the subject desires the object because the rival desires it. In desiring an object the rival alerts the subject to the

desirability of the object." See Girard's discussion of mimetic desire in *To Double Business Bound*, 125.

31 Cheah, *Spectral Nationality*, 1. If freedom is imagined, as Pheng Cheah has persuasively argued, as "the transcendence of finitude through rational purposive endeavor," then dying for the nation is a way to sacrifice one's individual life for the preservation of one's permanent existence as a free moral being in the sensible world.

32 Benedict Anderson suggests that the endurance of the nation as a political community ought to be thought of in terms of the quasi-religious moral pathos of purification through death. According to Anderson, "The great wars of this century are extraordinary not so much in the unprecedented scale on which they permitted people to kill, as in the colossal numbers persuaded to lay down their lives.... The idea of the ultimate sacrifice comes only with an idea of purity, through fatality." Anderson suggests that the political community of the nation conjoins a more religious discourse on purity; the nation becomes the moral terrain in the service of which one can transcend one's own mortality and finitude. See Anderson, *Imagined Communities*, 132.

33 Jammu and Kashmir came under the Armed Forces (Jammu and Kashmir) Special Powers Act (AFSPA) in July 1990. According to Suvir Kaul, the AFSPA has its origins in British colonial law. In August 1942, when, in the face of the Quit India Movement, Lord Linlithgow, then viceroy, enacted the Armed Forces (Special Powers) Ordinance, which allowed without impunity police and army brutality against civilians. In 1958, postcolonial India passed the ordinance into the AFSPA to again provide the army impunity against military operations targeted against civilians. See Kaul, "Indian Empire (and the Case of Kashmir)." See Erin Mee, *Theatre of Roots*, for a discussion on the ways in which Manipuri theatre directors have challenged the AFSPA in Manipur.

34 An important Kashmiri musician, dancer and playwright, Moti Lal Kemmu's plays include *Teen Asangat Ekanki*, *Trunove*, *Tshai*, *Tota Ta Aana*, and *Aka Nandun*, among others. He has also actively worked to revive Dhamali, a Kashmiri dance. He is the recipient of

several awards that include the Sahitya Academy Award (1982) and the Sangeet Natak Akademi Award (1997).

35 Raina's artistic work is informed by his dynamic engagement in secular activism. He was one of the founding members of Sahmat, a cultural nongovernmental organization created in 1990 in the wake of the assassination of Safdar Hashmi, a street theatre director and activist. Through performances, films, exhibitions, and other cultural interventions, SAHMAT has creatively challenged recent attempts to proscribe plural cultural expression in India.

36 The Aristotelian concept of catharsis is derived from medical, ritual, and aesthetic functions: it refers to the emptying out of a cluttered mind, the purging of emotion through the viewing of tragedy. It draws on ideas of therapeutic cleansing or purgation, ritual purification, and cognitive resolution. Emotions were considered to be precisely that which we need to expel through the process of catharsis. Catharsis was deemed essential to the proper functioning of well-balanced soul. See Nuttall, *Why Does Tragedy Give Pleasure?* and Rehm, *Radical Theatre*.

37 *Badshah Pather* mimetically recalls Manipuri director Lokendra Arambam's adaptation of *Macbeth*, *Stage of Blood* (1997), another all-male tragedy that reflects upon the political turmoil in Manipur, a state in northeast India that has been subject to the draconian AFSPA.

38 Over the course of my stay I had the opportunity to witness a rehearsal of *Badshah Pather* as well watch performances of *Darza Pather* and *Shikargah*.

39 In *King Lear*, maps and women bear an analogous relationship to territory: Both are revealed as instruments of possession, the penetration of which will seize and mark territory as one's own. See Ramaswamy, *The Goddess and the Nation* for a discussion of the relationship between maps and gendering of territory.

40 Michael Warner's discussion on the discursive constitution of counterpublics has been especially fruitful here. See Warner, *Publics and Counterpublics*.

41 See Derrida, *Of Hospitality*, especially 141.

42 See Peer, *Curfewed Night*.

43 Shahzad Bashir notes that Sufi master Hamadani regards the ear as the bodily organ "with the most sensitive connection to the heart. Unlike the eye and the mouth, which can be closed to stop seeing or talking, the ear can be precluded from sensing only if one removes oneself completely to a place where no sound is being made at all." See Bashir, *Sufi Bodies*, 74.

44 The figure of the wise fool is a staple not only in Shakespearean tragedy but also in Sanskrit drama.

45 Raina, personal communication, June 2010.

46 Hazrat Amir Khusrau Dehlavi (AD 1253–1325) is widely regarded as the "father of Qawwali" and is a prolific classical poet associated with royal courts of more than seven rulers of the Delhi Sultanate.

47 Qureshi, *Sufi Music of India and Pakistan*, 1.

48 Sufism consists of diverse and heterogeneous orders, practices, and philosophies that are often irreconcilable with each other; the popular perception of Sufis as counterposed to textual knowledge is misleading given the large textual production in the arena of Sufism. I thank Shahzad Bashir for pointing this out to me.

49 Sufi music is not universally practiced: For example, the Naqshbandi and the Qadiri orders frown upon music and dance. The Suhrawadi order of Sufism, and Shaikh Hamza in particular, strongly disapproved of *sama*, which he considered "forbidden practice." His disciple, Baba Dawud, however, approved of *sama*. This gives us a glimpse into the tremendous internal diversity that existed even within a singular Sufic tradition: the Suhrawady order of Sufism. See Rafiqi, Sufism in Kashmir, 27.

50 Abbas, *The Female Voice in Sufi Ritual*.

51 Bashir notes that in the Persianate environment, *zikr* ran the gamut from a silent remembering of God to groups of individuals doing dances to music. See Bashir, *Sufi Bodies*, 51. Likewise, Carl Ernst reminds us that that the basic metaphor in Sufi rhetoric accords primacy to inner reality; Sufi practices offered a way to proceed from ordinary external life to find the inner reality of God. See Ernst, *The Shambala Guide to Sufism*, 26.

52 In the context of South Asia, Priya Kumar discusses hospitality drawn from Derrida's work as an analytical category to think through ethnic violence in India; see her *Limiting Secularism*. For an analysis of Derridean hospitality in the context of cosmopolitanism, and Australasian cultural politics, see Gilbert and Lo, *Performance and Cosmopolitics*.

53 Raina, personal communication, June 2010.

54 Mahmud Gami (1765–1855) introduced the Persian forms of the *masnavi* and *ghazal* into Kashmiri language. He is noted for his work *Yusuf Zulaikha*, the first and the most popular *masnavi* in Kashmiri.

55 Rush Rehm reminds us that "tragedy draws together the natural world and the built environment of the polis, forging a deep connection between art and audience, between fiction and reality, between culture and nature." See Rehm, *Radical Theatre*, 27. This is especially appropriate in this context where the plays are performed in the daylight, transforming the audience into a community of witnesses.

56 The year 2010 was the third consecutive one of protests in Kashmir. In 2008, Kashmiris protested against the state government's acquisition of land for the pilgrimage to Amarnath. In 2009, the rape and murder of two young women in Shopian, in which the security forces were accused, led to another massive round of protests.

7 Afterword

1 Said, *The World, the Text and the Critic*.

2 Ibid., 6.

3 As quoted in Willett, *Brecht on Theatre*, 197.

Bibliography

Abbas, Shemeem Burney. *The Female Voice in Sufi Ritual: Devotional Practices of Pakistan and India.* Austin: University of Texas Press, 2002.

Adorno, Theodor W. *Aesthetic Theory.* Minneapolis: University of Minnesota Press, 1998.

Afzal-Khan, Fawzia. *A Critical Stage: The Role of Secular Alternative Theatre in Pakistan.* Kolkata: Seagull Books, 2005.

Agarwal, Bina. *A Field of One's Own: Gender and Land Rights in South Asia.* Cambridge University Press, 1995.

Aggarwal, Ravinda. *Beyond Lines of Control: Performance and Politics on the Disputed Borders of Ladakh, India.* Durham, NC: Duke University Press, 2004.

Agnivesh, Swami and Valson Thampu. *Harvest of Hate: Gujarat under Siege.* New Delhi: Rupa and Co., 2002.

Ahmad, Aijaz. "Many Roads to Kargil." *Frontline* 16:14 (July 3, 1999).

Ahmad, Rukhsana. *Black Shalwar.* Unpublished manuscript, 1998.

Ajneya, S.H. "Postbox." *Stories about the Partition of India.* Ed. Alok Bhalla. New Delhi: HarperCollins, 1994.

Ali, Agha Shahid. "Farewell." *The Country without a Post Office: Poems.*London: W.W. Norton, 1998.

Ali, Agha Shahid and Sara Suleri. *Ravishing DisUnitites: Real Ghazals in English.* Hanover, NH: University Press of New England, 2000.

Alter, Joseph S. *The Wrestler's Body: Identity and Ideology in North India.* Berkeley: University of California Press, 1992.

Alter, Stephen. *Amritsar to Lahore: A Journey across the India-Pakistan Border.* Philadelphia: University of Pennsylvania Press, 2001.

Amin, Shahid. *Event, Metaphor, Memory: Chari Chaura, 1922–1992.* Berkeley: University of California Press, 1995.

Amin, Shahid and Dipesh Chakrabarty, eds. *Subaltern Studies IX: Writings on South Asia and Society.* New Delhi: Oxford University Press, 1996.

Anderson, Benedict. *Imagined Communities: Reflections on the Origin and Spread of Nationalism.* London and New York: Verso, 1983.

Ankersmith, F.R. *Aesthetic Politics: Political Philosophy beyond Fact and Value.* Stanford University Press, 1997.

Ansari, Sarah. *Life after Partition: Migration, Community, and Strife in Sindh: 1947–1962.* Oxford University Press, 2005.

Antharjanam, Lalithambika. "A Leaf in the Storm." *Stories about the Partition of India.* Ed. Alok Bhalla. New Delhi: HarperCollins, 1994.

Appadurai, Arjun. *Fear of Small Numbers: An Essay on the Geography of Anger.* Durham, NC: Duke University Press, 2006.

—— *Modernity at Large: Cultural Dimensions of Globalization.* Minneapolis: University of Minnesota Press, 1996.

Arendt, Hannah. *The Human Condition.* University of Chicago Press, 1998.

—— *Men in Dark Times.* Orlando, FL: Harcourt Brace, 1968.

Asad, Talal. *Formations of the Secular: Christianity, Islam, Modernity.* Palo Alto, CA: Stanford University Press, 2003.

Askew, Kelly. *Performing the Nation: Swahili Music and Cultural Politics in Tanzania.* University of Chicago Press, 2002.

Auden, W.H. "Partition." *Collected Poems.* New York: Random House, 1976.

Auslander, Phillip. *Liveness: Performance in a Mediatized Culture.* London and New York: Routledge, 1999.

Austin, J.L. *How to Do Things with Words.* Cambridge, MA: Harvard University Press, 1962.

Bacchetta, Paola. "Reinterrogating Partition Violence: Voices of Women/ Children/Dalit in India's Partition." *Feminist Studies* 26.3 (2000): 567–585.

Bagchi, Jasodhara. "Freedom in an Idiom of Loss." *The Trauma and the Triumph: Gender and Partition in Eastern India*. Eds. Jasodhara Bagchi and Subhoranjan Dasgupta. Kolkata: Stree, 2003.

Bagchi, Jasodhara and Subhoranjan Dasgupta. "Introduction." *The Trauma and the Triumph: Gender and Partition in Eastern India*. Eds. Jasodhara Bagchi and Subhoranjan Dasgupta. Kolkata: Stree, 2003.

Baldwin, Shauna Singh. *What the Body Remembers*. New York: Anchor Books, 2001.

Bajwa, K.S. *The Falcon in My Name: A Soldier's Diary*. New Delhi: South Asia Publications, 2000.

Banerjee, Shampa, ed. *Ritwik Ghatak*. New Delhi: Directorate of Film Festivals of India, 1981.

Banerjee, Sikata. "Civic and Cultural Nationalism in India." *Competing Nationalisms in South Asia*. Eds. Paul Brass and Achin Vinaik. Hyderabad: Orient Longman, 2002.

Bashir, Shahzad. *Messianic Hopes and Mystical Visions: The Nurbakhshiya between Medieval and Modern Islam*. Columbia: University of South Carolina Press, 2003.

—— *Sufi Bodies: Religion and Society in Medieval Islam*. New York: Columbia University Press, 2011.

Basu, Amrita and Atul Kohli, eds. *Community Conflicts and the State in India*. New Delhi: Oxford University Press, 1998.

Bayly, Chris. "The Pre-history of Communalism." *Modern Asian Studies* 19 (1985): 177–203.

Benegal, Shyam. Dir. Mammo. National Film Development Corporation of India, 1994. Film.

Benegal, Som. "A Panorama of Theatre in India." Mumbai: Popular Prakashan [for] Indian Council for Cultural Relations (ICCR), 1968.

Benjamin, Walter. *Illuminations: Essays and Reflections*. New York: Schocken, 1968.

—— "On the Mimetic Faculty." *Reflections*. New York: Schocken Books, 1986.

Bhabha, Homi K. "DissemiNation: Time, Narrative, and the Margins of the Modern Nation." *Nation and Narration*. Ed. Homi Bhabha. New York: Routledge, 1990.

—— *Location of Culture*. London and New York: Routledge, 1994.

Bhabha, Homi K. ed. *Nation and Narration*.London and New York: Routledge, 1990.

—— "The World and the Home." *Dangerous Liaisons: Gender, Nation, and Postcolonial Perspectives*. Eds. Anne McClintock, Aamir Mufti, and Ella Shohat. Minneapolis: University of Minnesota Press, 1997.

Bhalla, Alok. "Memory, History, and Fictional Representations of the Partition." *Economic and Political Weekly* 34.44 (October 30, 1999).

—— "The Politics of Translation: Manto's Partition Stories and Khalid Hasan's English Version," *Social Scientist* 29.7/8 (July–August 2001), 19–38.

Bhalla, Alok ed. *Stories about the Partition of India*. New Delhi: HarperCollins, 1994.

Bhandari, Vivek. "Civil Society and the Predicament of Multiple Publics." *Comparative Studies of South Asia, Africa and the Middle East* 26.1 (2006): 26–50.

Bhargava, Rajeev. "Giving Secularism Its Due." *Economic and Political Weekly* (July 9, 1994), 1784–1791.

Bhargava, Rajeev. ed. *Secularism and Its Critics*.New Delhi: Oxford University Press, 1998.

Bharucha, Rustom. *In the Name of the Secular: Contemporary Cultural Activism in India*. Delhi: Oxford University Press, 1998.

—— *The Politics of Cultural Practice: Thinking Theatre in an Age of Globalization*. Hanover and London: Wesleyan University Press, 2000.

Bhaskar, Ira. "Myth and Ritual: Ghatak's *Meghe Dhaka Tara*." *Journal of Arts and Ideas* 3 (April–June 1983): 43–50.

Bhat, Javaid Iqbal. "Loss of a Syncretic Theatrical Form." *Folklore: An Electronic Journal of Folklore* 34 (2006): 39–56.

Bhatia, Nandi. *Acts of Authority/Acts of Resistance: Theater and Politics in Colonial and Postcolonial India*. New Delhi: Oxford University Press, 2004.

Bhattacharjea, Ajit. *Countdown to Partition: The Final Days*. New Delhi: HarperCollins, 1997.

Bhuchar, Sudha and Kristine Landon-Smith. *A Tainted Dawn*. London: Nick Hern Books, 1999.

Blau, Herbert. "Universals of Performance; Or, Amortizing Play." *SubStance* 11.4 (1983): 140–161.

Bose, Sumantra. *The Challenge in Kashmir: Democracy, Self-Determination, and a Just Peace*. New Delhi: Sage, 1996.

—— *Kashmir: Roots of Conflict, Paths to Peace*. Cambridge, MA: Harvard University Press, 2003.

Breckenridge, Carol, Sheldon Pollock, Homi Bhabha, and Dipesh Chakrabarty, eds. *Cosmopolitanism*. Durham, NC, and London: Duke University Press, 2002.

Brennan, Timothy. "The National Longing for Form" in Homi BHabha ed., *Nation and Narration*. London: Routledge, 44–70.

—— *At Home in the World: Cosmopolitanism Now*. Cambridge, MA, and London: Harvard University Press, 1997.

Burki, Shahid Javed. *Pakistan: A Nation in the Making*. Boulder, CO: Westview Press, 1986.

Burton, Antoinette. *Dwelling in the Archive: Women Writing House, Home, and History in Late Colonial India*. Oxford and New York: Oxford University Press, 2003.

Butalia, Urvashi. *The Other Side of Silence: Voices from the Partition of India*. Durham, NC: Duke University Press, 2000.

Butler, Judith. *Bodies That Matter: On the Discursive Limits of "Sex."* New York and London: Routledge, 1993.

—— *Excitable Speech: A Politics of the Performative*. New York and London: Routledge, 1997.

—— *Precarious Life: The Power of Mourning and Violence*. London: Verso, 2004.

Calzadilla, Fernando. "Performing the Political Encapuchados in Venezuela." *TDR* 46.4 (2002): 104–125.

Caruth, Cathy. "Introduction." *Trauma: Explorations in Memory*. Ed. Cathy Caruth. Baltimore, MD, and London: Johns Hopkins University Press, 1995.

Caruth, Cathy, ed. *Trauma: Explorations in Memory*. Baltimore, MD, and London: Johns Hopkins University Press, 1995.

—— *Unclaimed Experience: Trauma, Narrative, and History*. Baltimore, MD, and London: Johns Hopkins University Press, 1996.

"Case Study: Genocide in Bangladesh, 1971." Gendercide Watch. www.gendercide.org/case_bangladesh.html. Accessed November 2, 2011.

Cavell, Stanley. *Philosophy the Day after Tomorrow*. Cambridge: Harvard University Press, 2005.

Chakrabarty, Dipesh. *Habitations of Modernity: Essays in the Wake of Subaltern Studies*. University of Chicago Press, 2002.

—— "Modernity and Ethnicity in India." *Politics of Violence: From Ayodhya to Behrampada*. Eds. John McGuire, Peter Reeves, and Howard Brasted. New Delhi: Sage Publications, 1996.

—— *Provincializing Europe: Postcolonial Thought and Historical Difference*. Princeton University Press, 2000.

Chakravartty, Gargi. *Coming Out of Partition: Refugee Women of Bengal*. New Delhi: Bluejay Books, 2005.

Chambers, Samuel. "Spectral History, Untimely Theory." *Theory & Event* 3.4 (1999).

Chari, V. K. "The Nature of Poetic Truth: Some Indian Views," *British Journal of Aesthetics* 19.3 (1979).

Chatterjee, Partha. *The Nation and Its Fragments: Colonial and Postcolonial Histories*. Princeton University Press, 1993.

—— Review of *Rows and Rows of Fences*. *Biblio: A Review of Books*. New Delhi: Brinda Datta, 2001.

—— "Secularism and Toleration."*A Possible India: Essays in Political Criticism*. New Delhi: Oxford University Press, 1998.

Chatterjee, Partha and Pradeep Jeganathan, eds. *Subaltern Studies XI: Community, Gender, and Violence*. New Delhi: Permanent Black, 2000.

Chatterjee, Partha and Gyanendra Pandey, eds. *Subaltern Studies VII: Writings on South Asian History and Society.* New Delhi: Oxford University Press, 1992.

Chatterjee, Sudipto. "Man of the Heart." Developed at the University of California, Berkeley, 2005. Performance.

Chatterji, Joya. "The Fashioning of a Frontier." *Modern Asian Studies* 33.1 (1999): 1947–1952.

—— *The Spoils of Partition: Bengal and India, 1947–1967.* Cambridge University Press, 2007.

Chaturvedi, Vinayak. *Mapping Subaltern Studies and the Postcolonial.* London and New York: Verso, 2000.

Cheah, Pheng. *Spectral Nationality: Passages of Freedom from Kant to Postcolonial Literatures of Liberation.* New York: Columbia University Press, 2003.

Chester, Lucy. "The 1947 Partition: Drawing the Indo-Pakistani Boundary." *American Diplomacy* 7:1 (February2002): www.unc.edu/depts/diplomat/archives_roll/2002_01-03/chester_parti-tion/chester_partition.html. Accessed May 30, 2004.

—— *Borders and Conflict in South Asia: The Radcliffe Boundary Commission and the Partition of Punjab.* Manchester University Press, 2009.

Clifford, James. *Routes: Travel and Translation in the Late Twentieth Century.* Cambridge, MA: Harvard University Press, 1997.

Conquergood, Dwight. "Performance Studies: Interventions and Radical Research." *The Drama Review* 46.2 (2002): 145–156.

Constituent Assembly Debates, 1949. Delhi: Government of India Publications.

Constituent Assembly Debates, 1947–52. Delhi: Government of India Publications.

Cooper, Pravina and Ritwik Ghatak. "Between the Messianic and the Material." *Asian Cinema* 10.2 (1999): 96–106.

Cossman, Brenda and Ratna Kapur. *Secularism's Last Sigh? Hindutva and the (Mis)Rule of Law.* New Delhi: Oxford University Press, 1999.

Dahbour, Omar and Micheline R. Ishay. *The Nationalism Reader.* New Jersey: Humanities Press, 1995.

Daiya, Kavita. *Violent Belongings: Partition, Gender, and National Culture in Postcolonial India*. Philadelphia: Temple University Press, 2008.

Dalmia, Vasudha. *Poetics, Plays, and Performance: The Politics of Modern Indian Drama*. New York: Oxford University Press, 2008.

Das, Veena. *Critical Events: An Anthropological Perspective on Contemporary India*. New Delhi: Oxford University Press, 1995.

———. *Life and Words: Violence and the Descent into the Ordinary*. Berkeley: University of California Press, 2007.

Das, Veena, ed. *Mirrors of Violence: Communities, Riots, and Survivors in South Asia*. New Delhi: Oxford University Press, 1994.

Dasgupta, Chidananda. "Cinema, Marxism, and the Mother Goddess." *India International Centre Quarterly* 28 (2001 Special Commemorative Issue): 122–133.

Dattani, Mahesh. "Final Solutions." *Collected Plays*. New Delhi: Penguin, 2000.

Davis, Richard. *Picturing the Nation: Iconographies of Modern India*. Andhra Pradesh: Orient Longman, 2007.

DeCerteau, Michel. *The Practice of Everyday Life*. Trans. Steven Rendall. Berkeley: University of California Press, 1984.

———. *The Writing of History*. Trans. Tom Conley. New York: Columbia University Press, 1988.

Deiller, Jean Herve. "Theatre of War." *Things Asian* (May 2003): www.thingsasian.com/goto_article/article.2323.html. Accessed May 30, 2004.

Deleuze, Gilles and Félix Guattari. *A Thousand Plateaus: Capitalism and Schizophrenia*. Trans. Brian Massumi. Minneapolis: University of Minnesota Press, 1987.

Derrida, Jacques. *Limited, Inc.* Trans. Samuel Weber. Evanston, IL: Northwestern University Press, 1988.

———. *Of Hospitality (Cultural Memory in the Present)*. Stanford University Press, 2000.

———. *Specters of Marx: The State of the Debt, the Work of Mourning, and the New International*. Trans. Peggy Kamuf. New York and London: Routledge, 1994.

Devi, Jyotimoyee. *The River Churning: A Partition Novel*. Trans. Enakshi Chatterjee. New Delhi: Kali for Women, 1995.

Dharwadker, Aparna. "Diaspora, Nation, and the Failure of Home: Two Contemporary Indian Plays."*Theatre Journal* 50.1 (1998): 71–94.

—— *Theatres of Independence: Drama, Theory, and Urban Performance in India since 1947*. Iowa City: University of Iowa Press, 2005.

Diamond, Elin, ed. *Performance and Cultural Politics*. London and New York: Routledge, 1996.

Didur, Jill. "Fragments of Imagination: Re-Thinking the Literary in Historiography through Narratives of India's Partition." *Jouvert: A Journal of Postcolonial Studies* 1.2 (1997): http://social.chass.ncsu.edu/jouvert/v1i2/con12.htm. Accessed May 30, 2004.

—— *Unsettling Partition: Literature, Gender, Memory*. University of Toronto Press, 2006.

Din, Ayub Khan. *East Is East*. London: Nick Hern Books, 1997.

A Division of Hearts. Dirs. Satti Khanna and Peter Chappell. Mistral, 1987. Film.

Dolan, Jill. "Rehearsing Democracy: Advocacy, Public Intellectuals, and Civic Engagement in Theatre and Performance Studies." *Theatre Topics* 11.1 (2001): 1–17.

Dutta, Ella. "Taking a Role Call." *Hindustan Times*, December 16, 2002.

Dutta, Krishna and Andrew Robinson. *Rabindranath Tagore: An Anthology*. New York: St. Martin's Griffin Press, 1997.

Dwyer, Rachel and Chris Pinney, eds. *Pleasure and the Nation: The History, Politics, and Consumption of Public Culture in India*. New Delhi: Oxford University Press, 2001.

Eagleton, Terry. *Ideology of the Aesthetic*. Malden, MA: Blackwell, 1990.

Eaton, Natasha. "Between Mimesis and Alterity: Art, Gift, and Diplomacy in Colonial India, 1770–1800." *Society for Comparative Study of Society and History* 46.4 (October 2004): 816–844.

Ebron, Paulla. *Performing Africa*. Princeton University Press, 2002.

Elam, Harry J. *The Past as Present in the Drama of August Wilson.* Ann Arbor: University of Michigan Press, 2004.

Ernst, Carl. *The Shambala Guide to Sufism.* Boston: Shambala Publications, 1997.

Evans, Alexander. "Reducing Tension Is Not Enough." *The Washington Quarterly* 24.2 (2001): 181–193.

Faiz, Faiz Ahmed. *The Rebel's Silhouette: Selected Poems.* Trans. Agha Shahid Ali. Amherst: University of Massachusetts Press, 1991.

Felman, Shoshana. *The Scandal of the Speaking Body: Don Juan with J. L. Austin, or Seduction in Two Languages.* Palo Alto: Stanford University Press, 2002.

Feldman, Allen. *Formations of Violence: The Narrative of the Body and Political Terror in Northern Ireland.* University of Chicago Press, 1991.

Felman, Shoshana. "Education and Crisis, or the Vicissitudes of Teaching." *Trauma: Explorations in Memory.* Ed. Cathy Caruth. Baltimore, MD: Johns Hopkins University Press, 1995.

Flemming, Leslie. *Another Lonely Voice: The Urdu Short Stories of Saadat Hasan Manto.* Berkeley: University of California Press, 1979.

Foucault, Michel. *Discipline and Punish.* New York: Vintage Books, 1977.

Freitag, Sandria. *Collective Action and Community: Public Arenas and the Emergence of Communalism in North India.* Berkeley: University of California Press, 1989.

——— "Visions of the Nation: Theorizing the Nexus between Creation, Consumption, and Participation in the Public Sphere." *Pleasure and the Nation: The History, Politics, and Consumption of Public Culture in India.* Eds. Rachel Dwyer and Chris Pinney. New Delhi: Oxford University Press, 2001.

Freud, Sigmund. *Beyond the Pleasure Principle.* Trans. James Strachey. New York and London: W.W. Norton and Company, 1961.

—— "The 'Uncanny.'" *The Standard Edition of the Complete Psychological Works of Sigmund Freud*, vol. 17. Ed. and trans. James Strachey. London: Hogarth and the Institute of Psychoanalysis, 1955.

Ganesh, Kamala. "Mother Who Is Not a Mother: In Search of the Great Indian Goddess." *Economic and Political Weekly* 25.42/43 (October 20–27, 1990): WS58–WS64.

Garm Hawa. Dir M.S. Sathyu. M.M. Video, 1973. Film.

Gandhi, Mohandas. *The Collected Works of Mahatma Gandhi*, vol. 90. New Delhi: Publications Division, Ministry of Information and Broadcasting, Govt. of India, 1984.

Gebauer, Gunter and Christioph Wulf. *Mimesis: Culture – Art – Society*. Berkeley: University of California Press, 1996.

Geertz, Clifford. *The Negara State: The Theatre State in Nineteenth Century Bali*. Princeton University Press, 1980.

George, Rosemary Marangoly. *The Politics of Home: Postcolonial Relocations and Twentieth Century Fiction*. Berkeley: University of California Press, 1999.

Ghatak Ritwik. *Rows and Rows of Fences*. Calcutta: Seagull Books, 2000.

—— dir. *Subarnarekha*. India: J.J. Films, 1965. Film.

Ghosh, Amitav. *Shadow Lines*. New York: Penguin, 1990.

Gilbert, Helen and Jacqueline Lo. *Performance and Cosmopolitics: Cross-Cultural Transactions in Australasia*. New York: Palgrave Macmillan, 2009.

Girard, Rene. *Violence and the Sacred*. Trans. Patrick Gregory. New York: Continuum, 1998.

Glover, William. *Making Lahore Modern: Constructing and Imagining a Colonial City*. Minneapolis: University of Minnesota Press, 2007.

Goethals, Helen. "Poetry and History in the Context of W.H. Auden's Poem 'Partition.'" *4e colloque du SAHIB :La Route des Indes*, September 3–4, 1999: http://nte.univ-lyon2.fr/~goethals/decolonization/decolonization_auden.html. Accessed May 30, 2004.

Goffman, Erwing. *The Presentation of Self in Everyday Life*. Garden City: Doubleday Anchor Books, 1959.

Gopal, Priyamvada, *Literary Radicalism in India: Gender, Nation and the Transition to Independence.* New York: Routledge, 2005.

Gopal, Sarvepalli, ed. *Anatomy of a Confrontation: The Babri Masjid-Ramjanmabhumi Issue.* London: Zed Books, 1991.

Gould, Timothy. "The Unhappy Performative." *Performance and Performativity.* Eds. Andrew Parker and Eve Sedgwick. New York and London: Routledge, 1995.

Green, Jeffrey. *The Eyes of the People: Democracy in an Age of Spectatorship.* Oxford University Press, 2010.

Grewal, Inderpal and Caren Kaplan, eds. *Scattered Hegemonies: Postmodernity and Transnational Feminist Practices.* Minneapolis and London: University of Minnesota Press, 1994.

Gunew, Sneja. "The Melting Pot of Assimilation." *Transnational Asia Pacific: Gender, Culture, and the Public Sphere.* Eds. Shirley Geok-lin Lim, Larry E. Smith, and Wimal Dissanayake. Urbana: University of Illinois Press, 1999.

Gupta, Akhil. "Blurred Boundaries: The Discourse of Corruption, the culture of Politics, and the Imagined State." *American Ethnologist* 22.2 (May 1995).

——— "The Song of the Non-Aligned World: Transnational Identities and the Reinscription of Space in Late Capitalism."*Culture, Power, Place: Explorations in Critical Anthropology.* Eds. Akhil Gupta and James Ferguson. Durham, NC: Duke University Press, 1997.

Gupta, Akhil and James Ferguson, eds. *Culture, Power, Place: Explorations in Critical Anthropology.* Durham, NC: Duke University Press, 1997.

Gupta, Charu. *Sexuality, Obscenity, Community: Women, Muslims, and the Hindu Public in Colonial India.*New York: Palgrave, 2002.

Hall, Stuart. "The Local and The Global: Globalization and Ethnicity." *Culture, Globalization and the World-System.* Ed. Anthony D. King. London: Macmillan, 1991.

Halliwell, Stephen. *Aesthetics of Mimesis: Ancient Texts and Modern Problems*. Princeton University Press, 2002.

Hannerz, Ulf. "The World inCreolization." *Africa* 57.4 (1987): 546–559.

Hansen, Thomas Blom. "Politics as Permanent Performance." *The Politics of Cultural Mobilization in India*. Eds. John Zavos, Andrew Wyatt, and Vernon Hewitt. New Delhi: Oxford University Press, 2004.

—— *The Saffron Wave: Democracy and Hindu Nationalism in Modern India*. New Delhi: Oxford University Press, 1999.

—— *Wages of Violence: Naming and Identity in Postcolonial Bombay*. Princeton University Press, 2001.

Haqqani, Abdul Basit. "Love, Hate, Display." *The Daily Times*, December 29, 2003.

Hartman, Saidiya. "Seduction and the Ruses of Power." *Between Woman and Nation: Nationalisms, Transnational Feminisms, and the State*. Eds. Caren Kaplan, Norma Alarcon, and Minoo Moallem. Durham, NC: Duke University Press, 1999.

Hasan, Mubashir. "Bus to Delhi." *The Nation* (October 8, 2003).

Hasan, Mushirul, ed. *India's Partition: Process, Strategy, and Mobilization*. New Delhi: Oxford University Press, 1993.

—— *Inventing Boundaries: Gender, Politics, and the Partition of India*. New Delhi: Oxford University Press, 2000.

Hasan, Mushirul, "Prologue."*Inventing Boundaries: Gender, Politics, and the Partition of India*. Ed. Mushirul Hasan. New Delhi: Oxford University Press, 2000.

Hasan, Zoya, ed. *Forging Identities: Gender, Communities, and the State*. New Delhi: Oxford University Press, 1994.

—— *Politics and the State in India: Readings in Indian Government and Politics*.New Delhi: Sage, 2000.

—— "Minority Identity, State Policy, and Political Process." *Forging Identities: Gender, Communities, and the State*. Ed. Zoya Hasan. New Delhi: Oxford University Press, 1994.

Hashmi, Jamila. "The Exile." *Stories about the Partition of India*. Ed. Alok Bhalla. New Delhi: HarperCollins, 1994.

Hebdige, Dick. *Cut 'N' Mix: Culture, Identity, and Caribbean Music.* London: Methuen, 1987.

Hewitt, Vernon. *Reclaiming the Past: The Search for Political and Cultural Unity in Contemporary Jammu and Kashmir.* London: Portland Books, 1995.

Hobsbawm, Eric and Terence Ranger, eds. *The Invention of Tradition.* Cambridge University Press, 1983.

Hosain Attia. "After the Storm." *Stories about the Partition of India.* Ed. Alok Bhalla. New Delhi: HarperCollins, 1994.

India Ministry of Information and Broadcasting. *Millions on the Move: The Aftermath of Partition.* Modern India Series. New Delhi: Ministry of Information and Broadcasting, 1956.

Irigaray, Luce. *The Irigaray Reader.* Ed. Margaret Whitford. Cambridge: Basil Blackwell, 1991.

Jalal, Ayesha. *Self and Sovereignty: Individual and Community in South Asian Islam since 1850.* London: Routledge, 2000.

——— "Secularists, Subalterns, and the Stigma of 'Communalism': Partition Historiography Revisited." *Modern Asian Studies* 30.3 (1996): 681–737.

——— *The Sole Spokesman: Jinnah, The Muslim League, and the Demand for Pakistan.* Cambridge University Press, 1985.

Jeelani, Mehboob. "The Insurgent." *The Caravan* 3.10 (September 2011): *Caravanmagazine.in.* www.caravanmagazine.in/ Story/1050/The-Insurgent.html. Accessed October 27, 2011.

Jinnah, M.A.K. "An Extract from the Presidential Address of M.A. Jinnah – Lahore, 1940."*India's Partition: Process, Strategy, and Mobilization.* Ed. Mushirul Hasan. New Delhi: Oxford University Press, 1993.

——— "Presidential Address to the Constituent Assembly of Pakistan, 11 August 1947":*Pakistani.org,* www.pakistani.org/paki-stan/legislation/constituent_address_11aug1947.html. Accessed July 14, 2003.

John, Mary E. and Janaki Nair. *A Question of Silence? Sexual Economics in Modern India.* New Delhi: Zed Books, 2001.

Joshi, Ahbijat. *A Shaft of Sunlight*. London: Nick Hern Books, 1999.

Kak, Siddharth. *The Bhands of Kashmir*.Cinema Vision India, nd. Documentary film.

Kalra, Virinder and Navtej Purewal. "The Strut of the Peacocks: Partition, Travel, and the Indo-Pak Border."*Travel Worlds: Journeys in Contemporary Cultural Politics*. Eds. Raminder Kaur and John Hutnyk. London: Zed Books, 1999.

Kamra, Sukeshi. *Bearing Witness: Partition, Independence, End of the Raj*.Calgary, Alberta: Calgary University Press, 2001.

Kaplan, Caren, Norma Alarcon, and Minoo Moallem, eds. *Between Woman and Nation: Nationalisms, Transnational Feminisms, and the State*.Durham, NC, and London: Duke University Press, 1999.

Kapur, Anuradha. *Actors, Pilgrims, Kings, and Gods: The Ramlila at Ramnagar*. Calcutta: Seagull Press, 1990.

Kaul, Suvir. "Indian Empire (and the Case of Kashmir)." *Economic and Political Weekly* 46.13 (March 26, 2011): 66–75.

Kaul, Suvir, ed. *The Partitions of Memory: The Afterlife of the Division of India*. New Delhi: Permanent Black, 2001.

Kaur, Raminder. *Performative Politics and the Cultures of Hinduism: Public Uses of Religion in Western India*. London: Anthem Press, 2005.

Kaviraj, Sudipta "The Imaginary Institution of India." *Subaltern Studies VII: Writings on South Asian History and Society*. Eds. Partha Chatterjee and Gyanendra Pandey. New Delhi: Oxford University Press, 1992.

Kaviraj, Sudipta, ed. *Politics in India: Oxford in India Readings in Sociology and Social Anthropology*.New Delhi: Oxford University Press, 1997.

Kazi, Seema. *Between Democracy and Nation: Gender and Militarisation in Kashmir*. Pakistan: Oxford University Press, 2010.

Kazmi, Basir Sultan. *Generations of Ghazals*. Trans. Debjani Chatterjee. West Yorkshire: Redbeck Press, 2003.

Kazmi, Fareed. "Muslim Socials and the Female Protagonist: Seeing a Dominant Discourse at Work." *Forging Identities: Gender,*

Communities, and the State. Ed. Zoya Hasan. New Delhi: Oxford University Press, 1994.

Kesavan, Mukul. "Urdu, Awadh, and the Tawaif: The Islamicate Roots of Hindi Cinema." *Forging Identities: Gender, Communities, and the State*. Ed. Zoya Hasan. New Delhi: Oxford University Press, 1994.

Khan, Angshutosh, Gautam Bose, and Debaprasad Chakrabarti. "Left Cultural Movement in West Bengal: An Analysis." *Social Scientist* 6.6/7 (January–February 1978 Special Number of West Bengal): 114–119.

Khan, Liaquat Ali. Constituent Assembly, January 19. *Kashmir and Inter-Dominion Relations: Statement by Prime Minister Liaquat Ali Khan*. Government of Pakistan: Publications Department, 1950.

Khan, Yasmin. *The Great Partition: The Making of India and Pakistan*. New Haven, CT: Yale University Press, 2007.

Khanna, Satti and Peter Chapell. *A Division of Hearts*. 1987. Translation mine. Film.

Khilnani, Sunil. *The Idea of India*. New York: Farrar Straus Giroux, 1997.

Kleinman, Arthur, Veena Das, and Margaret Lock, eds. *Social Suffering*. Berkeley: University of California Press, 1997.

Kondo, Dorinne. "Re-Visions of Race: Contemporary Race Theory and the Cultural Politics of Racial Crossover in Documentary Theatre." *Theatre Journal* 52.1 (2000): 81–107.

Krishna, Maj. Ashok. *India's Armed Forces: Fifty Years of War and Peace*. New Delhi: Lancer Publishers, 1998.

Kumar, Amitava. "Splitting the Difference." *Transition Magazine* 11:1, 89 (2002): 44–55.

Kumar, Pankaj Rishi. *Pather Chujaeri*. Public Service Broadcasting Trust, 2001. Documentary Film.

Kumar, Priya. *Limiting Secularism: The Ethics of Coexistence in Indian Literature and Film*. Minneapolis: University of Minnesota Press, 2008.

Lal, Vinay. "The Mother in the Father of the Nation." *Manushi: A Journal of Women and Society* 91 (1995): 27–30.

Levinas, Emmanuel. *Otherwise Than Being: Or Beyond Essence*.Pittsburgh: Duquesne University Press, 1998.

Limaye, Satu P. "Mediating Kashmir: A Bridge Too Far." *The Washington Quarterly* 26.1 (2002–2003): 157–167.

Lindholm, Charles. "Prophets and Pirs: Charismatic Islam in the Middle East and South Asia." *Embodying Charisma: Modernity, Locality, and the Performance of Emotion in Sufi Cults.* Eds. Pnina Werbner and Helene Basu. Albany: State University of New York Press, 2006.

Loomba, Ania. *Colonialism/Postcolonialism*. London and New York: Routledge, 1998.

Loomba, Ania, Suvir Kaul, Matti Bunzl, Antoinette Burton, and Jed Esty, eds. *Postcolonial Studies and Beyond*. Durham, NC: Duke University Press.

Ludden, David, ed. *Contesting the Nation: Religion, Community, and the Politics of Democracy in India*.Philadelphia: University of Pennsylvania Press, 1996.

——— *Making India Hindu: Religion, Community, and the Politics of Democracy in India*. New York: Oxford University Press, 2005.

——— "Orientalist Empiricism: Transformations of Colonial Knowledge." *Orientalism and the Postcolonial Predicament: Perspectives from South Asia*. Eds. Carol Breckenridge and Peter van der Veer. Philadelphia: University of Pennsylvania Press, 1993.

Lugones, Maria. "Playfulness, World-Traveling, and Loving Perception." *Haciendo Caras/Making Face, Making Soul: Creative and Critical Perspectives by Women of Color*. Ed. Gloria Anzaldua. San Francisco: Aunt Lute, 1990.

Madan, T.N. *Modern Myths, Locked Minds: Secularism and Fundamentalism in India*. New Delhi: Oxford University Press, 1998.

——— "Secularism in Its Place." *Politics in India*.Ed. Sudipta Kaviraj. New Delhi: Oxford University Press, 1997.

Mahmood, Saba. *The Politics of Piety*. Princeton University Press, 2004.

Malkki, Liisa H. "National Geographic: The Rootings of Peoples and the Territorialization of National Identity among Scholars and Refugees." *Culture, Power, Place: Explorations in Critical Anthropology.* Eds. Akhil Gupta and James Ferguson. Durham, NC: Duke University Press, 1997.

Mani, Lata. "Contentious Traditions: The Debate on Sati in Colonial India." *Re-Casting Women: Essays in Colonial History.* Ed. Kumkum Sangari and Sudesh Vaid. New Delhi: Kali for Women, 1989.

Mankekar, Purnima. *Screening Culture, Viewing Politics: An Ethnography of Television, Womanhood, and Nation in Postcolonial India.* Durham, NC, and London: Duke University Press, 1999.

Mannes, Marya. *Subverse: Rhymes for Our Times.* New York: Braziller, 1959.

Manor, James. "Making Federalism Work." *Journal of Democracy* 9.3 (1998): 21–35.

Manto, Saadat Hasan. "Mozel."*Stories about the Partition of India.* Ed. Alok Bhalla. New Delhi: HarperCollins, 1999.

—— "Open It." *Stories about the Partition of India.* Ed. Alok Bhalla. New Delhi: HarperCollins, 1999.

—— *Partition: Sketches and Stories.* Trans. Khalid Hasan. New Delhi: Viking, 1991.

—— "Sorry." *Stories about the Partition of India.*Ed. Alok Bhalla. New Delhi: HarperCollins, 1999.

Martin, Biddy and Chandra Talpade Mohanty. "Feminist Politics: What's Home Got to Do with It?"*Feminist Studies, Critical Studies.* Ed.Teresa De Lauretis. Bloomington: Indiana University Press, 1986.

Marx, Karl. *Gundrisse: Foundations of the Critique of Political Economy.* Trans. Martin Nicolaus. London: Penguin, 1993.

Massignon, Louis and Herbert Mason. *The Passion of al-Hallaj.* Princeton, NJ: Princeton University Press, 1982.

McClintock, Anne. *Imperial Leather: Race, Gender, and Sexuality in the Colonial Context.* London and New York: Routledge, 1995.

McGuire, John, Peter Reeves, and Howard Blasted, eds. *Politics of Violence: From Ayodhya to Behrampada*. New Delhi: Sage, 1996.

Mehta, Suketu. "Reflections: A Fatal Love." *Himal: South Asian* (January 2004): www.himalmag.com/2004/january/reflections.htm. Accessed May 30, 2004.

Mehta, Uday Singh. "Nationalism's Mired Hopes: Partition, Cold War, and the Conflict in Kashmir." *The Boston Review* 28.1 (March 2003).

Menon, Jisha. "Rehearsing the Partition: Gendered Violence in *Aur Kitne Tukde*." *The Feminist Review* 84 (2006): 29–47.

——— "Unimaginable Communities." *Modern Drama* 48.2 (2005): 407–427.

Menon, Nivedita. *Recovering Subversion: Feminist Politics beyond the Law*. Urbana: University of Illinois Press, 2004.

Menon, Ritu and Kamla Bhasin. *Borders and Boundaries: Women in India's Partition*.New Brunswick, NJ: Rutgers University Press, 1998.

Metcalf, Thomas. *Ideologies of the Raj*. Cambridge University Press, 1995.

Mohanty, Chandra. *Feminism without Borders: Decolonizing Theory, Practicing Solidarity*. Durham, NC: Duke University Press, 2003.

——— "Under Western Eyes: Feminist Scholarship and Colonial Discourses." *Colonial Discourse and Postcolonial Theory*. Eds. Patrick Williams and Laura Chrisman. New York: Columbia University Press, 1994.

Mufti, Aamir R. *Enlightenment in the Colony: The Jewish Question and the Crisis of Postcolonial Culture*. Princeton University Press, 2007.

——— "A Greater Story-Writer Than God: Genre, Gender, and Minority in Late Colonial India." *Community, Gender, and Violence: Subaltern Studies XI*. Eds. Partha Chatterjee and Pradeep Jeganatha. New York: Columbia University Press, 2000.

Murphy, Richard. "Performing Partition in Lahore." *The Partitions of Memory: The Afterlife of the Division of India*. Ed. Suvir Kaul. New Delhi: Permanent Black, 2001.

Musafir, Gurmukh Singh. "The Abandoned Child." *Stories about the Partition of India.* Ed. Alok Bhalla. New Delhi: HarperCollins, 1994.

Nadeem, Shahid. "Border-Border." Unpublished manuscript.

Naim, C.M. "Consequences of the Indo-Pakistani War for Urdu Language and Literature: A Parting of Ways?"*Journal of Asian Studies* 28.2 (February 1969): 269–283.

Nair, Neeti. *Changing Homelands: Hindu Politics and the Partition of India.* Cambridge, MA: Harvard University Press, 2011.

Nair, Rukmini Bhaya. "Singing a Nation into Being." *Seminar* 491 (2001): www.india-seminar.com/2001/497/497%20ruk-mini%20bhaya%20nair.htm Accessed November 8, 2011.

Nandy, Ashis. "The Days of the Hyaena: A Foreword."*Mapmaking: Partition Stories from the Two Bengals.* Ed. Debjani Sengupta. New Delhi: Srishti Publishers & Distributors, 2003.

—— "History's Forgotten Doubles." *The Romance of the State: And the Fate of Dissent in the Tropics.* New Delhi: Oxford University Press, 2002.

—— "Nationalism, Genuine and Spurious." *Economic and Political Weekly* (New Delhi, August 12, 2006): 3500–3504.

—— "Politics of Secularism and the Recovery of Religious Tolerance." *Mirrors of Violence: Communities, Riots, and Survivors in South Asia.* Ed. Veena Das. New Delhi: Oxford University Press, 1990.

Nehru, Jawaharlal. Constituent Assembly (Legislative). New Delhi, November 25, 1947.

—— Speech to Lok Sabha. September 17, 1953, *Parliamentary Debates* 3:34.

Nijhawan, Dina Nath and R.D. Chopra. *Exhaustive Commentary on The Displaced Persons (Compensation and Rehabilitation) Act 1954 and The Displaced Persons (Compensation and Rehabilitation) Rules 1955.* New Delhi: Federal Law Depot, 1980.

Niranjana, Tejaswini and Susie Tharu. "Problems for a Contemporary Theory of Gender." *Subaltern Studies IX.* Eds. Shahid

Amin and Dipesh Chakrabarty. New Delhi: Oxford University Press, 1996.

Nora, Pierre. "Between Memory and History: Les Lieux des Memoires." *History and Memory in African-American Culture.* Eds. Geneviève Fabre and Robert O'Meally. New York and London: Oxford University Press, 1994.

Nuttall, Anthony. *Why Does Tragedy Give Pleasure?* Oxford University Press, 1996.

Oberoi, Surinder. "Fear and Loathing in Kashmir." *The Washington Quarterly* 24.2 (2001): 195–199.

O'Donnell, Erin. "'Woman' and 'Homeland' in Ritwik Ghatak's Films: Constructing Post-Independence Bengali Cultural Identity." *JumpCut: A Review of Contemporary Media* 45 (2005).

O'Hanlon, Rosalind. "Recovering the Subject: Subaltern Studies and Histories of Resistance in Colonial South Asia." *Mapping Subaltern Studies and the Postcolonial.*Ed. Vinayak Chaturvedi. London and New York: Verso, 2000.

O'Hanlon, Rosalind and David Washbrook. "After Orientalism: Culture, Criticism, and Politics in the Third World." *Mapping Subaltern Studies and the Postcolonial.* Ed. Vinayak Chaturvedi. London and New York: Verso, 2000.

Organiser, July 10, 1947.

Pandey, Gyanendra. *The Construction of Communalism in Colonial North India.* New Delhi: Oxford University Press, 1990.

—— "The Prose of Otherness."*Subaltern Studies VIII: Essays in Honour of Ranajit Guha.* Ed. David Arnold and David Hardiman. New Delhi: Oxford University Press, 1994.

—— *Remembering Partition: Violence, Nationalism, and History in India.* Cambridge University Press, 2001.

—— "Voices from the Edge: The Struggle to Write Subaltern Histories." *Mapping Subaltern Studies and the Postcolonial.* Ed. Vinayak Chaturvedi. London and New York: Verso, 2000.

Parker, Andrew and Eve Kosofsky-Sedgwick, eds. *Performance and Performativity.* New York and London: Routledge, 1995.

Patel, Geeta. *Lyrical Movements, Historical Hauntings: On Gender, Colonialism, and Desire in Miraji's Urdu Poetry.* Stanford University Press, 2001.

Patil, V.T. and Asiananda. *Healing the Subcontinent: In-depth Psychoanalysis of Partition and Kashmir.* New Delhi: Minerva, 2002.

Patraka, Vivian. *Spectacular Suffering: Theatre, Fascism, and the Holocaust.* Bloomington: Indiana University Press, 1999.

Pawar, Yogesh. *"The Lion Still Roars."* The Indian Express, September 9, 1998.

Peer, Basharat. *Curfewed Night: One Kashmiri Journalist's Frontline Account of Life, Love, and War in His Homeland.* New York: Scribner, 2010.

Perera, Jayantha. *Land and Cultural Survival: The Communal Land Rights of Indigenous Peoples in Asia.* Metro Manila, Philippines: Asian Development Bank, 2009.

Phelan, Peggy. "Converging Glances: A Response to Cathy Caruth's 'Parting Words.'" *Cultural Values* 5.1 (2001): 27–40.

—— *Mourning Sex: Performing Public Memories.* London and New York: Routledge, 1997.

—— *Unmarked: The Politics of Performance.* London and New York: Routledge, 1993.

Philips, C.H. and Mary Doreen Wainwright, eds. *The Partition of India: Policies and Perspectives, 1935–1947.* London: Allen & Unwin, 1970.

Plato. *The Republic.* Trans. Desmond Lee. New York: Penguin Classics, 2007.

Povinelli, Elizabeth. "A Flight from Freedom" *Postcolonial Studies and Beyond.* Eds. Ania Loomba, Suvir Kaul, Matti Bunzl, Antoinette Burton, and Jed Esty. Durham, NC: Duke University Press, 2005.

Prabhakar, Vishnu. "I Shall Live." *Stories about the Partition of India.* Ed. Alok Bhalla. New Delhi: HarperCollins, 1994.

Prakash, Gyan. "Can the Subaltern Ride? A Reply to O'Hanlon and Washbrook." *Mapping Subaltern Studies and the*

Postcolonial. Ed. Vinayak Chaturvedi. London and New York: Verso, 2000.

—— "Writing Post-Orientalist Histories of the Third World: Perspectives from Indian Historiography." *Mapping Subaltern Studies and the Postcolonial.* Ed. Vinayak Chaturvedi. London and New York: Verso, 2000.

Pritam, Amrita. (trans. Khushwant Singh), *The Skeleton and Other Writings.* Bombay: Jaico Publishing House, 1964.

Pritchett, Frances. *Nets of Awareness: Urdu Poetry and Its Critics.* Berkeley: University of California Press, 1994.

Qasmi, Ahmad Nadeem. "Parmeshwar Singh." *Stories about the Partition of India.* Ed. Alok Bhalla. New Delhi: HarperCollins, 1994.

Qureshi, Regula. *Sufi Music of India and Pakistan: Sound, Context, and Meaning in Qawwali.* University of Chicago Press, 1986.

Rafiqi, Abdul Qaiyum. *Sufism in Kashmir: From Fourteenth to Sixteenth Century.* New Delhi: Bharatiya Publishing House, 1972.

Raina, M.K. "The Bhand Panther of Kashmir": www.koausa.org/BhandPather/index.html. Accessed November 1, 2011.

Rajadhyaksha, Ashish. *Ritwik Ghatak: A Return to the Epic.* Bombay: Screen Unit, 1982.

Rajadhyaksha, Ashish and Amrit Gangar. *Ritwik Ghatak: Arguments, Stories.* Bombay: Screen Unit, 1987.

Rajagopal, Arvind. *Politics after Television: Religious Nationalism and the Reshaping of the Indian Public.* Cambridge University Press, 2001.

—— "Thinking through Emerging Markets: Brand Logics and the Cultural Forms of Political Society in India." *Social Text* 17.3 (1999): 131–149.

Rajan, Rajeswari Sunder. *Real and Imagined Women: Gender, Culture, and Postcolonialism.* London and New York: Routledge, 1993.

—— *The Scandal of the State: Women, Law, and Citizenship in Postcolonial India.* Durham, NC, and London: Duke University Press, 2003.

Rajan, Rajeswari Sunder, ed. *Signposts: Gender Issues in Post-Independence India*. New Delhi: Kali for Women, 1999.

Rakesh, Mohan. "The Owner of Rubble." *Stories about the Partition of India*.Vol. 3. Ed. Alok Bhalla. New Delhi: Indus/Harper, 1994.

Ramaswamy, Sumathi. *Beyond Appearances: Visual Practices and Ideologies in Modern India*. Thousand Oaks, CA: Sage Publications, 2003.

—— *The Goddess and the Nation: Mapping Mother India*. Durham, NC: Duke University Press, 2010.

Rayner, Alice. *Ghosts: Death's Double and the Phenomena of Theatre*. University of Minnesota Press, 2006.

Rehm, Rush. *Radical Theatre: Greek Tragedy and the Modern World*.London: Gerald Duckworth and Co., 2003.

Renan, Ernest. "What Is a Nation?" *Nation and Narration*. Ed. Homi Bhabha. London and New York: Routledge, 1990.

Roach, Joseph. *Cities of the Dead: Circum-Atlantic Performance*. New York: Columbia University Press, 1996.

Robinson, Andrew. *Satyajit Ray: The Inner Eye*. Berkeley: University of California Press, 1990.

Rokem, Freddie. *Performing History: Theatrical Representations of the Past*. University of Iowa Press, 2000.

Roy, Arundathi. *The Cost of Living*. New York: The Modern Library, 1999.

—— "Democracy: Who's She When She's at Home?" *Harvest of Hate*. Eds. Swami Agnivesh and Valson Thampu. New Delhi: Rupa & Co., 2002.

Roy, Asim. "The High Politics of India's Partition: The Revisionist Perspective." *India's Partition: Process, Strategy, and Mobilization*. Ed. Mushirul Hasan. New Delhi: Oxford University Press, 1993.

Roy, Bhaskar. *An Escape into Silence*. New Delhi: New Century Publications, 2002.

Rushdie, Salman. *Shalimar, the Clown*. RandomHouse: New York, 2005.

Said, Edward W. *Orientalism*. New York: Vintage Books, 1979.

—— *The World, the Text, and the Critic*. Cambridge, MA: Harvard University Press, 1983.

Sangari, Kumkum and Sudesh Vaid. "Politics of Diversity: Religious Communities and Multiple Patriarchies." *Economic and Political Weekly* 30.51 (1995): 3287–3310.

—— *Re-Casting Women: Essays in Colonial History*.New Delhi: Kali for Women, 1989.

Sarkar, Bhaskar. *Mourning the Nation: Indian Cinema in the Wake of Partition*. Durham, NC: Duke University Press, 2009.

Sarkar, Sumit. "The Decline of the Subaltern in Subaltern Studies." *Mapping Subaltern Studies and the Postcolonial*. Ed. Vinayak Chaturvedi. London and New York: Verso, 2000.

—— "Orientalism Revisited: Saidian Frameworks in the Writing of Modern Indian History." *Mapping Subaltern Studies and the Postcolonial*. Ed. Vinayak Chaturvedi. London and New York: Verso, 2000.

—— *Writing Social History*. New Delhi: Oxford University Press, 1997.

Sarkar, Tanika. "Foreword." *Coming Out of Partition: Refugee Women of Bengal*.New Delhi: Bluejay Books, 2005.

Sawhney, Simona. *The Modernity of Sanskrit*. University of Minnesota Press, 2008.

Schechner, Richard. *Between Theatre and Anthropology*. Philadelphia: University of Pennsylvania Press, 1985.

Schmitt, Karl. *The Concept of the Political*. University of Chicago Press, 2007.

Schneider, Rebecca. *Performance Remains: Art and War in Times of Theatrical Reenactment*. New York: Routledge, 2011.

Schofield, Victoria. *Kashmir in the Cross-Fire*. London: Harvill, 1996.

Scott, Joan. "Experience." *Feminists Theorize the Political*. Eds. Judith Butler and Joan Scott. New York and London: Routledge, 1989.

Sengupta, Anindya. "The Face of the Mother: Woman as Image and Bearer of the Look in Ritwik Ghatak's Films." *Journal of the Moving Image* 3 (June 2004): 168–186.

Settar, S. and Indira Baptista Gupta. *Pangs of Partition, Volume II: The Human Dimension.* New Delhi: Manohar, 2002.

Shahani, Kumar. "Violence and Responsibility." *Framework* 30/31 (1986): 79–83.

Shaheed-e-Mohabbat. Prod. Manjeet Mann. Dir. Manoj Panj. DEI/EROS, 1999. Film.

Shaikh, Farzana. *Making Sense of Pakistan.* New York: Columbia University Press, 2009.

—— "Muslims and Political Representation in Colonial India: The Making of Pakistan." *India's Partition: Process, Strategy, and Mobilization.* Ed. Mushirul Hasan. New Delhi: Oxford University Press, 1993.

Sharpe, Jenny. "The Unspeakable Limits of Rape: Colonial Violence and Counter-Insurgency." *Colonial Discourse and Postcolonial Theory.* Ed. Patrick Williams and Laura Chrisman. New York: Columbia University Press, 1994.

Shimakawa, Karen. *National Abjection: The Asian-American Body on Stage.* Durham, NC: Duke University Press, 2002.

Sidhwa, Bapsi. *Ice-Candy Man.* New Delhi: Penguin, 1988.

Siegal, Lee. *The Nation..* September 15, 2005.

Sikand, Yoginder. *The Role of Kashmiri Sufis in the Promotion of Social Reform and Communal Harmony.* Mumbai: Center for Study of Society and Secularism, 1999.

Singh, Amritjit Singh, Joseph T. Skerret, Jr., and Robert E. Hogan, eds. *Memory and Cultural Politics: New Approaches to American Ethnic Literatures.* Boston: Northeastern University Press, 1996.

Singh, Harkirat. "Wagah, Wagah." *Rediff on the Net* (February 1999): http://rediff.com/news/1999/feb/16waga.htm. Accessed May 30, 2004.

Singh, Khushwant. *Train to Pakistan.* New Delhi: Ravi Dayal, 1988.

Singh, Kirpal, ed. *Select Documents on Partition of Punjab, 1947.* New Delhi: National Book Shop, 1991.

Sinha, Mrinalini. *Colonial Masculinity: The "Manly Englishman" and the "Effeminate Bengali" in the Late Nineteenth Century.* Manchester University Press, 1995.

253

———— *Specters of Mother India: The Global Restructuring of an Empire.* Durham, NC: Duke University Press, 2007.

Sobti, Krishna, "Where Is My Mother?"*Stories about the Partition of India.* Ed. Alok Bhalla. New Delhi: HarperCollins, 1994.

Solomon, Rakesh. "Culture, Imperialism, and Nationalist Resistance: Performance in Colonial India." *Theatre Journal* 46 (1994): 323–337.

Som, Reba. *Rabindranath Tagore: The Singer and His Song.* New Delhi: Penguin, 2009.

Spivak, Gayatri. "Can the Subaltern Speak?" *Colonial Discourse and Postcolonial Theory.* Eds. Patrick Williams and Laura Chrisman. New York: Columbia University Press, 1994.

———— "The New Subaltern: A Silent Interview." *Mapping Subaltern Studies and the Postcolonial.*Ed. Vinayak Chaturvedi. London and New York: Verso, 2000.

Stephens, Paul and Robert Hardwick Weston. "Free Time: Overwork as an Ontological Condition." *Social Text* 26.1 (Spring 2008): 137–164.

Strauss, Julia and Donal Cruise O'Brien, eds. *Staging Politics: Power and Performance in Asia and Africa.* London: Tauris, 2007.

Strong, Roy. *Art and Power.* Berkeley: University of California Press, 1984.

Suleri, Sara. "Woman, Skin, Deep." *Colonial Discourse and Postcolonial Theory.* Eds. Patrick Williams and Laura Chrisman. New York: Columbia University Press, 1994.

Talbot, Ian. *Divided Cities: Partition and Its Aftermath in Lahore and Amritsar, 1947–57.* New Delhi: Oxford University Press, 2006.

———— *Pakistan: A Modern History.*New York: St. Martin's Press, 1998.

Talbot, Ian and Gurharpal Singh. *The Partition of India.* Cambridge University Press, 2009.

Talbot, Ian and Darshan Singh Tatla, eds. *Epicentre of Violence: Partition Voices and Memories from Amritsar.* New Delhi: Permanent Black, 2006.

Taussig, Michael. *Mimesis and Alterity: A Particular History of the Sense.* London and New York: Routledge, 1993.

Taylor, Diana. *The Archive and the Repertoire: Performing Cultural Memory in the Americas.* Durham, NC: Duke University Press, 2007.

—— *Disappearing Acts: Spectacles of Gender and Nationalism in Argentina's "Dirty War."* Durham, NC: Duke University Press, 1997.

Tendulkar, D.G. *Mahatma.* Bombay: Jhaveri and Tendulkar, 1952.

Thapar, Romila. "The Verdict on Ayodhya: A Historian's Perspective." *The Hindu,* October 2, 2010.

Thorold, Crispin. BBC Radio 4, March 13, 2004.

The Tribune. "Heated Exchange at Wagah during Retreat Ceremony." October 21, 2002.

Turner, Victor. *The Anthropology of Performance.* New York: PAJ Publications, 1986.

Varshney, Ashutosh. *Ethnic Conflict and Civic Life: Hindus and Muslims.* New Haven, CT, and London: Yale University Press, 2002.

—— "India, Pakistan, and Kashmir: Antinomies of Nationalism." *Asian Survey* (November 1991): 997–1019.

—— "Why Democracy Survives." *Journal of Democracy* 9:3 (July 1998): 36–50.

Vasudevan, Ravi. "A Response to the Discussion on Visual Culture." Available at: www.cscban.org.

Veer, Peter van der, ed. *Nation and Migration: The Politics of Space in the South Asian Diaspora.* Philadelphia: University of Pennsylvania Press, 1995.

Vinaik, Achin. *The Furies of Indian Communalism: Religion, Modernity, and Secularization.* London and New York: Verso, 1997.

—— "Situating Threat of Hindu Nationalism: Problems with Fascist Paradigm." *Economic and Political Weekly* (July 9, 1994): 1729–1748.

Viswanathan, Gauri. *Outside the Fold: Conversion, Modernity, and Belief.* Princeton University Press, 1998.

Visweswaran, Kamala. "Small Speeches, Subaltern Gender: Nationalist Ideology and Its Historiography." *Subaltern Studies IX: Writings on South Asia and Society.* Eds. Shahid Amin and Dipesh Chakrabarty. New Delhi: Oxford University Press, 1996.

Wajahat, Asghar. *Jis Lahore Nai Dekhya O Jamya Nai*. New Delhi: Vani Prakashan, 2001.

Warner, Michael. *Publics and Counterpublics*. Brooklyn, NY: Zone Books, 2002.

Werbner, Pnina and Helene Basu. *Embodying Charisma: Modernity, Locality, and the Performance of Emotion in Sufi Cults*. New York: Routledge, 1998.

Widmalm, Sten. *Kashmir in Comparative Perspective: Democracy and Violent Separatism in India*. Oxford University Press, 2002.

————— "The Rise and Fall of Democracy in Jammu and Kashmir." In *Community Conflicts and the State in India*. Ed. Amrita Basu and Atul Kohli. New Delhi: Oxford University Press, 1998.

Willett, John, trans. *Brecht on Theatre*. London: Methuen, 1978.

Williams, Patrick and Laura Chrisman, eds. *Colonial Discourse and Postcolonial Theory*. New York: Columbia University Press, 1994.

Wilmer, Steve. *Theatre, Society, and the Nation: Staging American Identities*. Cambridge University Press, 2002.

Zamindar, Vazira Fazila-Yacoobali. *The Long Partition and the Making of Modern South Asia: Refugees, Boundaries, Histories*. New York: Columbia University Press, 2007.

Zutshi, Chitralekha. *Languages of Belonging: Islam, Regional Identity, and the Making of Kashmir*. Oxford University Press, 2004.

Index

For EU product safety concerns, contact us at Calle de José Abascal, 56–1°, 28003 Madrid, Spain or eugpsr@cambridge.org.

www.ingramcontent.com/pod-product-compliance
Ingram Content Group UK Ltd.
Pitfield, Milton Keynes, MK11 3LW, UK
UKHW020333140625
459647UK00018B/2134